COMMON CORE ACHIEVE

Mastering Essential Test Readiness Skills

HiSET™ Exercise Book

READING & WRITING

Mc
Graw
Hill
Education

Bothell, WA • Chicago, IL • Columbus, OH • New York, NY

MHEonline.com

Send all inquiries to:
McGraw-Hill Education
8787 Orion Place
Columbus, OH 43240

ISBN: 978-0-02-143274-5
MHID: 0-02-143274-0

Printed in the United States of America.

1 2 3 4 5 6 7 8 9 RHR 17 16 15 14

Table of Contents

Congratulations! If you are using this book, it means that you are taking a key step toward achieving an important new goal for yourself. You are preparing to take the HiSET™ in order to earn your high school diploma, one of the most important steps in the pathway toward career, educational, and lifelong well-being and success.

Common Core Achieve: Mastering Essential Test Readiness Skills is designed to help you learn or strengthen the skills you will need when you take the HiSET™. The *Reading & Writing Exercise Book* provides you with additional practice with the key concepts and core skills required for success on test day and beyond.

How to Use This Book

This book is designed to follow the same lesson structure as the Core Student Module. Each lesson in the *Reading & Writing Exercise Book* is broken down into the same sections covering key concepts as the core module, with a page or more devoted to the topics covered in each section. Each lesson contains at least one Test-Taking Tip, which helps you prepare for a test by giving you hints such as how to determine where to find the answer to a question, or strategies such as how to eliminate unnecessary information. At the back of this book, you will find the answer key for each lesson. Not only are the answers provided, but there are also rationales for each concept-based question that gives explanations of why each answer choice is correct. If you get an answer incorrect, please return to the appropriate lesson and section in the online or the print Core Student Module to review the specific content.

About the HiSET™ Language Arts–Reading and Language Arts–Writing Tests

The HiSET™ Reading Test assesses across two content categories—application of concepts, analysis, synthesis, and evaluation involving Literary Texts and Informational Texts. Approximately 60% of the test is dedicated to literary texts and 40% to informational texts. There are a total of 40 questions on the test, all of which are in multiple-choice format. Test-takers have 65 minutes to complete all the questions.

The HiSET™ Writing Test assesses across three content categories—Organization of Ideas, Language Facility, and Writing Conventions. Approximately 20% of the test is dedicated to organization of ideas, 25% to language facility, and 55% to writing conventions. There are 50 questions on part 1 of the test and an essay question on part 2 of the text. Test-takers have 75 minutes to complete part 1 and 45 minutes to complete part 2.

Item Formats

Multiple-Choice Items
All the questions on the HiSET™ Reading test and part 1 of the Writing test are in multiple-choice format. Each multiple-choice question contains four answer choices, of which there is only one correct answer. When you encounter a multiple-choice question, eliminate any possible answers that cannot be correct based on the information given so you can focus on the relevant information to answer the question.

Essay Question
The Writing Practice in each lesson is designed to help you prepare for part 2 of the HiSET™ Writing test. Writing prompts guide you to produce responses that reflect the types of writing addressed in the essay question. Your essay response will be scored based on the development of your main idea through supporting reasons, examples, and details; clear organization of ideas; language use; and clarity and correctness of writing conventions. The Writing Practice activities will help you practice and master these areas of writing competency.

Strategies for Test Day

There are many things you should do to prepare for test day, in addition to studying. Other ways to prepare you for the day of the test include preparing physically, arriving early, and recognizing certain strategies that can help you succeed during the test. Some of these strategies are listed below.

- **Prepare physically.** Make sure you are rested, both physically and mentally on the day of the test. Eating a well-balanced meal will also help you concentrate while you take the text. Staying stress-free as much as possible on the day of the test will make you more likely to be focused than you would be if you are stressed.

- **Arrive early.** Arrive at the testing center at least 30 minutes before the beginning of the test. Give yourself enough time to get seated and situated in the room. Keep in mind that many testing centers will not admit you if you are late.

- **Think positively.** Studies have shown that a positive attitude can help with success, although studying helps even more.

- **Relax during the test.** Stretching and deep breathing can help you relax and refocus. Try doing this a few times during the test, especially if you feel frustrated, anxious, or confused.

- **Read the test directions carefully.** Make sure you understand what the directions are asking you to do and complete the activity appropriately. If you have any questions about the test or how to answer a specific item using the computer, ask them before the test begins.

- **Know the time limit for each test.** The Reading test has a time limit of 65 minutes (1 hour 5 minutes) and the Writing test has a time limit of 75 minutes (1 hour 15 minutes) for part 1 and 45 minutes for part 2. Try to work at a manageable pace. If you have extra time, go back and check your answers and finish any questions you might have skipped.

- **Have a strategy for answering questions.** For each question, read through the question prompt, identifying the important information to answer the question. If it is necessary, reread the information provided as well as any answer choices provided.

- **Don't spend a lot of time on difficult questions.** If you are unable to answer a question or are not confident in your answer, move on and come back to it later. If you are taking the paper-and-pencil version of the HiSET™, you may use the scrap paper with which you are provided to keep track of questions you want to review. If you are taking the computer-based version of the HiSET™, use the "mark and review" feature of the testing software to mark the question and move on to the next question. Answer easier questions first. At the end of the test, you will be able to answer and review any questions you marked, if time permits. Whether you skipped questions or not, you should try to finish with approximately 10–15 minutes left so you have time to answer questions you marked and to check all your answers.

- **Answer every question on the test.** If you do not know the answer, try to narrow down the possible answers and then make your best educated guess. You will lose points leaving questions unanswered, but making a guess could possibly help you gain points.

Good luck with your studies, and remember: you are here because you have chosen to achieve important and exciting new goals for yourself. Every time you begin working within the materials, keep in mind that the skills you develop in *Common Core Achieve: Mastering Essential Test Readiness Skills* are not just important for passing the HiSET™; they are keys to lifelong success.

This lesson will help you practice determining the main ideas and supporting details in two types of texts. Use it with Core Lesson 1.1 *Determine the Main Idea* to reinforce and apply your knowledge.

Key Concept

The main idea is the most important idea in a paragraph or passage. A main idea can be found in many different kinds of text.

Main Idea in Informational Text

Informational texts explain, describe, instruct, or try to persuade. The main idea often states the purpose of the document. The supporting details of the text give facts, opinions, examples, and explanations to support the main idea.

This office memo is about a company's new purchasing system. The text explains to company employees how to use the system when making purchases for their departments.

To All Employees,

As you should be aware, the Purchasing Tracker (PT) system has been rolled out and must now be used for all purchasing. This new system will allow our company to easily organize and track all orders in one system and to cut back on the number of steps required to process an order. As with any
5   new system, it will take some time to perfect the operation. However, to ensure that we realize the full benefit of PT, please start using these guidelines immediately.

Use of PT

Use of PT is mandatory for all new service orders. If you feel you have a special situation that cannot be accommodated in the system, let the PT team know immediately so the problem can be
10   solved in a way that does not delay the project.

Purchase orders to vendor prior to project start

Corporate policy mandates that suppliers may not start work on a project without a fully approved PT purchase order. A contract does not replace this requirement. If a contract is required for the project, it must be attached to the PT order. Suppliers can start the project only after receiving the
15   approved purchase order (with attached contract, if applicable).

Use of rates in PT

If a service category in PT has associated rates, then the PT order must be built using the applicable rate-based line items. This means the order should include a line specific to each rate-based item. Lump sums, combined totals, or use of "miscellaneous" items are not acceptable. Proper breakout
20   of the order ensures that the company has full visibility of what we are purchasing and that our reporting is meaningful.

Change orders

Orders should be created based on your original estimate. If the project specs or scope change, the order should be updated via the Change Order process before the supplier submits an invoice.
25   Suppliers may not begin work on additional scope items until they have received the updated purchase order. Do not pad your requisitions in an attempt to avoid change orders. Additional funds on a purchase order open the door for the supplier to invoice for these funds.

1 Which text feature best helps you identify the main idea of each section?

   A   Passage title

   B   Headings

   C   First sentence

   D   Last sentence

2 Which detail supports the main idea that vendors must have a purchase order before starting work?

   A   "let the PT team know immediately so the problem can be solved in a way that does not delay the project"

   B   "suppliers may not start work on a project without a fully approved PT purchase order"

   C   "Lump sums, combined totals, or use of 'miscellaneous' items are not acceptable."

   D   "Additional funds on a purchase order open the door for the supplier to invoice for these funds."

3 What is the main idea of the section titled "Use of rates in PT"?

   A   PT must be used for all service requests.

   B   Contracts do not replace purchase orders.

   C   Rates must be listed for each rate-based item.

   D   Orders should be based on estimates.

4 In which section would you expect to find a detail about additional work to a project?

   A   "Use of PT"

   B   "Purchase orders to vendor prior to project start"

   C   "Use of rates in PT"

   D   "Change orders"

5 "Employees must follow the guidelines for using the PT system" is a

   A   supporting detail.

   B   point of view.

   C   perspective.

   D   main idea.

6 Why might the writer of this informational text state the topic sentence at the beginning of the passage?

   A   To make sure the reader knows what the passage is about

   B   To provide information in least-important to most-important order

   C   So that the reader does not have to read the entire passage to understand it

   D   Because the reader would not understand the passage without the topic sentence

Main Idea in Literary Text

Fiction writers invent a self-contained world where imaginary events unfold. The writers also create characters who play roles in these events. Main ideas are presented in paragraphs and longer passages. As you read, look for the main idea and details. The main idea may be stated in a topic sentence, but it is more likely to be implied in a longer passage.

"To Build a Fire" is a short story by Jack London. It chronicles the adventures of a man as he hikes through Alaska in winter in an attempt to make a claim on a gold mine.

But all this—the mysterious, far-reaching hair-line trail, the absence of sun from the sky, the tremendous cold, and the strangeness and weirdness of it all—made no impression on the man. It was not because he was long used to it. He was a newcomer in the land, a *chechaquo*, and this was his first winter. The trouble with him was that he was without imagination. He was quick and alert in the things
5   of life, but only in the things, and not in the significances.

Fifty degrees below zero meant eighty-odd degrees of frost. Such fact impressed him as being cold and uncomfortable, and that was all. It did not lead him to meditate upon his frailty as a creature of temperature, and upon man's frailty in general, able only to live within certain narrow limits of heat and cold; and from there on it did not lead him to the conjectural field of immortality and man's place
10   in the universe. Fifty degrees below zero stood for a bite of frost that hurt and that must be guarded against by the use of mittens, ear-flaps, warm moccasins, and thick socks. Fifty degrees below zero was to him just precisely fifty degrees below zero. That there should be anything more to it than that was a thought that never entered his head. . . .

At the man's heels trotted a dog, a big native husky, the proper wolf-dog, gray-coated and without
15   any visible or temperamental difference from its brother, the wild wolf.

The animal was depressed by the tremendous cold. It knew that it was no time for travelling. Its instinct told it a truer tale than was told to the man by the man's judgment. In reality, it was not merely colder than fifty below zero; it was colder than sixty below, than seventy below. It was seventy-five below zero. Since the freezing-point is thirty-two above zero, it meant that one hundred and seven
20   degrees of frost obtained.

The dog did not know anything about thermometers. Possibly in its brain there was no sharp consciousness of a condition of very cold such as was in the man's brain. But the brute had its instinct. It experienced a vague but menacing apprehension that subdued it and made it slink along at the man's heels, and that made it question eagerly every unwonted movement of the man as if expecting him to
25   go into camp or to seek shelter somewhere and build a fire. The dog had learned fire, and it wanted fire, or else to burrow under the snow and cuddle its warmth away from the air.

Excerpt from "To Build a Fire" by Jack London

7 **What is the main idea of this excerpt?**

   A The dog has survival instincts that the man lacks.

   B The man has more knowledge than the dog.

   C The man and dog are dependent on each other.

   D The man and dog share the same experiences.

8 **Which detail shows that the man is not prepared for the environment?**

   A "he was long used to it"

   B "he was without imagination"

   C "He was quick and alert in the things of life"

   D "Such fact impressed him as being cold"

9 **What is the main idea of paragraph 4, (lines 16–20)?**

   A The dog is like a wild wolf.

   B The dog can tolerate the cold.

   C The dog trusts the man's judgment.

   D The dog knows how cold it really is.

10 **Which phrase would best summarize the main idea of the passage?**

   A Instinct or knowledge

   B Experience or inexperience

   C Mortality or immortality

   D Happiness or sadness

11 **What is the meaning of "tremendous" in lines 2 and 16?**

   A Large

   B Extreme

   C Excellent

   D Vast

12 **Which of the following statements is true about the main idea of the passage?**

   A The writer does not include a main idea.

   B The writer wants the reader to provide the main idea.

   C The main idea is obvious and, therefore, does not need to be stated.

   D The reader can infer the main idea through details.

✔ Test-Taking Tip

The more you practice reading different types of texts of different lengths, the better prepared you will be to read and understand passages presented in reading tests. A good way to practice is to read as much as you can about subjects that interest you. Not only will you become a better reader when you are taking a test, you will also increase your enjoyment of reading.

Language Practice

Commas are used in a number of situations, for example to separate items in a series, to set off introductory information, to separate independent ideas, and to separate text that provides additional details.

Read quickly through the draft feature article in the box below. Then go to the spread-out version and consider the suggestions for revision.

---

1   Reality television is not a new phenomenon. In fact reality shows like *Candid Camera* and *What's My Line* were hits in television's earliest days. PBS broke new ground in 1973 with *An American Family* by following the Loud family as they went about their everyday life and when the Louds decided on camera to divorce, millions of viewers were shocked.

2   By the 2000s reality television shows were common on nearly every network. The shows were clearly entertaining to viewers but they were also cheaper to make than scripted shows. A typical reality show uses a smaller crew, hires fewer performers, needs fewer sets, and requires very few writers. These less-expensive shows give networks a larger profit margin so hit reality shows mean big money.

---

1   Reality television is not a new

phenomenon. <u>In fact reality shows</u> like
                    1

Candid Camera and *What's My Line* were

hits in television's earliest days. PBS broke

new ground in 1973 with *An American*

Family by following the Loud family as they

went about <u>their everyday life and when the</u>
                          2

Louds decided on camera to divorce, millions

of viewers were shocked.

2   By the 2000s reality television shows

were common on nearly every network. The

shows were clearly <u>entertaining to viewers</u>
                          3

<u>but they</u> were also cheaper to make than
 3

scripted shows. A typical reality show uses a

smaller crew, hires fewer performers, needs

fewer sets, and requires very few writers.

These less-expensive shows give networks a

<u>larger profit margin so hit reality</u> shows mean
             4

big money.

1 **A** *(No change)*
   B In fact, reality shows
   C In fact reality shows,
   D In fact reality, shows

2 **A** *(No change)*
   B their everyday life, and, when the
   C their everyday life, and when the
   D their everyday life. And, when the

3 **A** *(No change)*
   B entertaining to viewers, but they
   C entertaining to viewers but, they
   D entertaining to viewers, but, they

4 **A** *(No change)*
   B larger profit margin. So, hit reality
   C larger profit margin so, hit reality
   D larger profit margin, so hit reality

✔ Test-Taking Tip

Some language questions might have partial sentences in the answer choices. Each answer choice might have very subtle differences such as the placement of a comma. Scan each answer choice to see how they differ. Then read the answer choices in the context of the passage to find the correct answer.

Writing Practice

Some people have nicknames that describe their appearance or abilities. For instance, Hall of Fame basketball player Hakeem "The Dream" Olajuwon earned his nickname for his amazing talents on the court. He was considered a "dream" athlete because he was such a talented player in all aspects of the game.

Write a brief paragraph in which you explain how someone received a nickname. You may write about yourself, a friend, a relative, or a famous person. Think about your **main idea**. You may state the main idea in a topic sentence or imply the main idea through the details. Make sure all the key details support the main idea.

This lesson will help you practice identifying supporting details in two informational texts. Use it with Core Lesson 1.2 *Identify Supporting Details* to reinforce and apply your knowledge.

Supporting details are concrete ideas that develop the main idea in a passage. There are many types of supporting details.

Identifying Supporting Details

The main idea of a passage is its most important idea. Supporting details are ideas in sentences and paragraphs that support this main idea. The supporting details in a text may include facts, examples, reasons, and descriptions.

The Fertile Crescent is an area in the Middle East that is of great historical importance. Many early civilizations developed in and around the Fertile Crescent.

The Middle East and the coastal regions of the Mediterranean Sea, as well as the Nile Delta, were the locations for the beginning of many early civilizations, including Egyptian, Babylonian, Sumerian, Phoenician, Persian, and Greek. The close proximity of these civilizations allowed for trade and also created competition for land and resources. The interaction among various cultures created changes in
5   and exchanges of traditions and technology.

The classical civilizations that had the largest impact on the world's cultural development are the Greek and Roman Empires. Greek civilization continued the Egyptian priorities of art, literature, music, theater, architecture, and the sciences. The first major citizen participation in government occurred in ancient Athens, a powerful Greek city-state. All male citizens participated in the assembly,
10   which determined laws and policies.

During the golden age of ancient Greece (500 BCE to 300 BCE, before the common era), many great philosophers and educators such as Socrates, Plato, and Aristotle shared their wisdom with the world. For the first time, the improvement of the mind and the body was viewed as an important priority for society. The challenge of improved physical fitness was the reason why the Olympic Games began in
15   ancient Greece.

Eventually the Romans conquered the Greeks, copying their architecture, art forms, and poetry, and even some of their mythological gods. The Greeks and the Romans had maintained early people's practice of using myth to explain natural phenomena such as seasonal changes, flooding and severe weather, and success in agriculture. To make the myths easier to understand and appreciate, the
20   Greeks and Romans had gods with human attributes. Greek and Roman mythology has continued to exist even after our understanding of the universe had outgrown the need for storylike explanations. Many of the planets, including Jupiter, Neptune, Mars, Venus, and Mercury, were named for Roman gods.

(continued)

25   The Romans were interested in military strength and acquiring land for the empire. Thus, athletic competition and training for combat as a form of entertainment developed in Rome. The Roman government differed from the Athenian model. One, two, or sometimes three consuls were chosen by the Roman senate, a group of the wealthiest landholders, or patricians. The vast majority of the citizens were plebeians—the small farmers, tradesmen, artisans, and merchants.

30   Wealth and connections among family members thus determined position in the social classes within Roman culture. This status determined whether a member of the society was considered to be worthy of having a vote. The Roman system of government was called a republic. The lower class of slaves and the common class of farmers and tradesmen were limited in their rights of marriage partners and land ownership.

35   One lasting contribution of the Romans was the calendar introduced by Julius Caesar in 46 BCE. Caesar made the months of unequal days and added leap years to make the reckoning more equal to an actual year. This Julian calendar, with some modifications, is still in use today.

1 Which term describes the type of details used to provide information about mythology and the calendar?

   A   Main
   B   Precise
   C   Supporting
   D   Insignificant

2 Which detail supports the main idea that Greek and Roman empires contributed to the culture of the surrounding area?

   A   "The interaction among various cultures created changes in and exchanges of traditions and technology."
   B   "For the first time, the improvement of the mind and the body was viewed as an important priority for society."
   C   "The challenge of improved physical fitness was the reason why the Olympic Games began in ancient Greece."
   D   "The vast majority of citizens were plebeians—the small farmers, tradesmen, artisans, and merchants."

3 Which detail could be added to paragraph 4 (lines 16–23) to support the main idea of the paragraph?

   A   When the Romans conquered the Greeks, much of Greek culture was destroyed.
   B   The Romans' astronomical discoveries included the discovery of several planets and the constellations.
   C   Although Roman and Greek gods shared similar stories, they had different names and personalities.
   D   The Romans made many contributions to culture, including a series of roadways and aqueducts.

4 In which paragraph would you expect to find a supporting detail about the Greek government?

   A   Paragraph 1 (lines 1–5)
   B   Paragraph 2 (lines 6–10)
   C   Paragraph 3 (lines 11–15)
   D   Paragraph 4 (lines 16–23)

5 Which detail could be cited to support an idea about the structure of Roman society?

   A   "To make the myths easier to understand and appreciate, the Greeks and Romans had gods with human attributes."
   B   "Thus, athletic competition and training for combat as a form of entertainment developed in Rome."
   C   "One, two, or sometimes three consuls were chosen by the Roman senate, a group of the wealthiest landholders, or patricians."
   D   "One lasting contribution of the Romans was the calendar introduced by Julius Caesar in 46 BCE."

Using Details to Make Generalizations

Writers use many types of details to help the reader understand a passage. By thinking carefully about these details, the reader can make generalizations, or broad statements about the text.

***The Pioneers* is a historical novel published in 1823. This excerpt is set in New York about the time when the frontier was expanding in that area.**

Amongst the sportsmen was to be seen the tall, gaunt form of Leatherstocking. . . .

The reports of the fire-arms became rapid, whole volleys rising from the plain, as flocks of more than ordinary numbers darted over the opening, covering the field with darkness, like an interposing cloud; and then the light smoke of a single piece would issue from among the leafless bushes on the
5   mountain, as death was hurled on the retreat of the affrighted birds, who would rise from a volley, for many feet into the air, in a vain effort to escape the attacks of man. Arrows, and missiles of every kind, were seen in the midst of the flocks. . . .

So prodigious was the number of the birds, that the scattering fire of the guns, with the hurling of missiles, and the cries of the boys, had no other effect than to break off small flocks from the immense
10   masses that continued to dart. . . . None pretended to collect the game, which lay scattered over the fields in such profusion, as to cover the very ground with the fluttering victims.

Leather-stocking was a silent, but uneasy spectator of all these proceedings, but was able to keep his sentiments to himself. . . .

"This comes of settling a country," he said—"here have I known the pigeons to fly for forty long
15   years, and, till you made your clearings, there was nobody to scare or to hurt them. I loved to see them come into the woods, for they were company to a body; hurting nothing; being, as it was, as harmless as a garter-snake. But now it gives me sore thoughts when I hear the frighty things whizzing through the air, for I know it's only a motion to bring out all the brats in the village at them. Well! The Lord won't see the waste of his creaters for nothing, and right will be done to the pigeons, as well as others, by-
20   and-by.—There's Mr. Oliver, as bad as the rest of them, firing into the flocks as if he was shooting down nothing but the Mingo warriors."

Among the sportsmen was Billy Kirby, who, armed with an old musket, was loading, and, without even looking into the air, was firing, and shouting as his victims fell even on his own person. He heard the speech of Natty, and took upon himself to reply—

25   "What's that, old Leather-stocking!" he cried; "grumbling at the loss of a few pigeons! If you had to sow your wheat twice, and three times, as I have done, you wouldn't be so massyfully feeling'd to'ards the divils.—Hurrah, boys! Scatter the feathers. This is better than shooting at a turkey's head and neck, old fellow."

"It's better for you, maybe, Billy Kirby," returned the indignant old hunter, "and all them as don't
30   know how to put a ball down a rifle-barrel, or how to bring it up ag'in with a true aim; but it's wicked to be shooting into flocks in this wastey manner; and none do it, who know how to knock over a single bird. If a body has a craving for pigeon's flesh, why! It's made the same as all other creaters, for man's eating, but not to kill twenty and eat one. When I want such a thing, I go into the woods till I find one to my liking, and then I shoot him off the branches without touching a feather of another, though there
35   might be a hundred on the same tree. But you couldn't do such a thing, Billy Kirby—you couldn't do it if you tried. . . ."

Excerpt from *The Pioneers* by James Fenimore Cooper

6 Which generalization can be drawn from the details in the first two paragraphs (lines 1–7)?

   A Many local residents hunted birds.

   B The people were hungry and shot the birds for survival.

   C The birds were a health threat to the people of the community.

   D The people were trying to protect the native birds in the area.

7 Which detail supports the generalization that the hunting expedition was unnecessary?

   A "This comes of settling a country," he said—"here have I known the pigeons to fly for forty years . . ."

   B "I loved to them come into the woods, for they were company to a body . . ."

   C ". . . for I know it's only a motion to bring out all the brats in the village at them."

   D "The Lord won't see the waste of his creaters for nothing . . ."

8 Which detail provides an example to support the generalization that the shooting of the pigeons was justified?

   A "If you had to sow your wheat twice, and three times, as I have done, you wouldn't be so massyfully feeling'd to'ards the divils."

   B "It's better for you, maybe, Billy Kirby," returned the indignant old hunger, "and all them as don't know how to put a ball down a rifle-barrel . . ."

   C "If a body has a craving for pigeon's flesh, why! It's made the same as all other creaters, for man's eating, but not to kill twenty and eat one."

   D "When I want such a thing, I go into the wood till I find one to my liking, and then I shot him off the branches without touching a feather of another . . ."

9 Which of the following meanings associated with the word "fire" seems most intended in line 8?

   A Light and heat from burning

   B Shooting of guns

   C Being under attack

   D To terminate someone's employment

Language Practice

A complete sentence must have a subject and predicate. It must be able to stand alone. When you write, check your text for sentence fragments.

Read quickly through the draft feature article in the box below. Then go to the spread-out version and consider the suggestions for revision.

As a scuba diver, I enjoy looking at the amazing underwater animals. One of my favorites is the distinctive octopus. What makes it so special? A gigantic head attached to eight wiggly arms, large eyes, spotted skin, and incredible flexibility. However, what fascinates me most is its behavior. Using specialized pigment cells, changing the color of its skin to match its environment. I, as well as its predators, have often swum by the octopus without noticing it. When it is discovered, great, thick clouds of black ink. This startles the predator, allowing the octopus a chance to escape.

As a scuba diver, I enjoy looking at the amazing underwater animals. One of my favorites is the distinctive octopus. What
<u>   </u>
        1
makes it so special? A gigantic head attached to eight wiggly arms, <u>large eyes, spotted</u>
        2
<u>skin, and incredible flexibility.</u> However,
     2
what fascinates me most is its behavior.

Using specialized pigment cells, <u>changing the</u>
         3
<u>color of its skin to match its environment.</u>
       3
I, as well as its predators, have often swum by the octopus without noticing it. When it is discovered, <u>great, thick clouds of black</u>
         4
<u>ink.</u> This startles the predator, allowing the
 4
octopus a chance to escape.

1 **A** *(No change)*
    B among the thousands of creatures I have seen.
    C although it is hard to choose.
    D the incredibly flexible octopus.

2 **A** *(No change)*
    B makes the octopus different from many animals.
    C not to mention its squishy, flexible body.
    D and the fact that it is found in oceans around the world.

3 **A** *(No change)*
    B located in the muscles of its skin.
    C creating a variety of colors and patterns.
    D it can blend in with almost any environment.

4 **A** *(No change)*
    B by a predator or even a diver like myself.
    C the octopus can release a puff of black ink.
    D which does not occur frequently.

✓ Test-Taking Tip

When you are taking a test, be an active reader. Underlining words in the passage or taking notes on scratch paper will help you find important details when you are answering questions. Later you can use your notes to determine a main idea or to make generalizations.

Writing Practice

There are many kinds of natural disasters, including hurricanes, tornados, forest fires, and earthquakes. Reporters who cover these events write to inform people about what happened. They must be able to give facts, descriptions, explanations, and reasons to help their readers understand the main idea.

Write a brief paragraph about a real or imagined natural disaster. Include a **generalization** that accurately describes the type of disaster. Use at least three types of **supporting details** in your paragraph to help the reader experience and understand what happened.

_____

_____

_____

_____

_____

_____

_____

_____

_____

_____

_____

_____

_____

_____

_____

_____

_____

_____

_____

_____

_____

_____

This lesson will help you practice identifying directly stated main ideas and implied main ideas from supporting details. Use it with Core Lesson 1.3 *Identify Direct and Implied Main Ideas* to reinforce and apply your knowledge.

Key Concept

The main idea may be stated directly in a topic sentence or sentences, or it may be implied. An implied main idea must be inferred from supporting details.

Direct and Implied Main Ideas

In some texts, the main idea may be directly stated. In others, the main idea is implied, or expressed indirectly, through the details in the text. To figure out the implied main idea, you need to think about what the details are about and how they are related to each other.

In the early years of the United States, new leaders were elected and the country expanded. This period spans the late 1700s through the middle of the 1800s, from Presidents George Washington to James Polk.

Early Domestic and Foreign Policy

The years between 1791 and 1803 saw the United States expand geographically. Between 1791 and 1796, Vermont, Kentucky, and Tennessee were admitted to the Union under the administration of George Washington, the first US president. In 1803, under President Thomas Jefferson, Ohio was
5   admitted to the Union, and the largest acquisition of land for the United States occurred with the Louisiana Purchase. By paying France $15 million for the territory, Jefferson doubled the size of the country. He subsequently appointed Lewis and Clark to explore the acquired territory.

The Monroe Doctrine

A strong sense of nationalism developed after the War of 1812. For the first time the United States
10   could afford to look inward and pay less attention to European affairs. As a result, US westward expansion continued, with victories over several Native American tribes.

In 1823, President James Monroe proclaimed to the world that European powers would no longer be allowed to colonize the Americas. He indicated that the United States would remain neutral in European conflicts as long as the European powers left the emerging republics in North and South
15   America alone. Known as the Monroe Doctrine, this foreign policy statement marked the appearance of the United States on the world political stage.

Jacksonian Democracy and the Mexican War

After Monroe left office, sectionalism became a problem for the United States. Sectionalism refers to the political, cultural, and economic differences among regions of the country—in this case the
20   agricultural South and West and the industrial Northeast. The conflicting demands that each section put upon the government caused great political turmoil.

(continued)

The first US president elected to office as a result of these factional differences was Andrew Jackson in 1828. A Southerner and hero in the War of 1812, Jackson was considered to be a populist, a man who represented the interests of the common people. He believed that *all* people, not just the
25   propertied few, should have a voice in deciding how the government should be run.

As the champion of the common people, Jackson opposed the establishment of a national bank because he believed that it would benefit only the wealthy and because he feared the Eastern merchants and industrialists would control it. Under Jacksonian democracy, farmers and craftspeople gained a louder voice in government than they had had under previous administrations. Despite
30   pressure to annex Texas during his second term, Jackson refused, fearing a war with Mexico.

President James Polk, Jackson's successor, had no such fear. Congress, agreeing to the demands of the Texans, annexed the Texas Republic in 1845. Thus, the expansionist fervor in the United States was renewed. Manifest Destiny—the drive to extend the US borders to the Pacific Ocean—became a rallying cry. When President Polk was unable to purchase the territory that included New Mexico and
35   California, the United States declared war on Mexico in 1846 as a result of a territorial dispute between the two countries.

The Treaty of Guadalupe Hidalgo that ended the war in 1848 resulted in the United States gaining the land that would later become California, Utah, Nevada, and parts of Colorado, New Mexico, Arizona, and Wyoming. Thus, the United States had set its continental boundaries.

1   **Which sentence best describes how the main idea is expressed?**

   A   It is implied through details.

   B   It is stated explicitly.

   C   There is no main idea.

   D   The reader creates the main idea.

2   **Which sentence best expresses the main idea of the entire passage?**

   A   The Louisiana Purchase doubled the size of the country.

   B   Exploration of new lands was a priority of early Americans.

   C   Relationships between the United States and Mexico were strained.

   D   US domestic and foreign policies have changed through the years.

3   **Which sentence best expresses the main idea of the first paragraph?**

   A   "The years between 1791 and 1803 saw the United States expand geographically."

   B   "In 1803, . . . the largest acquisition of land for the United States occurred with the Louisiana Purchase."

   C   "By paying France $15 million for the territory, Jefferson doubled the size of the country."

   D   "He subsequently appointed Lewis and Clark to explore the acquired territory."

4   **Which part of the passage best implies the main idea that the United States expanded through a territorial war?**

   A   "Early Domestic and Foreign Policy" section (lines 1–7)

   B   "The Monroe Doctrine" section (lines 9–16)

   C   Paragraphs 5–6 (lines 22–30)

   D   Paragraphs 7–8 (lines 31–39)

Implied Main Ideas and Supporting Details

The main idea of a text may be directly stated, but it is often implied. To identify an implied main idea, look for sentences that contain key phrases and details. Think about how these details are related.

Fables are fictional stories that are written to teach real-world lessons. In "The Golden Windows," a boy sets out to unravel the mystery of a house with diamond and gold windows.

All day long the little boy worked hard, in field and barn and shed . . . but at sunset there came an hour that was all his own, for his father had given it to him. Then the boy would go up to the top of a hill and look across at another hill that rose some miles away. On this far hill stood a house with windows of clear gold and diamonds. They shone and blazed so that it made the boy wink to look at
5   them: but after a while the people in the house put up shutters, as it seemed, and then it looked like any common farmhouse. . . .

One day the boy's father called him and said: "You have been a good boy, and have earned a holiday. . . .

The boy . . . started off to find the house with the golden windows. . . .

After a long time he came to a high green hill; and when he had climbed the hill, there was the
10   house on the top; but it seemed that the shutters were up, for he could not see the golden windows. He came up to the house, and then he could well have wept, for the windows were of clear glass, like any others, and there was no gold anywhere about them.

A woman came to the door, and looked kindly at the boy, and asked him what he wanted.

"I saw the golden windows from our hilltop," he said, "and I came to see them, but now they are
15   only glass." . . .

"We are poor farming people," she said, "and are not likely to have gold about our windows; but glass is better to see through."

She bade the boy sit down on the broad stone step at the door . . . and bade him rest; then she called her daughter, a child of his own age. . . .

20   She led the boy about the farm. . . . Then when they had eaten an apple together, and so had become friends, the boy asked her about the golden windows. The little girl nodded, and said she knew all about them, only he had mistaken the house. . . .

"Come with me, and I will show you the house with the golden windows, and then you will see for yourself."

25   They went to a knoll that rose behind the farmhouse, and as they went the little girl told him that the golden windows could only be seen at a certain hour, about sunset. . . .

When they reached the top of the knoll, the girl turned and pointed; and there on a hill far away stood a house with windows of clear gold and diamond, just as he had seen them. And when they looked again, the boy saw that it was his own home.

(continued)

30 Then he told the little girl that he must go. . . . He kissed her, and promised to come again, but he did not tell her what he had learned; and so he went back down the hill, and the little girl stood in the sunset light and watched him. . . .

It was dark before the boy reached his father's house; but the lamplight and firelight shone through the windows, making them almost as bright as he had seen them from the hilltop; and when he opened
35 the door, his mother came to kiss him, and his little sister ran to throw her arms about his neck, and his father looked up and smiled from his seat by the fire. . . .

"[H]ave you learned anything?" asked his father.

"Yes!" said the boy. "I have learned that our house has windows of gold and diamond."

Excerpt from *The Pig Brother and Other Fables and Stories* by Laura E. Richards

5 **The boy's words and his actions at the top of both hills can help you determine**

  A the main idea.

  B the writer's point of view.

  C figurative language.

  D the author's perspective.

6 **Which sentence best describes how the main idea is presented in this passage?**

  A The main idea is stated as a topic sentence.

  B The main idea is stated at the end of the story.

  C The writer wants the reader to provide the main idea.

  D The reader can infer the main idea through the details.

7 **Which statement best describes the main idea of this passage?**

  A Things are not always the way we see them.

  B Hard work always pays off in the end.

  C Sometimes friends are the best kind of family.

  D Home is not always the easiest place to stay.

8 **Identify the excerpt from the passage that best supports the main idea.**

  A "One day the boy's father called him and said: "You have been a good boy, and have earned a holiday. . . .""

  B "She bade the boy sit down on the broad stone step at the door . . . and bade him rest; then she called her daughter, a child of his own age. . . ."

  C "The little girl nodded, and said she knew all about them, only he had mistaken the house. . . ."

  D "It was dark before the boy reached his father's house; but the lamplight and firelight shone through the windows. . . ."

9 **In line 7, the word "holiday" most nearly means**

  A a celebration.

  B a time of relaxation.

  C a date on a calendar.

  D a religious feast day.

✓ Test-Taking Tip

Keep an eye on the time as you are taking the test. Plan ahead. Think about how much time you should spend on each section or on each question. Allow time at the end of the test to check your answers. Check periodically to make sure that you are on target to finish.

Writing Practice

You walk into a dark room. What is the first thing you do? Do you turn on a light? We use lights to help us work, play, drive, and stay safe. A standard lightbulb is relatively simple—it's just a filament and a glass covering—yet it's hard to imagine our lives without this amazing invention.

Write a brief paragraph about a real or imagined invention. Before beginning to write, determine your main idea. You may **directly state the main idea** in a topic sentence or **imply the main idea** through the details. Make sure the key details are related and support the main idea.

_____

_____

_____

_____

_____

_____

_____

_____

_____

_____

_____

_____

_____

_____

_____

_____

_____

_____

_____

_____

_____

_____

_____

_____

_____

This lesson will help you practice summarizing details in two passages. Use it with Core Lesson 1.4 *Summarize Details* to reinforce and apply your knowledge.

Key Concept

Explaining the most important ideas in a passage in a concise way is called summarizing. A summary includes the main idea and the key supporting details.

Summarizing Key Information

To write a concise and effective summary, you must first identify the most important points. Begin by identifying the main idea. Then identify the most important supporting details. After these details are identified, paraphrase the main idea and important supporting details in your own words.

"The Watchers" was written by William Stanley Braithwaite (1878–1962), an American writer and poet.

Two women on the lone wet strand
(The wind's out with a will to roam)
The waves wage war on rocks and sand,
(And a ship is long due home.)

5 The sea sprays in the women's eyes—
(Hearts can writhe like the sea's wild foam)
Lower descend the tempestuous skies,
(For the wind's out with a will to roam.)

"O daughter, thine eyes be better than mine,"
10 *(The waves ascend high as yonder dome)*
"North or south is there never a sign?"
(And a ship is long due home.)

They watched there all the long night through—
(The wind's out with a will to roam)
15 Wind and rain and sorrow for two,—
(And heaven on the long reach home.)

"The Watchers" by William Stanley Braithwaite

1 Which statement best paraphrases the main idea of the poem?

   A   Storms can be dangerous for ships.

   B   Storms can last a long time and cause sorrow.

   C   A mother and daughter wait for a missing ship.

   D   A mother and daughter share memories as they wait in a storm.

2 Which supporting detail should be included in a summary of the poem?

   A   There are rocks and sand by the shore.

   B   The ship was long overdue to be home.

   C   They looked north and south to find the ship.

   D   The sand was wet where they stood.

3 Which line should be paraphrased and included in a summary of the poem?

   A   *"The wind's out with a will to roam."*

   B   *"The sea sprays in the women's eyes—"*

   C   *"O daughter, thine eyes be better than mine"*

   D   *"And heaven on the long reach home."*

4 Which of the following meanings associated with the word "sign" seems most intended in line 11?

   A   A hand motion or signal

   B   A public notice

   C   Something that indicates what is to come

   D   Marks or symbols used in place of words

✓ Test-Taking Tip

Many tests provide reading passages followed by questions. One helpful strategy for planning your time is to take the total time allotted for the test and divide it by the number of passages. This tells you how much time to spend on each section of the test.

Summarizing a Text

To create an effective summary, identify the main idea and the most important supporting details. Paraphrase these in concise statements to tell what the passage is about. Often related details can be grouped into a single statement.

The US Department of State offers advice to people who are traveling internationally. This bulletin offers advice for travel during hurricane season.

Travel Alert

U.S. DEPARTMENT OF STATE

Bureau of Consular Affairs

Hurricane Season

5   May 30, 2013

      The Department of State alerts U.S. citizens to the upcoming hurricane season in the Atlantic, the Caribbean, and the Gulf of Mexico. Hurricane season in the Atlantic begins June 1 and ends November 30.

      The National Oceanic and Atmospheric Administration's (NOAA) Climate Prediction Center . . .
10   expects to see an active or extremely active season in the Atlantic Basin this year. [There is] a 70 percent chance of 13 to 20 named storms, of which seven to eleven are predicted to strengthen to a hurricane. . . . Of those, three to six are expected to become major hurricanes. . . . NOAA recommends that those in hurricane-prone regions begin preparations for the upcoming season now.

(continued)

15 During and after some previous storms, U.S. citizens traveling abroad encountered dangerous and often uncomfortable conditions. [These conditions] lasted for several days while awaiting transportation back to the United States. In the past, many U.S. citizens were forced to delay travel . . . due to infrastructure damage to airports and limited flight availability. Roads were also washed out or obstructed by debris. [This damage adversely affected] access to airports and land routes out of affected areas. Reports of looting and sporadic violence in the aftermath of natural
20 disasters have occurred. Security personnel may not always be readily available to assist. In the event of a hurricane, travelers should be aware that they may not be able to depart the area for 24–48 hours or longer.

If you travel to these areas during hurricane season, we recommend you obtain travel insurance to cover unexpected expenses during an emergency. [You may be in a situation that] requires
25 an evacuation from an overseas location. [If so,] the U.S. Department of State will work with commercial airlines to ensure that U.S. citizens are repatriated as safely and efficiently as possible. Commercial airlines are the Department's primary source of transportation in an evacuation. [O]ther means of transport are utilized only as a last resort. The U.S. Department of State will not provide no-cost transportation, but does have the authority to provide repatriation loans to those
30 in financial need.

If you live in or are traveling to storm-prone regions, prepare for hurricanes and tropical storms by organizing a kit in a waterproof container that includes a supply of bottled water, non-perishable food items, a battery-powered or hand-crank radio, any medications taken regularly, and vital documents. . . . Emergency shelters often provide only very basic resources and may have limited
35 medical and food supplies. NOAA and the Federal Emergency Management Agency (FEMA) have additional tips on their websites.

Excerpt from "Travel Alert" by the United States Department of State

5 Read the following statement.

Hurricane season in the Atlantic runs through the summer and part of the fall. The area affected includes the Atlantic, the Caribbean, and the Gulf of Mexico. US citizens should read the following advice from the Department of State.

The statement above is

A a critique of the first paragraph.

B a paraphrase of the first paragraph.

C a direct quotation from the first paragraph.

D a supporting detail from the first paragraph.

6 Which of the following sentences best paraphrases the main idea of the whole passage?

A People should use caution when they are traveling to other countries.

B The upcoming hurricane season will be active and destructive.

C As hurricane season approaches, people should make preparations.

D NOAA and FEMA are good sources of hurricane information.

7 Which supporting detail is most important to include in a summary?

A "[There is] a 70 percent chance of 13 to 20 storms . . ."

B "Of those, three to six are expected to become major hurricanes."

C "[These conditions] lasted for several days while awaiting transportation back to the United States."

D "[W]e recommend you obtain travel insurance to cover unexpected expenses during an emergency."

8 Which sentence best summarizes the details in the third paragraph (lines 14–22)?

A Risks to travelers include delays, unsafe travel conditions, and risks to personal safety.

B U.S. citizens often experience hardships, such as looting and violence, when they are traveling to other countries.

C Drivers should be cautious during hurricane season as roadways might be washed away or have obstacles.

D Security personnel might be too busy with other issues to help U.S. citizens who are traveling in hurricane-prone areas.

9 Which text feature identifies important information that should be included in a summary of this passage?

A Boldfaced headings

B Italicized text

C Date

D Paragraph breaks

10 Read the following statements, which paraphrase the passage's main idea and supporting details.

i. During hurricane season, travelers should be prepared for emergencies.

ii. Purchasing traveler's insurance can help travelers with the unexpected expense of emergency evacuation.

iii. The NOAA does not recommend travel to other countries during hurricane season.

iv. Hurricane season affects certain regions from June through November.

v. Travelers should consider bringing a well-stocked emergency kit.

vi. Travelers should be prepared for unsafe and uncomfortable conditions after a hurricane.

vii. It is likely that 13 to 20 named storms will occur this season.

Which combination of statements should be included in a summary of the travel alert?

A ii, iii, v, vi, vii

B i, ii, iv, v, vi

C i, iii, iv, v, vii

D ii, iv, v, vi, vii

✔ Test-Taking Tip

When you are reading test passages, it is tempting to read the questions and then skim the passage to find the answers. Unfortunately, when you do not read the entire passage, you might miss important ideas or details. The gaps can cause confusion, especially with questions that ask you to perform higher-level thinking skills such as summarizing or synthesizing information. Always take time to read the passage thoroughly. Later you can skim the passage to find the details that are needed to answer questions.

Writing Practice

When you tell a friend about a favorite book or movie, you are providing a summary. Your summary might explain what problems the characters face, how a problem is solved, or why certain events are important. A summary that includes only the most important details will be precise and effective.

Write a **summary** of a movie that you have seen or a book that you have read. Begin with a paraphrase of the main idea. Then briefly describe key details that will help the reader understand important aspects of the movie or book.

_____

_____

_____

_____

_____

_____

_____

_____

_____

_____

_____

_____

_____

_____

_____

_____

_____

_____

_____

_____

_____

_____

_____

_____

_____

This lesson will help you practice identifying a theme in two different passages. Use it with Core Lesson 1.5 *Identify a Theme* to reinforce and apply your knowledge.

Key Concept

The theme is the underlying meaning of a story. An author reveals the theme in a work of fiction through characters, setting, language, and other literary elements.

Using Fictional Elements to Determine Theme

The theme is the central message of a text, and it may express the author's belief or opinion about life. The theme, however, is not always directly stated; it may be implied. The author may reveal the theme through the narrator's or characters' comments or actions.

This passage is a folktale that offers an explanation for how El Capitan, a rock formation in Yosemite Valley, was created.

Here were once two little boys living in the valley who went down to the river to swim. After paddling and splashing about to their hearts' content, they went on shore and crept up on a huge boulder which stood beside the water. They lay down in the warm sunshine to dry themselves, but fell asleep. They slept so soundly that they knew nothing, though the great boulder grew day by day,
5   and rose night by night, until it lifted them up beyond the sight of their tribe, who looked for them everywhere.

The rock grew until the boys were lifted high into the heaven, even far up above the blue sky, until they scraped their faces against the moon. And still, year after year, among the clouds they slept.

Then there was held a great council of all the animals to bring the boys down from the top of the
10   great rock. Every animal leaped as high as he could up the face of the rocky wall. Mouse could only jump as high as one's hand; Rat, twice as high. Then Raccoon tried; he could jump a little farther. One after another of the animals tried, and Grizzly Bear made a great leap far up the wall, but fell back. Last of all Lion tried, and he jumped farther than any other animal, but fell down upon his back. Then came tiny Measuring-Worm, and began to creep up the rock. Soon he reached as high as Raccoon had
15   jumped, then as high as Bear, then as high as Lion's leap, and by and by he was out of sight, climbing up the face of the rock. For one whole snow, Measuring-Worm climbed the rock, and at last he reached the top. Then he wakened the boys, and came down the same way he went up, and brought them down safely to the ground. Therefore the rock is called Tutokanula, the measuring worm. But white men call it El Capitan.

Excerpt from "Legend of Tu-Tok-A-Nu'-La (El Capitan)" from *Myths and Legends of California and the Old Southwest* edited by Katherine Berry Judson

1 The actions of the Measuring-Worm express the story's central message, or

   A theme.
   B main idea.
   C perspective.
   D topic sentence.

2 Which sentence below best states the theme of the passage?

   A When you work together, you can solve a problem.
   B Never judge someone by the way he or she looks.
   C By making a continued effort, you will finish the job.
   D The strongest person will survive in the end.

3 Which detail from the passage helps you understand the theme?

   A "And still, year after year, among the clouds they slept."
   B "Then there was held a great council of all the animals to bring the boys down from the top of the great rock."
   C "Every animal leaped as high as he could up the face of the rocky wall."
   D "For one whole snow, Measuring-Worm climbed the rock, and at last he reached the top."

4 Which of the following meanings associated with the word "creep" seems most intended in line 13?

   A A hateful, mean, or unpleasant person
   B A feeling of things crawling on your body
   C Spreading out or growing on a surface
   D Moving, slowly, low to the ground

Synthesizing Multiple Main Ideas to Determine Theme

To determine the theme of a text, synthesize information from fictional elements such as setting, plot, characterization, point of view, language, and conflict. As you read, also think about the main idea of each paragraph and synthesize these to state the theme.

This story is a satire that tells about an encounter between a king and a clever "inventor."

Having obtained an audience of the King an Ingenious Patriot pulled a paper from his pocket, saying:

May it please your Majesty, I have here a formula for constructing armour-plating which no gun can pierce. If these plates are adopted in the Royal Navy our warships will be invulnerable, and therefore invincible. Here, also, are reports of your Majesty's Ministers, attesting the value of the
5   invention. I will part with my right in it for a million tumtums."

After examining the papers, the King put them away and promised him an order on the Lord High Treasurer of the Extortion Department for a million tumtums.

"And here," said the Ingenious Patriot, pulling another paper from another pocket, "are the working plans of a gun that I have invented, which will pierce that armour. Your Majesty's Royal Brother, the
10   Emperor of Bang, is anxious to purchase it, but loyalty to your Majesty's throne and person constrains me to offer it first to your Majesty. The price is one million tumtums."

Having received the promise of another check, he thrust his hand into still another pocket, remarking:

"The price of the irresistible gun would have been much greater, your Majesty, but for the fact that its missiles can be so effectively averted by my peculiar method of treating the armour plates with a
15   new—"

(continued)

"The King signed to the Great Head Factotum to approach.

"Search this man," he said, "and report how many pockets he has."

"Forty-three, Sire," said the Great Head Factotum, completing the scrutiny.

"May it please your Majesty," cried the Ingenious Patriot, in terror, "one of them contains tobacco."

20   "Hold him up by the ankles and shake him," said the King; "then give him a check for forty-two million tumtums and put him to death. Let a decree issue declaring ingenuity a capital offence."

Excerpt from "The Ingenious Patriot" from *Fantastic Fables* by Ambrose Bierce

5 How does determining the point of view of the story help you understand the theme?

A From the king's perspective, you understand how difficult it is to protect one's kingdom.

B From the patriot's perspective, you learn the dangers of greed with those in authority.

C From the perspective of the Great Head Factotum, you learn a lesson about money.

D From the narrator's perspective, you understand the lessons the king and the patriot learned.

6 How is the author's characterization of the main character as a patriot helpful in understanding the theme?

A The character presents himself as a trusted and wise adviser to the king.

B The character calls himself loyal, but his actions show otherwise.

C The character acts with cunning and enriches himself by doing so.

D The character is penalized for his ingenuity and sales tactics.

7 Which sentence is the best statement of the theme of the passage?

A Rulers are not always fair.

B Weapons are dangerous.

C You can't always trust what a person says.

D You should always listen to wise advice.

8 Information from the characterization of the king and the patriot, the language used in the dialog, and the outcome of the interaction between the characters allow you to determine the theme by

A stating the information.

B quoting the information.

C synthesizing the information.

D summarizing the information.

✔ **Test-Taking Tip**

Some test answers can be found directly in a passage. For others, such as identifying theme and implied main ideas, you may need to synthesize information from several places. When you synthesize, make a list of important ideas. Mark out any that are not relevant. Then look for ways that the ideas are connected.

Writing Practice

There are many different types of short stories. Satires, such as "The Ingenious Patriot," reveal problems in society in a humorous way. Fables, such as "Legend of Tu-Tok-A-Nu'-La," are another type of short story. Fables sometimes explain how something was created and often have a moral. Topics for short stories range from solving a mystery to going on a magical adventure to explaining how bluebonnets came to Texas.

Write a short story. You may invent your own or retell a story you have read in your own words. Your short story should have a beginning, middle, and end. It should have a **theme** that is stated or implied, with details to support the theme.

_____

_____

_____

_____

_____

_____

_____

_____

_____

_____

_____

_____

_____

_____

_____

_____

_____

_____

_____

_____

_____

_____

This lesson will help you practice determining the sequence of events in two types of texts. Use it with Core Lesson 2.1 *Sequence Events* to reinforce and apply your knowledge.

Key Concept

The sequence of events is the order in which the events in a text occur.

Sequence of Time

To fully comprehend narrative passages and procedural texts, readers need to understand the order of events or steps. When you are reading a passage, use transitions and text features to help determine the sequence of events.

***Pride and Prejudice*, a novel written by English author Jane Austen, was published in 1813. The main characters of Austen's novels are often strong young women who confront social expectations, such as those related to marriage and social class.**

"In vain I have struggled. It will not do. My feelings will not be repressed. You must allow me to tell you how ardently I admire and love you."

Elizabeth's astonishment was beyond expression. She stared, coloured, doubted, and was silent. This he considered sufficient encouragement; and the avowal of all that he felt, and had long felt
5   for her, immediately followed. He spoke well; but there were feelings besides those of the heart to be detailed; and he was not more eloquent on the subject of tenderness than of pride. His sense of her inferiority—of its being a degradation—of the family obstacles which had always opposed to inclination, were dwelt on with a warmth which seemed due to the consequence he was wounding, but was very unlikely to recommend his suit.

10   In spite of her deeply rooted dislike, she could not be insensible to the compliment of such a man's affection, and though her intentions did not vary for an instant, she was at first sorry for the pain he was to receive; till, roused to resentment by his subsequent language, she lost all compassion in anger. She tried, however, to compose herself to answer him with patience, when he should have done. He concluded with representing to her the strength of that attachment which, in spite of all his
15   endeavours, he had found impossible to conquer; and with expressing his hope that it would now be rewarded by her acceptance of his hand. As he said this, she could easily see that he had no doubt of a favourable answer. He spoke of apprehension and anxiety, but his countenance expressed real security. Such a circumstance could only exasperate farther, and, when he ceased, the colour rose into her cheeks, and she said:

20   "In such cases as this, it is, I believe, the established mode to express a sense of obligation for the sentiments avowed, however unequally they may be returned. It is natural that obligation should be felt, and if I could feel gratitude, I would now thank you. But I cannot—I have never desired your good opinion, and you have certainly bestowed it most unwillingly. I am sorry to have occasioned pain to anyone. It has been most unconsciously done, however, and I hope will be of short duration. The
25   feelings which, you tell me, have long prevented the acknowledgment of your regard, can have little difficulty in overcoming it after this explanation."

Mr. Darcy, who was leaning against the mantelpiece with his eyes fixed on her face, seemed to catch her words with no less resentment than surprise. His complexion became pale with anger, and the disturbance of his mind was visible in every feature. He was struggling for the appearance of
30   composure, and would not open his lips till he believed himself to have attained it. The pause was to Elizabeth's feelings dreadful.

Excerpt from *Pride and Prejudice* by Jane Austen

1 Which pair of words or phrases in lines 11–13 are transitions that signal the time sequence?

A "instant" and "at first"

B "instant" and "till"

C "at first" and "till"

D "till" and "roused"

2 Which transition phrase in the text signals that something happened just before "the colour rose into [Elizabeth's] cheeks" in lines 18–19?

A "As he said"

B "but his countenance"

C "Such a circumstance"

D "when he ceased"

3 In the statement "<u>As he said this</u>, she could easily see that he had no doubt of a favourable answer," which phrase could logically replace the underlined text and convey the intended meaning?

A While he was saying this

B After he had said this

C Until he said this

D Subsequent to saying this

4 Which of the following meanings associated with the word "apprehension" seems most intended in line 17?

A Understanding

B Nervousness

C Hesitation

D Detention

5 Which of these events is the second event in the passage?

A Mr. Darcy expresses his feelings.

B Elizabeth expresses her feelings.

C Mr. Darcy becomes angry.

D Elizabeth becomes angry.

Sequence in a Process

Transition words make it easy to understand the order of a procedure or a process. In some cases, text features such as headings can also help readers understand the order of events or actions.

The U.S. Energy Information Administration publishes a variety of information to help consumers. This article explains where natural gas comes from.

How Was Natural Gas Formed?

The main ingredient in natural gas is methane, a gas (or compound) composed of one carbon atom and four hydrogen atoms. Millions of years ago, the remains of plants and animals (diatoms) decayed and built up in thick layers. This decayed matter from plants and animals is called organic material—it
5 was once alive. . . . Pressure and heat changed some of this organic material into coal, some into oil (petroleum), and some into natural gas—tiny bubbles of odorless gas.

In some places, gas escapes from small gaps in the rocks into the air; then, if there is enough activation energy from lightning or a fire, it burns. When people first saw the flames, they experimented with them and learned they could use them for heat and light.

10 ### How Do We Get Natural Gas?

The search for natural gas begins with geologists, who study the structure and processes of the Earth. They locate the types of rock that are likely to contain gas and oil deposits.

(continued)

Today, geologists' tools include seismic surveys that are used to find the right places to drill wells. Seismic surveys use echoes from a vibration source at the Earth's surface (usually a vibrating pad under a truck built for this purpose) to collect information about the rocks beneath. Sometimes it is necessary to use small amounts of dynamite to provide the vibration that is needed.

Scientists and engineers explore a chosen area by studying rock samples from the earth and taking measurements. If the site seems promising, drilling begins. Some of these areas are on land, but many are offshore, deep in the ocean. Once the gas is found, it flows up through the well to the surface of the ground and into large pipelines.

Some of the gases that are produced along with methane, such as butane and propane (also known as "by-products"), are separated and cleaned at a gas processing plant. The by-products, once removed, are used in a number of ways. For example, propane can be used for cooking on gas grills.

Dry natural gas is also known as consumer-grade natural gas. In addition to natural gas production, the U.S. gas supply is augmented by imports, withdrawals from storage, and by supplemental gaseous fuels.

Most of the natural gas consumed in the United States is produced in the United States. Some is imported from Canada and shipped to the United States in pipelines. A small amount of natural gas is shipped to the United States as liquefied natural gas (LNG).

We can also use machines called "digesters" that turn today's organic material (plants, animal wastes, etc.) into natural gas. This process replaces waiting for millions of years for the gas to form naturally.

Excerpt from "Natural Gas Basics" by the U.S. Energy Information Administration

6 The sequence of events noted in the section "How Was Natural Gas Formed?" describes a

A   process.

B   flashback.

C   transition.

D   feature.

7 Which description best explains how this text is arranged?

A   Two processes described in order of importance

B   Two processes described with interrupting flashbacks

C   Two processes described, each in reverse chronological order

D   Two processes described, each in chronological order

8 Which text feature helps indicate that the process of forming natural gas comes before the process of obtaining it?

A   Visual graphics

B   Title

C   Boldfaced headings

D   Underlined phrases

9 On the basis of information from the section "How Do We Get Natural Gas?," which transition phrase would accurately complete the following sentence: "Scientists study samples and take measurements . . ."

A   before taking a seismic survey.

B   after taking a seismic survey.

C   while taking a seismic survey.

D   until taking a seismic survey.

Test-Taking Tip

When you read a passage, take note of section headings that organize the passage. These headings can also help you find the correct answer to a test question. Later, when you read the questions, notice whether a question tells you where in the passage to look for an answer. Going straight to that section will help you find the information quickly.

Writing Practice

Sometimes when telling stories about a past event, events are described out order. When you do this, it is important to use transition words to indicate that you are breaking from chronological order.

Write a paragraph about an experience in which you taught someone how to do something. For example, it could be about teaching a younger sibling how to ride a bike or showing your grandfather how to write an e-mail. Your **process** should have at least four steps. Include at least one detail that is **out of sequence**, and use **transition** words to indicate at which point in the process this step occurred.

_____

_____

_____

_____

_____

_____

_____

_____

_____

_____

_____

_____

_____

_____

_____

_____

_____

_____

_____

_____

_____

_____

_____

This lesson will help you practice inferring relationships within two literary texts. Use it with Core Lesson 2.2 *Infer Relationships between Events, People, and Ideas* to reinforce and apply your knowledge.

Key Concept

Making an inference is determining the most likely explanation for the given information.

Inferring a Writer's Meaning

To make inferences about a text, use a combination of explicit details and implied information as clues. Then combine this information with your personal knowledge to draw conclusions about the relationships among characters, events, setting, and ideas in a text.

"Dick Baker's Cat" is a short story by Mark Twain, an American author who wrote many stories about larger-than-life characters. This story, about the relationship between a miner and his cat in the old West, is told in dialect—language used by a specific group of people.

One of my comrades . . . was one of the gentlest spirits. . . . Dick Baker, pocket-miner of Dead-Horse Gulch. He was forty-six, grey as a rat, earnest, thoughtful, slenderly educated, slouchily dressed and clay-soiled, but his heart was finer metal than any gold his shovel ever brought to light.

5   Whenever he was . . . a little downhearted, he would fall to mourning over the loss of a wonderful cat he used to own. . . . [H]e always spoke of the strange sagacity of that cat with the air of a man who believed in his secret heart that there was something human about it—maybe even supernatural.

I heard him talking about this animal once. He said:

"Gentlemen, I used to have a cat by the name of Tom Quartz . . . and he was the remarkablest cat *I* ever see. . . . [H]e had more hard, natchral sense than any man in this camp. . . . He knowed more about 10 mining . . . than any man *I* ever, ever see. . . . He would dig out after me an' Jim when we went over the hills prospect'n', and he would trot along behind us for as much as five mile. . . . [I]f the ground suited him, he would lay low . . . till the first pan was washed. . . . [T]hen he would sidle up 'n' take a look, an' if there was about six or seven grains of gold he was satisfied. . . . Then he would lay down on our coats and snore like a steamboat till we'd struck the pocket, an' then get up 'n' superintend. . . .

15   "Well, by an' by, up comes this yer quartz excitement. Everybody was into it—everybody was . . . pick'n' 'n' blast'n' instead of shovelin' dirt on the hillside—everybody was putt'n' down a shaft instead of scrapin' the surface. Noth'n' would do Jim, but we must tackle the ledges, too, 'n' so we did. We commenced putt'n' down a shaft. . . . Tom Quartz . . . hadn't ever seen any mining like that before, 'n' he was all upset. . . . *You* know how it is with old habits. But by an' by Tom Quartz begin to git sort of 20 reconciled a little, though he never could altogether understand that eternal sinkin' of a shaft an' never pannin' out anything. At last he got to comin' down in the shaft, hisself to try to cipher it out. An' he would curl up on a gunny-sack in the corner an' go to sleep. . . .

(continued)

"Well, one day when the shaft was down about eight foot, the rock got so hard that we had to put in a blast. . . . [W]e lit the fuse 'n' clumb out 'n' got off 'bout fifty yards—'n' forgot . . . Tom Quartz sound
25 asleep on the gunny-sack. In 'bout a minute we seen a puff of smoke bust up out of the hole. [A]bout four million ton of rocks 'n' dirt 'n' smoke 'n' splinters shot up 'bout a mile an' a half into the air. . . .

". . . right in the dead centre of it was old Tom Quartz a-goin' end over end, an' a-snortin' an' a-sneez'n. . . . An' that was the last we see of *him* for about two minutes 'n' a half. . . . [T]hen all of a sudden it begin to rain rocks . . . an' directly he come down ker-whoop. . . . One ear was sot back on
30 his neck, 'n' his tail was stove up, 'n' his eye-winkers was singed off. . . . [H]e was all blacked up with powder an' smoke, an' all sloppy with mud 'n' slush f'm one end to the other. . . . He took a sort of a disgusted look at hisself. . . . [T]hen he turned . . . 'n' marched off. . . ."

Excerpt from "Dick Baker's Cat" by Mark Twain

1   **Based on the narrator's description of Dick Baker at the beginning of the story, the reader can infer that the narrator considers Baker to be**

   A clever but ultimately cruel.

   B simple and uneducated but kind.

   C good at mining but bad with money.

   D well educated and a sharp dresser.

2   **The narrator explicitly states that Dick Baker believes his cat has near-human intelligence. What does the narrator imply about his own personal opinion of the cat's ability?**

   A The cat has amazing intelligence.

   B Dogs are more intelligent than cats.

   C Tom Quartz is smarter than Jim.

   D The cat's near-human intelligence is doubtful.

3   **Beginning with line 11 ("[I]f the ground suited him . . . ") through line 14, the cat's behavior would be best described as**

   A so unbelievable that it would seem supernatural to most observers.

   B impressive for a cat, but regarded by its owner as unremarkable.

   C normal for most cats, but interpreted by the owner as humanlike.

   D typical of a trained circus animal but not of a pet cat.

4   **Dick Baker describes the miners' enthusiasm for quartz. Based on his description and the choice of words, what can you infer about the cat?**

   A The cat hopes to find a large supply of quartz.

   B The cat does not think quartz is salable.

   C The cat prefers digging deep to searching the topsoil.

   D The cat thinks underground mining is not worthwhile.

5   **From the description of what happens to Tom Quartz after Dick lit the fuse, what can you infer about Dick's feelings about the event?**

   A It is devastating.

   B It is amusing.

   C It is pleasing.

   D It is frightening.

Citing Evidence

When making inferences about a text, a reader must look for evidence in the text. Evidence can include opinions, examples, and facts.

"The House in the Mist" is a short story by Anna Katharine Green. The narrator of this tale describes his first sight of a mysterious house shrouded in the mist and explains what made him go there.

It was a night to drive any man indoors. Not only was the darkness impenetrable, but the raw mist enveloping hill and valley made the open road anything but desirable to a belated wayfarer like myself.

Being young . . . I was not averse to adventure. . . . Consequently, when I saw a light shimmering through the mist . . . I resolved to make for it and the shelter it so opportunely offered.

5 But I did not realise then . . . that shelter does not necessarily imply refuge, or I might not have undertaken this adventure. . . . Yet who knows? The impulses of an unfettered spirit lean toward daring, and youth . . . seeks the strange, the unknown, and sometimes the terrible.

My path towards this light was by no means an easy one. After confused wanderings through tangled hedges . . . I arrived in front of a long, low building, which, to my astonishment, I found
10 standing with doors and windows open . . . save for one . . . through which the light shone from a row of candles. . . .

The quiet and seeming emptiness of this odd and picturesque building made me pause. I am not much affected by visible danger, but this silent room, with its air of sinister expectancy, struck me most unpleasantly. . . . I was about to reconsider my first impulse and withdraw again to the road,
15 when a second look . . . sent me straight toward the door which stood so invitingly open.

But half-way up the path my progress was again stayed by the sight of a man issuing from the house. . . . He seemed in haste, and . . . was engaged in replacing his watch in his pocket.

But he did not shut the door behind him, which I thought odd, especially as his final glance had been a backward one [at] the place he was so hurriedly leaving.

20 As we met he raised his hat. . . . Indeed, he was so little impressed by my presence there that he was for passing me without a word. . . . But this did not suit me. I was hungry, cold, and eager for creature comforts. . . . [T]he house before me gave forth, not only heat, but a savoury odour. . . . I therefore accosted the man.

"Will bed and supper be provided for me here?" I asked. "I am tired . . . and hungry enough to pay
25 anything in reason—."

I stopped, for the man had disappeared. . . . But at the break in my sentence his voice came back in good-natured tones. . . .

"Supper will be ready at nine, and there are beds for all. Enter, sir; you are the first to arrive, but the others cannot be far behind."

30 A queer greeting certainly. . . .

"Well," thought I. . . . "He invited me to enter, and enter I will."

(continued)

The house . . . was no ordinary farm-building, but a rambling old mansion. . . . Though furnished, warmed, and lighted with candles, . . . it had about it an air of disuse which made me feel myself an intruder, in spite of the welcome I had received. [E]re long I found myself inside the great room and
35 before the blazing logs whose glow had lighted up the doorway and added its own attraction to the other allurements of the inviting place.

Though the open door made a draught which was anything but pleasant, I did not feel like closing it, and was astonished to observe the effect of the mist through the square thus left open to the night. It was not an agreeable one. . . . I let my eyes roam over the . . . walls and . . . furniture which gave
40 such an air of old-fashioned richness to the place. . . . But the solitude . . . struck cold to my heart, and I missed the cheer rightfully belonging to such attractive surroundings.

Excerpt from *Room Number 3 and Other Detective Stories* by Anna Katharine Green

6 **In lines 1 and 2, the phrases "darkness [was] impenetrable" and "raw mist [was] enveloping hill and valley" are**

A opinions expressed by the narrator about weather conditions.

B inferences made by the reader about the story's setting.

C facts about weather conditions where the author lived.

D examples to illustrate the idea that it is not a good night to be outdoors.

7 **In line 6, the word "unfettered" most nearly means**

A unrestrained.

B unnatural.

C unguarded.

D unforgiving.

8 **Which statement from the passage could you cite to support the inference that the narrator feels uneasy in this setting?**

A "The house . . . was no ordinary farm-building, but a rambling old mansion."

B "Though furnished, warmed, and lighted with candles, . . . it had about it an air of disuse . . ."

C . . . which made me feel myself an intruder, in spite of the welcome I had received."

D "I found myself . . . before the blazing logs whose glow had . . . added its own attraction . . ."

9 **Which statement is a valid inference that a reader might make after reading the passage?**

A No one has ever lived in the house.

B The man leaving the house is the butler.

C Other people have been invited to the house.

D The narrator decides to leave the house immediately.

✓ **Test-Taking Tip**

Use your prior knowledge when making inferences about a passage on a test. Before reading the passage, read the title, study illustrations or graphics that accompany the text, and skim the passage for words that are highlighted or often repeated. Then use what you already know about these words and ideas to predict which topics are likely to be discussed in the passage. While you read, combine details in the text with what you already know to make inferences that help you understand what you are reading.

Writing Practice

When writing, authors do not explain everything they want readers to know. Many details are implicit; readers must make inferences to understand the meaning of the text.

Think of a person you find inspiring. Make a list of two facts and two opinions about that person. **Analyze** your details to see how they relate to one another. Next, figure out one more characteristic of the person that you could **imply** in your paragraph. Then write a paragraph that explicitly states the two facts and two opinions and implies the additional detail. Make sure that the additional detail is implied by the relationship between the stated facts and opinions.

This lesson will help you practice analyzing relationships among text elements in two literary passages. Use it with Core Lesson 2.3 *Analyze Relationships between Ideas* to reinforce and apply your knowledge.

Key Concept

Relationships exist between different text elements—between characters, between characters and setting, between plot and setting, or between ideas.

Identifying Literary Elements

Literary texts, especially stories, contain certain key elements that help build the narrative, or the story that is being told. The key elements include plot, setting, theme, and character. Writers use characterization to describe their characters through details such as dialogue, actions, and descriptions.

A Christmas Carol by Charles Dickens is a well-loved tale that introduces Ebenezer Scrooge, the man who hates Christmas, to readers around the world.

Once upon a time—of all the good days in the year, on Christmas Eve—old Scrooge sat busy in his counting-house. It was cold, bleak, biting weather: foggy withal: and he could hear the people in the court outside, go wheezing up and down, beating their hands upon their breasts, and stamping their feet upon the pavement stones to warm them. The city clocks had only just gone three, but it
5   was quite dark already—it had not been light all day—and candles were flaring in the windows of the neighbouring offices, like ruddy smears upon the palpable brown air. The fog came pouring in at every chink and keyhole, and was so dense without, that although the court was of the narrowest, the houses opposite were mere phantoms. To see the dingy cloud come drooping down, obscuring everything, one might have thought that Nature lived hard by, and was brewing on a large scale.

10   The door of Scrooge's counting-house was open that he might keep his eye upon his clerk, who in a dismal little cell beyond, a sort of tank, was copying letters. Scrooge had a very small fire, but the clerk's fire was so very much smaller that it looked like one coal. But he couldn't replenish it, for Scrooge kept the coal-box in his own room; and so surely as the clerk came in with the shovel, the master predicted that it would be necessary for them to part. Wherefore the clerk put on his white
15   comforter, and tried to warm himself at the candle; in which effort, not being a man of a strong imagination, he failed.

"A merry Christmas, uncle! God save you!" cried a cheerful voice. It was the voice of Scrooge's nephew, who came upon him so quickly that this was the first intimation he had of his approach.

"Bah!" said Scrooge, "Humbug!"

20   He had so heated himself with rapid walking in the fog and frost, this nephew of Scrooge's that he was all in a glow; his face was ruddy and handsome; his eyes sparkled, and his breath smoked again.

"Christmas a humbug, uncle!" said Scrooge's nephew. "You don't mean that, I am sure?"

"I do," said Scrooge. "Merry Christmas! What right have you to be merry? What reason have you to be merry? You're poor enough."

(continued)

25   "Come, then," returned the nephew gaily. "What right have you to be dismal? What reason have you to be morose? You're rich enough."

Scrooge having no better answer ready on the spur of the moment, said, "Bah!" again; and followed it up with "Humbug."

Excerpt from *A Christmas Carol: A Ghost Story of Christmas* by Charles Dickens

1 **Which detail from the passage describes the story's main character, Scrooge?**

A   He felt very cold.

B   He was in a bad mood.

C   He had a cheerful voice.

D   He did not have much money.

2 **The phrases "cold, bleak, biting weather: foggy withal" (line 2) and "it had not been light all day" (line 5) are details about the story's**

A   characters.

B   narrative.

C   setting.

D   theme.

3 **Which event is not part of the plot in this passage?**

A   Scrooge says, "Bah! Humbug!"

B   Scrooge walks through the fog to the counting house.

C   Scrooge's clerk tries to warm himself with heat from a candle.

D   Scrooge's nephew comes to visit his uncle on the morning of Christmas Eve.

4 **Which quotation from the passage is an example of characterization?**

A   "The city clocks had only just gone three . . ."

B   "candles were flaring in the windows of the neighbouring offices . . ."

C   "see the dingy cloud come drooping down . . ."

D   "his face was ruddy and handsome; his eyes sparkled . . ."

Analyzing Relationships in Text

The various relationships among the setting, characters, and events in the plot can help you understand or infer a story's theme.

A woman has reported a crime and given authorities a description of the place where the crime occurred. This excerpt from a work of fiction portrays the beginning of the investigation into the woman's allegations.

"What door is that? You've opened all the others; why do you pass that one by?"

". . . That's only Number 3. A mere closet, gentlemen," responded the landlord in a pleasant voice. . . . "Jake, the clerk you saw below, used it last night. But it's not on our regular list. Do you want a peep at it?"

5   "Most assuredly. . . ."

". . . There, gentlemen!" he cried, unlocking the door and holding it open. . . . "You see it no more answers the young lady's description than the others. . . . The old lady never put foot in this tavern."

The two men . . . peered into the shadowy recesses . . . , and one of them, a tall and uncommonly good-looking young man . . . , stepped softly inside. He was a gentleman farmer living near, recently
10   appointed deputy sheriff. . . .

(continued)

"I observe," he remarked . . . , "that the paper on these walls is not at all like that she describes. She . . . said that it was of a muddy pink colour and had big scrolls. . . . This paper is blue and striped. Otherwise—"

"Let's go below," suggested his companion. . . . "It's cold here, and there are several new questions
15 I should like to put to the young lady. Mr. Quimby,"—this to the landlord, "I've no doubt you are right, but we'll give this poor girl another chance. . . ."

"My reputation is in your hands, Coroner Golden," was the quiet reply. Then, as they both turned, "my reputation against the word of an obviously demented girl."

The words made their own echo. As the third man moved to follow the other two into the hall, . . .
20 he involuntarily cast another look behind him as if expectant of some contradiction reaching him from the bare and melancholy walls he was leaving. But no such contradiction came. . . . The dull blue paper . . . was . . . grimy with age. . . . Certainly he was a dreamer to doubt such plain evidences. . . . Yet—

. . . Had it occurred to him to turn again before rounding the corner—but no, I doubt if he would
25 have learned anything. . . . The closing of a door by a careful hand . . . what is there . . . to re-awaken curiosity and fix suspicion? Nothing, when the man concerned is Jacob Quimby; nothing. Better that he failed to look back; it left his judgment freer for the question confronting him in the room below.

Three Forks Tavern . . . was . . . situated just back of the highway . . . between the two towns of Chester and Danton in southern Ohio. It . . . had all the picturesquesness of age and the English
30 traditions of its original builder. Though so near two thriving towns, it retained its own quality of apparent remoteness. . . . This in a measure was made possible by the nearness of the woods which almost enveloped it; but the character of the man who ran it had still more to do with it, his sympathies being entirely with the old, and not at all with the new. . . . This, while it appealed to . . . summer boarders, did not so much meet the wants of the casual traveller, so that while the house might from
35 some reason or other be overfilled one night, it was just as likely to be almost empty the next. . . . The building itself was of wooden construction . . . with gables . . . projecting here and there. . . . These gables were new, that is, they were only a century old; the portion . . . in . . . which we first found the men we have introduced to you, was the original house.

Excerpt from *Room Number 3 and Other Detective Stories* by Anna Katharine Greene

5 **Which statement best describes the relationship between the setting and plot of this passage?**

A Three men walk down a hallway of an old tavern.

B A man questions the sanity of a young woman involved in a crime.

C A conversation between three men reveals information about a crime.

D A man makes observations about a room possibly involved in a crime.

6 **Which statement describes the relationship between the characters and events in this passage?**

A A coroner convinces a suspicious deputy sheriff to investigate a local tavern owner.

B A tavern owner cooperates with the investigation by a coroner and a deputy sheriff.

C A coroner and a deputy sheriff discover that a tavern owner is the prime suspect in a crime.

D A demented young woman tells a deputy sheriff that a tavern owner committed a crime.

7 Which phrase best describes the relationship between Three Forks Tavern and its owner, as explained in the last paragraph (lines 28–38)?

A The owner is indifferent to the tavern

B The tavern has an impact on the owner's mood.

C The owner wants to keep the tavern from changing.

D The tavern is important in changing the owner's life.

8 A key detail that ties the story's plot to its setting is

A the gable on the building.

B the striped blue wallpaper in Room 3.

C the fact that Room 3 is where Jake slept.

D the closeness of the tavern to Danton, Ohio.

9 What does "retained" in line 30 mean?

A Employed

B Restrained

C Preserved

D Remembered

10 The deputy sheriff's thoughts could be evidence to support which of these themes?

A The importance of being truthful about one's objectives

B The importance of considering other people's point of view

C The importance of considering everyone to be a suspect at first

D The importance of intuition and careful observations in judgments

Test-Taking Tip

Understanding what a question is asking is an important part of taking a test. Unfortunately not all questions are simple and easy to understand. When you come across a long or complex question, especially one referring to a passage, read it carefully. Then try separating the question into parts. For example: Does part of the question tell you where to look for the answer? What is the question asking you about the passage you read? What is the question asking or telling you about the answer options? Does the question throw in a "twist," such as asking which answer does <u>not</u> relate to the text?

Writing Practice

All narratives have a setting, and the setting often plays an important role in the events that occur in a narrative. For example, the place where a wedding is held might make the event romantic, memorable, or even comical. A journey might be exciting because of the surprises that come from experiencing a new place. The events that unfold might be affected as much by the setting as by the characters involved.

Write a paragraph describing an important event in your life that happened in a memorable place. Be sure to describe the **setting** as well as the event. Make it clear why the place was important for this particular event.

This lesson will help you practice determining implicit relationships between ideas in two types of texts. Use it with Core Lesson 2.4 *Determine Implicit Relationships between Ideas* to reinforce and apply your knowledge.

Key Concept

Just as ideas are sometimes implied by writers, so are the relationships between ideas. When this occurs, readers must find clues in the text to help them understand how the ideas connect.

Interpreting Implied Relationships between Ideas

Authors sometimes present explicit ideas with implicit relationships among them. Readers often need to make inferences about these relationships for a full understanding of a text. Readers can use language structure, punctuation, and the proximity of words and ideas to support their inferences.

As Earth spins on its axis, it is heated unevenly. This uneven heating creates a variety of temperatures and moisture levels in air masses. These differences affect Earth's water cycle— the continuous movement of water from Earth's surface to the atmosphere and back again, through evaporation, condensation, and precipitation.

Humidity and Temperature Affect Air Masses

Humidity and temperature affect how masses of air interact in the atmosphere. Air masses are created when a body of air takes on characteristics from the land or water over which it forms. The central region of Canada usually creates cold and dry air masses. Air masses over the Gulf of Mexico
5   are warm and humid. The Pacific Northwest has cool air masses that are also humid. Air masses over the southwestern region of the United States are often dry, but warm. Air masses that move across the United States from west to east help meteorologists predict the weather.

Cold air masses are usually unstable and turbulent, and they move faster than warm air masses. When a cold air mass comes into contact with a warm air mass, the warmer air is forced upwards. Any
10   moisture in that air condenses quickly, forming cumulus clouds—puffy clouds that look like cotton balls. If the warm air has a lot of moisture, it forms cumulonimbus or thunderhead clouds, storm clouds that drop a heavy load of precipitation quickly. Often the quick rush of moist air separates the electric charges within the cloud, creating lightning. This release of charged particles superheats individual air particles. They expand so fast that small sonic booms, or thunder, are heard.

15   Warm air masses are usually stable, with steady wind. Clouds formed by warm air masses are stratus clouds—low-lying, level clouds that bring precipitation in the form of drizzle in warm weather. As the warm air continues to move up and over the cooler air mass, the clouds become higher and thinner. The high, wispy clouds are cirrus clouds; they do not hold enough moisture to form precipitation.

(continued)

20   **Air Masses Cause Fronts**

A front occurs when two air masses collide, forming a boundary between them. Strong fronts generally bring precipitation. When cold air pushes warm air, a cold front forms. If the warm air pushes the cold air away, a warm front forms. Sometimes, the boundary between the two air masses does not move; the front becomes stationary. Stationary fronts bring conditions similar to those of a warm front,
25   but precipitation that results is usually milder and lasts longer.

More commonly, these fronts take place at the change of seasons. In the central part of the United States, spring brings collisions of newly arriving warm, moist air from the Gulf of Mexico with retreating dry, cold air from central Canada. This generates conditions that can cause a tornado, the result of a very isolated strong updraft of warm, moist air. Because of Earth's rotation, the updraft
30   has a counterclockwise spin. (This is known as the Coriolis Effect, a force that affects all wind and water currents in both hemispheres. It is the reason that trade vessels coming from Europe to North America must travel south to the equator instead of straight across the Atlantic.) Tornadoes may have wind speeds of up to 300 miles per hour and travel across the ground at up to 70 miles per hour. Most tornadoes are produced in a region known as Tornado Alley: an area from central Texas, northward to
35   northern Iowa, and from central Kansas and Nebraska east to western Ohio.

Hurricanes are also seasonal storms. Hurricane season is August through October, when conditions are right for the movement of large low-pressure circulation patterns fueled by warm ocean waters near the equator. All Atlantic and Gulf of Mexico coastal areas are at risk for hurricanes. The storms can produce winds of more than 155 miles, heavy rainfall, and damaging storm surges.

1   **In lines 1–7 , what information is implied by explicit details about air masses?**

   A   Air masses in the Southwest are dry.

   B   Humidity affects how air masses interact.

   C   Air masses over the Gulf of Mexico are warm.

   D   The weather in central Canada is usually cold and dry.

2   **The wording and sentence structure of lines 8 and 15 make it clear that the author is**

   A   comparing similar characteristics of warm and cold air masses.

   B   contrasting different characteristics of warm and cold air masses.

   C   explaining how warm air masses slowly become cold air masses.

   D   explaining how cold air masses slowly become warm air masses.

3   **The details about cold and warm air masses in the second and third paragraphs (lines 8–19) could lead a reader to infer that**

   A   gusty winds accompany warm air masses.

   B   puffy, cotton-like clouds indicate nice weather.

   C   cold air masses cause greater precipitation than warm air masses.

   D   rain occurs only when cold air masses come in contact with warm air masses.

4   **On the basis of text details about storms, readers can logically infer that**

   A   tornadoes happen most often over water.

   B   tornadoes occur most often in northwestern states, like Oregon.

   C   the Coriolis Effect causes hurricanes to have a clockwise spin.

   D   the Coriolis Effect causes hurricanes to have a counterclockwise spin.

Citing Evidence of Implied Relationships

When inferring the relationship between ideas, a reader must support inferences with evidence supporting the implied relationship. Based on this evidence, the reader can predict outcomes within the text or predict how this evidence may apply to other texts or to situations outside of one particular text.

The Importance of Being Earnest, **written in 1895 by Irish playwright Oscar Wilde, is a comedy about Victorian etiquette and social classes. The main character, Jack, creates an alter-ego named Ernest. In the following excerpt, Jack's deception threatens to catches up with him.**

JACK. . . . I would like to . . . take advantage of Lady Bracknell's temporary absence. . . .

GWENDOLEN. . . . I would certainly advise you to do so. Mamma has a way of coming back suddenly. . . .

5 **JACK.** . . . (*Nervously.*) Miss Fairfax, ever since I met you I have admired you more than any girl . . . I have ever met since . . . I met you.

GWENDOLEN. . . . Yes, I am quite well aware of the fact. . . . And I often wish that in public, at any rate, you had been more demonstrative. . . . Even before I met you I was far from indifferent to you. (JACK *looks at her in amasement.*) . . . [M]y ideal has always been to love someone of the name of Ernest. There is something in that name that inspires absolute confidence. The moment Algernon first
10 mentioned . . . a friend called Ernest, I knew I was destined to love you.

JACK. . . . You really love me, Gwendolen?

GWENDOLEN. . . . My own Ernest!

JACK. . . . But you don't really mean . . . that you couldn't love me if my name wasn't Ernest?

GWENDOLEN. . . . But your name is Ernest.

15 **JACK.** . . . Yes, I know it is. But supposing it was something else? Do you mean . . . you couldn't love me then?

GWENDOLEN. . . . (*Glibly*) Ah! That is clearly a metaphysical speculation, and has very little reference at all to the actual facts of real life. . . .

JACK. . . . Personally, darling . . . I don't think the name suits me at all.

20 **GWENDOLEN.** . . . It suits you perfectly. It is a divine name. It has a music of its own. It produces vibrations.

JACK. . . . I think there are . . . much nicer names. I think Jack, for instance, a charming name.

GWENDOLEN. . . . Jack? . . . No, there is very little music in the name Jack. . . . It produces absolutely no vibrations. . . . I have known several Jacks, and they all, without exception, were more
25 than usually plain. . . . The only really safe name is Ernest.

JACK. . . . Gwendolen, I must get christened at once—I mean we must get married at once. . . .

GWENDOLEN. . . . Married, Mr. Worthing?

JACK. . . . (*Astounded.*) Well. . . . You know that I love you, and you led me to believe, Miss Fairfax, that you were not absolutely indifferent to me.

30 **GWENDOLEN.** . . . I adore you. But you haven't proposed. . . .

JACK. . . . Gwendolen!

GWENDOLEN. . . . Yes, Mr. Worthing . . . ?

JACK. . . . Gwendolen, will you marry me? (*Goes on his knees.*)

GWENDOLEN. . . . Of course I will, darling. How long you have been about it! I am afraid you
35 have had very little experience in how to propose.

(continued)

(Enter LADY BRACKNELL.)

    LADY BRACKNELL. . . . Mr. Worthing! Rise, sir, from this semi-recumbent posture. It is most indecorous.

    GWENDOLEN. . . . Mamma! (*He tries to rise; she restrains him.*) I must beg you to retire. This is
40   no place for you. Besides, Mr. Worthing has not quite finished yet.

    LADY BRACKNELL. . . . Finished what, may I ask?

    GWENDOLEN. . . . I am engaged to Mr. Worthing, Mamma. (*They rise together.*)

    LADY BRACKNELL. . . . Pardon me, you are not engaged to anyone. When you do become engaged to someone, I, or your father . . . will inform you of the fact. An engagement should come on
45   a young girl as a surprise. . . . It is hardly a matter that she could be allowed to arrange for herself. . . . Gwendolen . . . wait for me below in the carriage.

      Excerpt from *The Importance of Being Earnest* by Oscar Wilde

5 The statement "Mamma has a way of coming back suddenly. . . ." is evidence to support which predicted outcome?

  A Gwendolen's mother will like Jack.

  B Gwendolen's mother is Jack's mother.

  C Gwendolen's mother is out shopping.

  D Gwendolen's mother will walk in any minute.

6 In line 39, the word "retire" most nearly means

  A to leave a career.

  B to go away.

  C to go to bed.

  D to take out of service.

7 Which of these statements is a logical inference a reader might make?

  A Algernon dislikes Jack and Gwendolen.

  B Jack does not know Algernon.

  C Algernon is Gwendolen's cousin.

  D Jack and Gwendolen both know Algernon.

8 The proximity of the statements "I must get christened at once" and "I mean we must get married at once" implies that

  A Jack wants to be christened, or named, Algernon.

  B Jack wants to be christened, or renamed, after he gets married.

  C Jack wants to change his name so he can get married as Ernest.

  D Jack wants to change Gwendolen's name before they get married.

✓ Test-Taking Tip

When you answer questions about a reading passage, you should search the passage for the answers. However, to save time, first read the question and answer choices carefully for clues so you can focus your search.

Writing Practice

When writing a text, an author can use structure and patterns to reveal his or her ideas without stating them. For example, an author can describe one item with very favorable language, and then describe the negative attributes of a similar item. It will then be inferred by the reader that the author prefers the item he or she described with more positive words.

Write a paragraph **comparing and contrasting** two different cities you have visited or lived in. Structure your sentences so that it is clear that you are comparing and contrasting these cities without saying so explicitly. Include at least two similarities and two differences. Include at least one statement that implies (but does not state) that one city is better than the other city.

This lesson will help you practice analyzing details to understand two types of complex texts. Use it with Core Lesson 2.5 *Analyze the Role of Details in Complex Texts* to reinforce and apply your knowledge.

Key Concept

The details in complex informational and literary texts provide clues to the main ideas, significance of events, and relationships implied by the author.

Examining Complex Literary Texts

Complex literary texts often contain challenging words, abstract ideas, or implicit purposes. In addition, the subject might be unfamiliar, the text might have more than one theme, and the text structure might be unusual. To understand complex literary texts, readers should scan the text to pick up clues from the title and key details, combine these clues with their knowledge, and draw from their life experiences.

The following passage is narrated by a man who explains his past to provide context for a "wild" story. It is from a short story by the American author Edgar Allan Poe.

For the most wild, yet most homely narrative which I am about to pen, I neither expect nor solicit belief. Mad indeed would I be to expect it in a case where my very senses reject their own evidence. Yet mad am I not—and very surely do I not dream. But tomorrow I die, and today I would unburthen my soul. My immediate purpose is to place before the world plainly, succinctly, and without comment,
5   a series of mere household events. In their consequences these events have terrified—have tortured— have destroyed me. Yet I will not attempt to expound them. To me they presented little but horror—to many they will seem less terrible than *baroques*. Hereafter, perhaps, some intellect may be found which will reduce my phantasm to the commonplace—some intellect more calm, more logical, and far less excitable than my own, which will perceive, in the circumstances I detail with awe, nothing more than
10   an ordinary succession of very natural causes and effects.

From my infancy I was noted for the docility and humanity of my disposition. My tenderness of heart was even so conspicuous as to make me the jest of my companions. I was especially fond of animals, and was indulged by my parents with a great variety of pets. With these I spent most of my time, and never was so happy as when feeding and caressing them. This peculiarity of character grew
15   with my growth, and in my manhood I derived from it one of my principal sources of pleasure. To those who have cherished an affection for a faithful and sagacious dog, I need hardly be at the trouble of explaining the nature or the intensity of the gratification thus derivable. There is something in the unselfish and self-sacrificing love of a brute which goes directly to the heart of him who has had frequent occasion to test the paltry friendship and gossamer fidelity of mere *Man*.

20   I married early, and was happy to find in my wife a disposition not uncongenial with my own. Observing my partiality for domestic pets, she lost no opportunity of procuring those of the most agreeable kind. We had birds, gold-fish, a fine dog, rabbits, a small monkey, and *a cat*.

This latter was a remarkably large and beautiful animal, entirely black, and sagacious to an astonishing degree. In speaking of his intelligence, my wife, who at heart was not a little tinctured
25   with superstition, made frequent allusion to the ancient popular notion which regarded all black cats as witches in disguise. Not that she was ever serious upon this point, and I mention the matter at all for no better reason than that it happens just now to be remembered.

Excerpt from "The Black Cat" by Edgar Allan Poe

1 By scanning the title and the first sentence of each paragraph, the reader can tell that the narrator is discussing

A his life and his cat.

B cats and superstitions.

C his childhood and relatives.

D marriage and fiction writing.

2 Choose the phrase that best completes the following summary of lines 1 through 10: The narrator says that perhaps readers will

A be persuaded to agree with the events he is about to describe.

B be terrified yet entertained by the events he is about to describe.

C determine a logical explanation for the events he is about to describe.

D understand why he has written about the events he is about to describe.

3 Which statement best summarizes the main idea of lines 20 through 22?

A The narrator's wife had pets of all different kinds.

B The narrator married someone who was agreeable.

C The narrator married someone who shared his loved of animals.

D The narrator's wife allowed him to get fish, birds, a dog, and a cat.

4 Which of the following meanings associated with the word "brute" seems most intended in line 18?

A Animal

B Monster

C Savage

D Thug

Understanding Complex Informational Texts

Complex informational texts can be challenging when the reader is not familiar with technical vocabulary and concepts. It is helpful to scan for recurring words, make predictions and connections based on prior knowledge, and visualize as you read. Paraphrase difficult words, concepts, and complex sentences using your own words, summarize the main points implied by the details, and try to identify the author's main ideas. As you read, think about how the details relate to the main ideas.

This passage is an excerpt from a speech about the affordability of college. It was delivered by President Barack Obama in August 2013.

A higher education is the single best investment you can make in your future. . . . And that's not just me saying it. Look, right now, the unemployment rate for Americans with at least a college degree is about one-third lower than the national average. The incomes of folks who have at least a college degree are more than twice those of Americans without a high school diploma. So more than ever
5 before, some form of higher education is the surest path into the middle class.

But what I want to talk about today is what's become a barrier and a burden for too many American families—and that is the soaring cost of higher education. . . .

Over the past three decades, the average tuition at a public four-year college has gone up by more than 250 percent. . . . Now, a typical family's income has only gone up 16 percent. So think about that—
10 tuition has gone up 250 percent; income gone up 16 percent. . . .

The average student who borrows for college now graduates owing more than $26,000. Some owe a lot more than that . . . a lot of these young people [have] done everything they're supposed to do—got good grades in high school, applied to college, did well in school—but now they come out, they've got this crushing debt. . . . It becomes hard to start a family and buy a home [or] start a business if you are
15 servicing $1,000 worth of debt every month. . . .

(continued)

So at a time when a higher education has never been more important or more expensive, too many students are facing a choice that they should never have to make: . . . say no to college and pay the price . . . or . . . go to college, but then you run the risk that you won't be able to pay it off. . . .

So . . . we've got a crisis in terms of college affordability and student debt. And over the past four
20 years . . . we enacted historic reforms to the student loan system, so taxpayer dollars stop padding the pockets of big banks and instead help more kids afford college. . . .

Because what was happening . . . through banks; they didn't have any risk because the federal government guaranteed the loans, but they were still taking billions of dollars out of the program. We said, well, let's just give the loans directly to the students. . . .

25 Then we set up a consumer watchdog. And [it] is already helping students and families navigate the financial options . . . without getting ripped off. . . .

Then, we . . . cap loan repayments at 10 percent of monthly income for many borrowers who are trying to responsibly manage their . . . debt. . . . So overall, we've made college more affordable for millions of students and families. . . . And then . . . Democrats and Republicans worked together to keep
30 student loan rates from doubling. . . .

So that's all a good start, but it's not enough . . . if the cost is going up by 250 percent, tax revenues aren't going up 250 percent -- and so [at] some point, the government will run out of money, which means more and more costs are being loaded on to students and their families.

The system's current trajectory is not sustainable . . . state legislatures are going to have to step
35 up. They can't just keep cutting support for public colleges and universities. . . . [Schools] are not going to be able to just keep on increasing tuition year after year. . . . Our economy can't afford the trillion dollars in outstanding student loan debt. . . . We can't price the middle class and everybody working to get into the middle class out of a college education. We're going to have to do things differently. We can't go about business as usual.

Excerpt from "Remarks by the President on College Affordability" by Barack Obama

5 Scan the introduction and the first two paragraphs. Which of the following is the main theme of this speech?

A   The cost of higher education is too high.

B   The incomes of college graduates need to increase.

C   The importance of higher education is overestimated.

D   The unemployment rate for college graduates is too high.

6 Which detail offers the strongest support for the idea that college tuition is no longer affordable to the average American?

A   Some college graduates owe more than $26,000 in loan debt.

B   It's hard to start a family if you have to pay $1000 in debt each month.

C   Federal tax revenues have not increased by 250 percent, but college costs have.

D   Average tuition increased 250 percent while average income increased 16 percent.

7 Which of the following could best help a reader visualize the main problem described in the text?

A   Picture someone driving a fancy car.

B   Picture a graduating class of students in caps and gowns.

C   Picture a long line of people at the unemployment office.

D   Picture a college graduate writing a check for $1000 to a bank each month.

8 Which of the following statements best summarizes all the technical information in lines 25 through 30?

A   The government offered tax credits and grants to make college more affordable.

B   The government took several steps to help and protect students who take out loans.

C   The government took lending away from the banks to offer more money to students.

D   The government's political parties worked together to keep loan rates from doubling.

9 Based on the lines 31 through 39, which of the following statements is the author's conclusion?

A   The old system was not sustainable, so changes were made.

B   The changes made will redirect the trajectory of the current system.

C   Some changes were made to the old system, but more must be made.

D   If the current system does not change, the government will run out of money.

Language Practice

Pronouns take the place of nouns or pronouns named earlier in the text. The antecedent is the word that the pronoun is replacing. The pronoun and antecedent should agree in number and gender.

Read quickly through the draft article in the box below. Then go to the spread-out version, and consider the suggestions for revision.

---

1   Customer Service is a major key to any restaurant's success. How well the host and waitstaff treat diners can make the difference between him returning or not.

2   Opportunities for good customer service start the moment that diners walk in a restaurant's door. The host should greet the customers as soon as they come in and either seat them or take down their names for the next available table. The host should make sure the party knows what the expected wait time should be.

3   Servers should also make customer service their first priority. A server should look their customers in the eyes and repeat orders to ensure accuracy. A server should also check on his or her customers as the meal progresses to ensure their needs have been met.

---

1   Customer Service is a major key to any

restaurant's success. How well the host and

waitstaff treat diners can make the difference

between <u>him</u> returning or not.
　　　　　　1

2   Opportunities for good customer service

start the moment that diners walk in a

restaurant's door. The host should greet the

customers as soon as <u>they</u> come in and either
　　　　　　　　　　　2

seat them or take down their names for the

next available table. The host should make

sure the party knows what the expected wait

time should be.

3   Servers should also make customer

service their first priority. A server should

look <u>their</u> customers in the eyes and repeat
　　　3

orders to ensure accuracy. A server should

also check on <u>his or her</u> customers as the
　　　　　　　　4

meal progresses to ensure their needs have

been met.

1   A   *(No change)*
　　B   her
　　C   them
　　D   they

2   A   *(No change)*
　　B   them
　　C   his
　　D   she

3   A   *(No change)*
　　B   they
　　C   them
　　D   his or her

4   A   *(No change)*
　　B   them
　　C   she
　　D   he

✔ Test-Taking Tip

The writing response portion of the test is used to assess numerous abilities. These include your organizational skills and stylistic choices, the effectiveness of your arguments, your use of evidence, and your grasp of standard English conventions. In other words, your score will take into account what you write and how you write it. Therefore, it's important to become comfortable with content and presentation.

Writing Practice

Not all English speakers use exactly the same vocabulary. We all learn new words through our daily experiences, our jobs, and our interests. Anyone who plays a sport, has a hobby, or works in a particular industry learns the specialized terms and procedures that go along with that activity. Sometimes without realizing it, in different areas of our lives, we communicate in ways that not all of our family and friends can understand.

Write a paragraph **explaining** a particular rule or procedure that pertains to your job, a sport you watch or play, or a hobby or special interest you have. Be sure to use clear writing, but include the words and ideas that are specific to that activity without defining them to your reader.

This lesson will help you practice determining connotative and figurative meanings in two types of texts. Use it with Core Lesson 3.1 *Determine Connotative and Figurative Meanings* to reinforce and apply your knowledge.

Key Concept

The connotative meaning of a word or phrase is the meaning suggested by the word. Figurative language includes words or phrases that imply more than their literal meanings.

Identifying Connotative and Figurative Meanings

Authors use connotative and figurative language to set the tone and mood of a text. The tone conveys the author's attitude about the subject. The mood is the emotion that the reader feels when reading the text. As you read, analyze the author's use of specific words and phrases to identify the text's tone and mood.

Edgar Allan Poe is known for gruesome imagery and chilling tales. In this poem, Poe portrays human life as a stage play. Humans are the actors; angels are the audience. As with much of Poe's work, the main characters come to a nasty end.

Lo! 't is a gala night
Within the lonesome latter years.
An angel throng, bewinged, bedight
In veils, and drowned in tears,
5   Sit in a theatre to see
A play of hopes and fears,
While the orchestra breathes fitfully
The music of the spheres.

Mimes, in the form of God on high,
10   Mutter and mumble low,
And hither and thither fly;
Mere puppets they, who come and go
At bidding of vast formless things
That shift the scenery to and fro,
15   Flapping from out their condor wings
Invisible Woe.

That motley drama—oh, be sure
It shall not be forgot!
With its Phantom chased for evermore
20   By a crowd that seize it not,
Through a circle that ever returneth in
To the self-same spot;
And much of Madness, and more of Sin,
And Horror the soul of the plot.

(continued)

25   But see amid the mimic rout

A crawling shape, intrude:

A blood-red thing that writhes from out

The scenic solitude!

It writhes—it writhes!—with mortal pangs

30   The mimes become its food,

And seraphs sob at vermin fangs

In human gore imbued.

Out—out are the lights—out all!

And over each quivering form

35   The curtain, a funeral pall,

Comes down with the rush of a storm,

While the angels, all pallid and wan,

Uprising, unveiling, affirm

That the play is the tragedy, "Man,"

40   And its hero, the Conqueror Worm.

"The Conqueror Worm" by Edgar Allan Poe

1 **Which phrase from the poem is an example of figurative language?**

    A "Lo! 't is a gala night"

    B "While the orchestra breathes fitfully"

    C "Mutter and mumble low"

    D "While the angels, all pallid and wan,"

2 **What is the mood of the poem?**

    A Haunting

    B Indifferent

    C Longing

    D Sympathetic

3 **What is the tone of the poem?**

    A Admiring

    B Angry

    C Cheerful

    D Distressed

4 **What metaphor does Poe use to describe death?**

    A A heavenly angel

    B A symphony's finale

    C A carnivorous worm

    D A never-ending circle

5 **Reread the second and third stanzas (lines 9–24). How does the speaker feel about humankind?**

    A The speaker celebrates human life.

    B The speaker thinks humans are silly fools.

    C The speaker pities humans' eventual death.

    D The speaker is proud of the human struggle.

6 **Which of the following words used in the poem has a negative connotation?**

    A Bewinged

    B Evermore

    C Writhes

    D Affirm

Understanding Connotative and Figurative Meanings in Various Texts

Connotative and figurative language add depth to literary texts. An author's descriptions and word choices indicate the author's attitude about the subject, and they influence how the reader might feel toward the characters and about the events in the story. As you read, reflect on the author's reason for using certain words and phrases.

Written in 1819, "Rip Van Winkle" is a short story about a man who falls asleep in the woods after playing a game with a group of strangers. He wakes up 20 years later. His children are grown, his wife has died, and the Revolutionary War has been won. This passage describes Rip's life before he fell asleep.

Rip Van Winkle was one of those happy mortals of foolish, pleasant dispositions who take the world easy, eat white bread or brown (which ever can be got with least thought or trouble), and would rather starve on a penny than work for a pound. He would have whistled life away in perfect contentment but for his wife's continual harping about his idleness, his carelessness, and the ruin he
5   was bringing on his family. Morning, noon, and night, her tongue was incessantly going. Every thing he said or did was sure to produce a torrent of criticism. Rip had but one way of replying to all lectures of the kind. He shrugged his shoulders, shook his head, cast up his eyes, but said nothing. This, however, always provoked a fresh volley from his wife. He was then forced to retreat to the outside of the house—the only side which, in truth, belongs to a henpecked husband.

10   Rip's sole domestic adherent was his dog Wolf, who was as much henpecked as his master. Dame Van Winkle regarded them as companions in idleness, looking upon Wolf with an evil eye as the cause of his master's so often going astray. True, he was as courageous an animal as ever scoured the woods—but what courage can withstand the terrors of a woman's tongue? The moment Wolf entered the house, his crest fell, his tail drooped to the ground, or curled between his legs. He sneaked about
15   with a gallows air, casting many a sidelong glance at Dame Van Winkle. At the least flourish of a broomstick or ladle, he flew to the door with a pre-emptive yelp.

Times grew worse and worse with Rip Van Winkle as years of matrimony rolled on. A tart temper never mellows with age, and a sharp tongue is the only edge tool that grows keener by constant use. For a long while he used to console himself by frequenting a kind of club of the sages, philosophers,
20   and other idle men of the village. Sessions were held on a bench before a small inn designated by a ruddy portrait of his majesty George the Third. Here they used to sit in the shade of a long lazy summer's day, talk listlessly over village gossip, or tell endless sleepy stories about nothing. . . .

The opinions of this band were completely controlled by Nicholas Vedder, a patriarch of the village and landlord of the inn. . . . It is true, he was rarely heard to speak, but smoked his pipe incessantly.
25   His adherents, however, (for every great man has his adherents) perfectly understood him and knew how to gather his opinions. When any thing that was read or related displeased him, he was observed to smoke his pipe vehemently and send forth short, frequent, and angry puffs. When pleased, he would inhale the smoke slowly and tranquilly, emitting it in light and placid clouds. Sometimes he would even deign to take the pipe from his mouth to let the fragrant vapour curl about his nose, gravely nodding
30   his head in token of approval.

From even this strong hold the unlucky Rip was at length thwarted by his unruly wife, who would suddenly break in upon the tranquility of the meeting and call the members all to task. That honourable personage, Nicholas Vedder himself, was hardly safe from the daring tongue of this terrible shrew who charged him outright with encouraging her husband in habits of idleness.

Excerpt from "Rip Van Winkle" by Washington Irving

7 On the basis of the language used in the passage, how do you think the author wants readers to feel about Rip Van Winkle?

    A Curious

    B Irritated

    C Neutral

    D Sympathetic

8 What is the meaning of "keener" as it is used in line 18?

    A Duller

    B Kinder

    C Sharper

    D Wiser

9 Review paragraphs 2 (lines 10–16) and 4 (lines 23–30). Which pair of words could replace "adherent" and "adherents"?

    A Enemy/enemies

    B Friend/friends

    C Pet/pets

    D Student/students

10 How does the mood change between paragraphs 4 (lines 23–30) and 5 (lines 31–34)?

    A It changes from calm to frenzied.

    B It changes from riotous to peaceful.

    C It changes from humorous to serious.

    D It changes from unpleasant to pleasant.

11 Which word best describes Dame Van Winkle?

    A Domineering

    B Flirtatious

    C Meek

    D Passive

12 From the context, what is the meaning of the word "henpecked" as it is used in line 9?

    A Enjoying lovely solitude

    B Taking pleasure in silence

    C Suffering constant nagging

    D Feeling spiritually fulfilled

✓ Test-Taking Tip

You may not know the definition of every word given as an answer choice, but you can often determine the meaning of an unfamiliar word. Examine the word's root, prefix, and suffix for clues as to what the word means. Eliminate answer choices that are clearly wrong. Sometimes, but not always, the correct answer is quite different from the other choices.

Language Practice

Homophones are words that sound the same but are spelled differently and have different meanings. Using the correct homophones is an important part of crafting a text that is clear and easy to understand.

Read quickly through the draft passage in the box below. Then go to the spread-out version and consider the suggestions for revision.

Courtney and Malik were a great pare. They had similar interests, accept when it came to food. Unlike Malik, Courtney loved seafood, especially mussels. Malik ate mostly vegetables. His favorites were leaks and karats. Courtney teased Malik that her palate was more sophisticated, but he wasn't sure whether she really believed that. One meal they could agree on was serial for breakfast. Every morning, they would each pour a big bowl to tied themselves over until lunch.

Courtney and Malik were a great <u>pare</u>.

1

They had similar interests, <u>accept</u> when it

1

came to food. Unlike Malik, Courtney loved

seafood, especially <u>mussels</u>. Malik ate mostly

2

vegetables. His favorites were <u>leaks</u> and

2

<u>karats</u>. Courtney teased Malik that her <u>palate</u>

2   3

was more sophisticated, but he wasn't sure

<u>whether</u> she really believed that. One meal

3

they could agree on was <u>serial</u> for breakfast.

4

Every morning, they would each <u>pour</u> a big

4

bowl to <u>tied</u> themselves over until lunch.

4

1 **A** *(No change)*
    B pair/except
    C pear/accept
    D pair/accept

2 **A** *(No change)*
    B mussels/leaks/carats
    C muscles/leeks/carrots
    D mussels/leeks/carrots

3 **A** *(No change)*
    B palette/whether
    C pallet/whether
    D palate/weather

4 **A** *(No change)*
    B serial/pore/tide
    C cereal/poor/tied
    D cereal/pour/tide

✔️ **Test-Taking Tip**

It is easy to stray off course in your writing while completing a response that is timed. Before you begin to write, reread the directions and jot down a brief outline of your main points. The outline will serve as a roadmap to keep you on track and help you use your time to answer the question thoroughly.

Writing Practice

Connotative and figurative language brings depth to your writing. This descriptive language adds interest while guiding the reader to react to the text in a specific way. For example, "Jaime was silent" simply says that Jaime didn't make any noise. "Jaime was as quiet as a mouse" is more descriptive. It describes Jaime as quiet, but it also makes Jaime seem small and meek.

Write a paragraph describing an emotional moment in your life. It can be a memory filled with happiness, sadness, anger, or humor. Use **connotative and figurative language** to give the reader a vivid description of the situation and the emotions you felt at the time.

_____

_____

_____

_____

_____

_____

_____

_____

_____

_____

_____

_____

_____

_____

_____

_____

_____

_____

_____

_____

_____

_____

_____

_____

This lesson will help you practice analyzing tone in two types of texts. Use it with Core Lesson 3.2 *Analyze Tone* to reinforce and apply your knowledge.

> ## Key Concept
>
> Tone is the expression of a writer's attitude through stylistic choices.

Identifying Author's Tone in an Informational Text

The tone an author conveys in a text is much like the tone of your voice when you speak. In writing, authors convey tone through word choice and sentence structure. The tone of an informational text should fit the author's purpose for writing, the topic, and the genre.

Customers communicate with companies for many reasons. A customer's purpose for writing may be to offer praise, to file a complaint, or to review a product. In this letter to a hotel manager, a customer describes what he experienced as a guest of the hotel.

Manager
Value Inn Hotel
122 Massachusetts Avenue
Washington, DC 20027

5   Dear Manager,

I am writing about a number of problems I had while staying at your hotel in May of this year. The headaches began at the front desk, where I had to wait in line for 10 minutes. When I finally reached the desk, the employee was unable to find my reservation even after I spelled my name several times and gave her my reservation number. She then said there were no more non-smoking rooms, even
10   though I had reserved one weeks ago. She also informed me that only rooms on the twenty-second floor were available despite the fact that I had reserved a lower-floor room.

Naturally, I had trouble with my room key and had to return to the desk, where more customers were in line. The clerk who checked me in wasn't there, and the new clerk huffily told me to wait in line with the others. I waited 15 more minutes to get a key to my room. When I finally entered my room, it
15   was nothing short of a disaster. I returned to the front desk for a third time. Imagine my surprise when the clerk offered me a nonsmoking room on a lower floor!

Despite the better room, my troubles were far from over. Your website clearly said that Internet access was free, yet I had to pay $9.95 to access it. When I made my reservation, I was told that the pool was open. Once at the hotel, however, I learned that the pool was not scheduled to open until the
20   following weekend, which was Memorial Day. As the cherry on top, the air conditioner in my room broke down during the night. I called the front desk, but the engineer was not successful in his attempt to repair it. Since there were no other rooms available (apparently not even those on the twenty-second floor), I had to sleep in a stuffy, uncomfortable room.

I complained to a desk clerk about all of these problems, but she said that there was nothing she
25   could do to solve them. Because of the problems I experienced, I would like the cost of my stay refunded to me.

Sincerely,

Charles Walters

1 How does the topic of this letter affect its tone?

A The topic, a compliment about a hotel stay, sets a tone of congratulations.

B The topic, a complaint about a hotel stay, sets an angry, frustrated tone.

C The topic, a compliment about a hotel stay, sets a neutral tone.

D The topic, a complaint about a hotel stay, sets a tone of disappointment.

2 Which sentence from lines 12–16 best expresses the tone in the letter?

A "Naturally, I had trouble with my room key and had to return to the desk."

B "I waited 15 more minutes to get a key to my room."

C "I returned to the front desk for a third time."

D "Imagine my surprise when the clerk offered me a nonsmoking room on a lower floor!"

3 Which word from lines 6–11 is a metaphor that conveys the tone in the letter?

A "headaches"

B "employee"

C "reservation"

D "informed"

4 How do the phrases "a number of problems" and "all of these problems" likely make the hotel manager feel when reading the letter?

A Satisfied

B Embarrassed

C Motivated

D Relieved

5 Which aspect of the sentence in lines 20–21 would be changed by replacing "As the cherry on top" with "Thankfully"?

A Tone

B Meaning

C Mood

D Purpose

✔ Test-Taking Tip

Before you begin a test, take a moment to assess the length of each passage and set of questions. Knowing the length of the passages and the number of questions will help you calculate how much time to spend on each section. Plan to spend more time on the longer passages. They require careful reading and interpretation. Shorter passages take less time. When you have reached your self-imposed time limit, move to the next section. If you finish some sections early, return to sections you did not finish.

Analyzing Tone in a Literary Text

Tone plays an important role in literary writing. It can help build suspense in a mystery story or create a sense of urgency in an adventure story. When writers carefully craft the details of a story, the words and phrases they choose help express the tone.

In "The Thief," a short story by Anna Katharine Greene, a valuable coin goes missing during a dinner party. The host remains gracious while speculating about his guests' guilt.

"And now, if you have all seen the coin and sufficiently admired it, you may pass it back. I make a point of never leaving it off the shelf for more than fifteen minutes."

The half dozen or more guests seated about the board of the genial speaker, glanced casually at each other as though expecting to see the object mentioned immediately produced.

5   . . . [N]o coin appeared.

"I have other amusements waiting," suggested their host, with a smile in which even his wife could detect no signs of impatience. "Now let Robert put it back into the cabinet."

Robert was the butler. . . .

"Perhaps it is in somebody's lap," timidly ventured one of the younger women. "It doesn't seem to
10 be on the table."

Immediately all the ladies began lifting their napkins and shaking out the gloves which lay under them, in an effort to relieve their own embarrassment and that of the gentlemen who had not even so simple a resource as this at their command.

"It can't be lost," protested Mr. Sedgwick, with an air of perfect confidence. "I saw it but a minute
15 ago in somebody's hand. Darrow, you had it; what did you do with it?"

"Passed it along."

"Well, well, it must be under somebody's plate or doily." And he began to move about his own and such dishes as were within reach of his hand.

Each guest imitated him, lifting glasses and turning over spoons till Mr. Sedgwick himself bade
20 them desist. "It's slipped to the floor," he nonchalantly concluded. "A toast to the ladies, and we will give Robert the chance of looking for it."

As they drank this toast, his apparently careless, but quietly astute, glance took in each countenance about him. The coin was very valuable and its loss would be keenly felt by him. Had it slipped from the table some one's eye would have perceived it, some hand would have followed it. Only
25 a minute or two before, the attention of the whole party had been concentrated upon it. Darrow had held it up for all to see, while he discoursed upon its history. He would take Darrow aside at the first opportunity and ask him—But—it! how could he do that? These were his intimate friends. He knew them well, more than well, with one exception, and he—Well, he was the handsomest of the lot and the most debonair and agreeable. . . .

30   "And now, some music!" he cheerfully cried, as with lingering glances and some further pokings about of the table furniture, the various guests left their places and followed him into the adjoining room.

(continued)

But the ladies were too nervous and the gentlemen not sufficiently sure of their voices to undertake the entertainment of the rest at a moment of such acknowledged suspense; and

35 notwithstanding the exertions of their host and his quiet but much discomfited wife, it soon became apparent that but one thought engrossed them all, and that any attempt at conversation must prove futile so long as the curtains between the two rooms remained open and they could see Robert on his hands and knees searching the floor and shoving aside the rugs. . . .

"No, sir; and it's not in the dining-room. I have cleared the table and thoroughly searched the floor."

40 Mr. Sedgwick knew that he had. He had no doubts about Robert. Robert had been in his employ for years and had often handled his coins and, at his order, sometimes shown them.

"Very well," said he, "we'll not bother about it any more to-night; you may draw the curtains."

Excerpt from *Number 3 and Other Detective Stories* by Anna Katherine Greene

6 **What tone can a reader expect from a story of this genre?**

A Disbelief

B Wonder

C Suspense

D Neutrality

7 **What does "futile" (line 37) mean?**

A Annoying

B Pointless

C Careless

D Useful

8 **The author uses short phrases and short sentences in lines 5–18 so the tone will**

A remain lighthearted and fun.

B show the confusion of the guests.

C serve to cast a suspecting shadow on the butler.

D build the reader's interest in what happens next.

9 **Which word best describes the tone of the story?**

A Intense

B Terrifying

C Friendly

D Frantic

10 **How does the paragraph beginning with line 22 affect the tone of the passage?**

A It helps build tension by revealing Mr. Sedgwick's suspicions.

B It slows down the pace of the story by telling how Robert searches for the coin.

C It misleads readers by naming Darrow as the culprit.

D It distracts from the theft by focusing on a description of one guest.

11 **Reread lines 9–10. Which word could replace "timidly"?**

A Boldly

B Hesitantly

C Loudly

D Proudly

> ✔ **Test-Taking Tip**
>
> Some test items are about specific words, phrases, paragraphs, or sections of a passage. Before answering a question about a text detail, always reread the related sentence or paragraph. As you reread, focus on what the question is about. For example, if the item is about the meaning of a word, think about how the word is used in that context.

Writing Practice

Connotative words, figurative language, and sentence structure are the building blocks that an author uses to express tone in a story. Think about the words you would use to tell a ghost story versus the words you would use to talk about an exciting baseball play. As a writer, expressing your tone can deepen the reader's interest in the story.

Write a paragraph in which you **describe** the adult responsibilities you now have that you did not have before. For example, perhaps you are now responsible for helping your children do their homework. Before you write, decide on your **purpose** for writing. Choose words, descriptions, and sentence structures that will convey your desired **tone**.

_____

_____

_____

_____

_____

_____

_____

_____

_____

_____

_____

_____

_____

_____

_____

_____

_____

_____

_____

_____

_____

_____

This lesson will help you practice analyzing word choices in two texts. Use it with Core Lesson 3.3 *Analyze Word Choice* to reinforce and apply your knowledge.

Key Concept

To communicate accurately, authors make careful decisions about the words they use.

Choosing the Right Word

An author's word choices determine the tone, mood, and impact of a text. Readers or listeners can gain a deeper understanding about what an author wants them to feel, think, and understand by analyzing word choices and writing style.

Royall Tyler wrote *The Contrast* in 1787. This play is about three women who are being wooed simultaneously by the same man, Billy Dimple. In this scene, Maria is trying to tell her father that she does not want to marry Billy even though they are engaged.

VAN ROUGH. What, Mary, always singing doleful ditties, and moping over these troublesome books.

MARIA. I hope, Sir, that it is not criminal to improve my mind with books; or to divert my melancholy with singing at my leisure hours.

VAN ROUGH. Pray, what right has a girl of your age to be in the dumps? Haven't you every thing 5 your heart can wish; ain't you going to be married to a young man of great fortune; ain't you going to have the quit-rent of twenty miles square?

MARIA. One hundredth part of the land, and a lease for life of the heart of a man I could love, would satisfy me.

VAN ROUGH. . . . A young woman should be very sober when she is making her choice, but when 10 she has once made it, as you have done, I don't see why she should not be as merry as a lark; . . . Why, there was your mother now; to be sure when I popp'd the question to her, she did look a little silly; but when she had once looked down on her apron-strings, as all modest young women us'd to do, and drawled out ye-s, she was as brisk and as merry as a bee.

MARIA. My honored mother, Sir, had no motive to melancholy; she married the man of her choice.

15 **VAN ROUGH.** The man of her choice! And pray, Mary, ain't you going to marry the man of your choice? . . . I'd have you to know, Mary, if you won't make young Van Dumpling the man of *your* choice, you shall marry him as the man of *my* choice.

MARIA. You terrify me, Sir. Indeed, Sir, I am all submission. My will is yours.

VAN ROUGH. Why, that is the way your mother us'd to talk. "My will is yours, my dear Mr. Van 20 Rough, my will is yours": but she took special care to have her own way though for all that.

MARIA. Do not reflect upon my mother's memory, Sir—

VAN ROUGH. Why not, Mary, why not? She kept me from speaking my mind all *her* life, and do you think she shall henpeck me now she is *dead* too? . . .

[*Enter* SERVANT.]

25 **SERVANT.** Sir, Mr. Transfer, the broker, is below. [*Exit.*]

VAN ROUGH. Well, Mary, I must go.—Remember, and be a good girl, and mind the main chance. [*Exit.*]

(continued)

MARIA [*Alone.*] How deplorable is my situation! How distressing for a daughter to find her heart warring with her filial duty! I know my father loves me tenderly, why then do I reluctantly
30 obey him? . . . With what reluctance I should oppose the will of a parent, or set an example of filial disobedience; at a parent's command I could wed awkwardness and deformity. Were the heart of my husband good, I would so magnify his good qualities with the eye of conjugal affection, that the defects of his person and manners should be lost in the emanation of his virtues. At a father's command, I could embrace poverty. Were the poor man my husband, I would learn resignation to my lot; I would enliven
35 our frugal meal with good humor, and chase away misfortune from our cottage with a smile. But to marry a depraved wretch, whose only virtue is a polished exterior; who is actuated by the unmanly ambition of conquering the defenceless. . . . Can he, who has no regard for the peace and happiness of other families, ever have a due regard for the peace and happiness of his own?

Excerpt from *The Contrast* by Tyler Royall

1 **How does Maria feel when the scene begins? How do you know?**

A She is relaxed; she uses the word "leisure" to describe the time she spends reading and singing.

B She is troubled; her father uses the word "troublesome" to describe the books she is reading.

C She is sad; she uses the word "melancholy" to describe the mood she is trying to chase away.

D She is happy; her father uses the word "merry" to describe the mood of women who get engaged.

2 **In line 14, the author has Maria use the word "honored" to show**

A the love Maria had for her mother.

B that Maria's mother was a good person.

C that Maria's mother was well-respected.

D Maria's bitter feelings about her mother's death.

3 **Which word reveals how Mr. Van Rough feels about Maria's mother?**

A Young

B Modest

C Submissive

D Henpeck

4 **In line 10, the phrase "merry as a lark" is an example of**

A a metaphor.

B a simile.

C personification.

D signal words.

5 **Based on Maria's description of Billy Dimple as a "depraved wretch" in line 36, how does Maria feel about her fiancé?**

A She tolerates him.

B She hates him.

C She loves him.

D She pities him.

Analyzing and Evaluating Word Choice in Various Texts

Word choice is particularly important when a text is written for the purpose of persuasion. The author's word choices, including connotative language and figurative language, inform the reader about how the writer wants him or her to feel about the topic.

In 1872 Susan B. Anthony was arrested for illegally voting in the 1872 federal election. After paying a $100 fine, she went on a speaking tour defending suffrage for women. This is an excerpt from Anthony's speech.

Friends and Fellow Citizens: I stand before you tonight under indictment for the alleged crime of having voted at the last presidential election, without having a lawful right to vote. It shall be my work this evening to prove to you that in thus voting, I not only committed no crime, but, instead, simply exercised my citizen's rights, guaranteed to me and all United States citizens by the National
5   Constitution, beyond the power of any State to deny.

Our democratic-republican government is based on the idea of the natural right of every individual member thereof to a voice and a vote in making and executing the laws. We assert the province of government to be to secure the people in the enjoyment of their unalienable rights. We throw to the winds the old dogma that governments can give rights. Before governments were organized, no one
10   denies that each individual possessed the right to protect his own life, liberty and property. And when 100 or 1,000,000 people enter into a free government, they do not barter away their natural rights; they simply pledge themselves to protect each other in the enjoyment of them, through prescribed judicial and legislative tribunals. They agree to abandon the methods of brute force in the adjustment of their differences, and adopt those of civilization. . . .

15   The preamble of the Federal Constitution says:

"We, the people of the United States, in order to form a more perfect union, establish justice, insure domestic tranquility, provide for the common defense, promote the general welfare, and secure the blessings of liberty to ourselves and our posterity, do ordain and establish this Constitution for the United States of America."

20   It was we, the people; not we, the white male citizens; nor yet we, the male citizens; but we, the whole people, who formed the Union. And we formed it, not to give the blessings of liberty, but to secure them; not to the half of ourselves and the half of our posterity, but to the whole people—women as well as men. And it is a downright mockery to talk to women of their enjoyment of the blessings of liberty while they are denied the use of the only means of securing them provided by this democratic-
25   republican government—the ballot.

Excerpt from "Is It a Crime for a Citizen of the United States to Vote?" by Susan B. Anthony

6 Susan B. Anthony gave this speech and chose her words to

A teach people that women have the right to vote.

B notify people that women have the right to vote.

C persuade people that women have the right to vote.

D warn people that women have the right to vote.

7 The speaker chose her words to influence which audience?

A Male landowners

B Women

C Politicians

D Average citizens

8 Which of the following meanings associated with the word "exercised" seems most intended in line 4?

A Eliminated

B Ignored

C Maintained

D Used

9 Which phrase from lines 6–14 is an example of figurative language?

A Unalienable rights

B Throw to the winds

C Governments can give rights

D Protect each other

10 Which idea is conveyed by the word "mockery" in lines 23–25?

A It is meaningless to talk of rights when women are not able to vote.

B It is silly to talk of rights when women are not able to vote.

C It is difficult to talk of rights when women are not able to vote.

D It is encouraging to talk of rights when women are not able to vote.

11 How did Anthony want her audience to feel as a result of her word choices?

A Hopeful

B Angry

C Depressed

D Excited

✔ Test-Taking Tip

Context clues can help you figure out the meaning of a word used in a test question. If you read a test question that has an unfamiliar word, search the rest of the question for clues to its meaning. You can also refer to the test's introduction and directions for context clues.

Writing Practice

Powerful writing comes from the heart. Authors convey their feelings about a particular subject through the use of carefully chosen words that are meant to evoke feelings or emotions in the reader. As a writer, it is important to bring your passion to life with connotative and figurative language, as well as with vivid descriptions. Your words should give the reader a clear picture of your feelings.

Write a paragraph describing your **viewpoint** on a current social or political topic such as forced school closings or mandatory health insurance. Choose words that will convey your point of view and **persuade** the reader to agree with you.

This lesson will help you practice analyzing the development of ideas with fiction and nonfiction texts. Use it with Core Lesson 4.1 *Analyze the Development of Ideas* to reinforce and apply that knowledge.

Key Concept

Every piece of writing has a structure. Writers develop their ideas in texts through organization.

Identifying Text Structure

Sequence is a common type of text structure. Stories and other narratives relate events in the order in which the events happened. Often these texts include words such as *first, second, next,* and *last.* Another way writers organize their writing is to compare and contrast two or more ideas by using words such as *although, both,* and *in contrast.* A third way to organize a text is through cause and effect. Words and phrases such as *so, therefore, since,* and *as a result* identify cause-and-effect structure. Description, the fourth type of structure, involves using vivid details to guide how a narrative unfolds. Using the description structure, writers often use terms that express spatial relationships: *above, to the right, next to.* Finally, writers who use the structure of problem and solution present a problem and one or more solutions. Texts written using this structure commonly include words and phrases such as *in order to* and *so that.*

The *Titanic* began its first voyage in 1912 from Southampton, England. The ship set sail for New York, but it sank four days after departure.

Ever was [an] ill-starred voyage more [promising] than when the *Titanic* . . . steamed majestically out of the port of Southampton. [The ship left] at noon on Wednesday, April 10th, bound for New York.

Elaborate preparations had been made for the maiden voyage. Crowds of eager watchers gathered to witness the departure. . . . [Everyone was] interested because of the notable people who were to
5   travel aboard her. Friends and relatives of many of the passengers were at the dock to bid Godspeed to their departing loved ones. The passengers themselves were unusually gay and happy.

Majestic and beautiful the ship rested on the water, marvel of shipbuilding, worthy of any sea. As this new queen of the ocean moved slowly from her dock, no one questioned her construction. . . . [She had] an elaborate system of water-tight compartments, calculated to make her unsinkable. She had
10   been pronounced the safest as well as the most [luxurious] Atlantic liner afloat.

There was silence just before the boat pulled out. . . . [Then] the heavy whistles sounded. The splendid *Titanic*, her flags flying and her band playing, churned the water and plowed heavily away.

Then . . . the people on board wav[ed] handkerchiefs and shout[ed] good-byes. . . . [Their voices] could be heard only as a buzzing murmur on shore. [Next, the *Titanic*] rode away on the ocean,
15   proudly [and] majestically. . . .

And so it was only her due that the *Titanic* steamed out of the harbor bound on her maiden voyage. . . . A thousand "God-speeds" were [called] after her, while [she dwarfed] every other vessel that she passed. . . .

In command of the *Titanic* was Captain E.J. Smith. . . . The next six officers, in the order of their
20   rank, were Murdock, Lightollder [sic], Pitman, Boxhall, Lowe and Moody. Dan Phillips was chief wireless operator, with Harold Bride as assistant.

(continued)

From the forward bridge, fully ninety feet above the sea, peered out the [kind] face of the ship's master. [He was] cool of aspect, deliberate of action, [and] impressive in [his confidence]. . . .

From far below the bridge sounded the strains of the ship's orchestra, playing a favorite air from
25 "The Chocolate Soldier." All went as merry as a wedding bell. Indeed, among that gay ship's company were two score or more at least for whom the wedding bells had sounded. . . . Some were on their honeymoon tours. Others were returning to their motherland. . . .

[Who] would have [predicted] that within the span of six days that stately ship . . . would lie at the bottom of the Atlantic . . . ?

Excerpt from *Sinking of the Titanic and Great Sea Disasters*, edited by Logan Marshall, 1912

1 **What is the structure of this passage?**

A Compare and contrast

B Problem and solution

C Sequence

D Cause and effect

2 **What purpose does the following sentence (lines 17–18) serve? "A thousand 'God-speeds' were [called] after her, while [she dwarfed] every other vessel that she passed. . . ."**

A To describe the cause of the Titanic's sinking

B To describe the effect of the Titanic's sinking

C To compare the Titanic with other ships

D To contrast the Titanic with other ships

3 **Which word in the paragraph that begins "Then . . . the people on board . . ." (lines 13–15) highlights the text structure of the passage?**

A On

B And

C Could

D Next

4 **Which excerpt from the passage provides a cause for large crowds to have gathered at the departure of the *Titanic*?**

A "Elaborate preparations had been made. . . . Crowds of eager watchers gathered to witness the departure."

B "Friends and relatives . . . were at the dock to bid Godspeed to their departing loved ones."

C "She had been pronounced the safest as well as the most [luxurious] Atlantic liner afloat."

D "Then . . . the people on board wav[ed] handkerchiefs and shout[ed] good-byes."

Variations in Organization

Chronological order (or time order) describes a sequence of events by relating what happened first, second, third, and so on. However, there are variations of this text structure. When writers interrupt the sequence to introduce events that took place before the story began, this is called *flashback*. Slow pacing adds details and descriptions so the plot moves along gradually. Fast pacing moves through events quickly to arrive at an important moment.

Sherlock Holmes is a famous fictional detective. He solves mysteries by combining seemingly insignificant clues.

Holmes had been seated for some hours in silence with his long, thin back curved over a chemical vessel in which he was brewing a particularly malodorous product. . . .

"So, Watson," said he, suddenly, "you do not propose to invest in South African securities?" . . .

"How on earth do you know that?" I asked. . . .

5   "Now, Watson, confess yourself utterly taken aback," said he.

"I am."

"I ought to make you sign a paper to that effect."

"Why?"

"Because in five minutes you will say that it is all so absurdly simple."

10   "I am sure I will say nothing of the kind."

"You see, my dear Watson, . . . it is not really difficult to construct a series of inferences, each dependent upon its predecessor and each simple in itself. If, after doing so, one simply knocks out all the central inferences and presents one's audience with the starting-point and the conclusion, one may produce a startling, though possibly a meretricious, effect. Now, it was not really difficult, by an

15   inspection of the groove between your left forefinger and thumb, to feel sure that you did *not* propose to invest your small capital in the gold fields."

"I see no connection."

". . . Here are the missing links of the very simple chain: 1. You had chalk between your left finger and thumb when you returned from the club last night. 2. You put chalk there when you play

20   billiards. . . . 3. You never play billiards except with Thurston. 4. You told me, four weeks ago, that Thurston had an option on some South African property which would expire in a month, and which he desired you to share with him. 5. Your check book is locked in my drawer, and you have not asked for the key. 6. You do not propose to invest your money in this manner."

"How absurdly simple!" I cried.

25   "Quite so!" said he, a little nettled. "Every problem becomes very childish once it is explained to you. Here is an unexplained one. See what you can make of that, friend Watson." He tossed a sheet of paper upon the table. . . . I looked with amazement at the absurd hieroglyphics upon the paper.

"Why, Holmes, it is a child's drawing," I cried.

"Oh, that's your idea!"

30   "What else should it be?"

"That is what Mr. Hilton Cubitt . . . is very anxious to know. . . . There's a ring at the bell, Watson. I should not be very much surprised if this were he."

(continued)

A heavy step was heard upon the stairs, and an instant later there entered a tall, ruddy, clean-
shaven gentleman. . . . Having shaken hands with each of us, he was about to sit down, when his eye
35   rested upon the paper with the curious markings. . . .

"Well, Mr. Holmes, what do you make of these?" he cried.

"At first sight it would appear to be some childish prank. It consists of a number of absurd little
figures dancing across the paper upon which they are drawn. Why should you attribute any importance
to so grotesque an object?"

40   "I never should, Mr. Holmes. But my wife does. It is frightening her to death. . . . That's why I want
to sift the matter to the bottom."

Holmes held up the paper so that the sunlight shone full upon it. It was a page torn from a
notebook. The markings were done in pencil. . . . [He] examined it for some time, and then, folding it
carefully up, he placed it in his pocketbook.

45   "This promises to be a most interesting and unusual case," said he.

Excerpt from "The Mystery of the Dancing Men" by Sir Arthur Conan Doyle

5   **Which text structure is used in the paragraph beginning with line 33?**

   A   Chronological order
   B   Compare and contrast
   C   Problem and solution
   D   Cause and effect

6   **What is the meaning of "inferences" as it is used in lines 11 and 13?**

   A   Statements
   B   Conclusions
   C   Evidence
   D   Reasoning

7   **What variation on time order is used in the paragraph that begins "Here are the missing links" (lines 18–23) organized?**

   A   Holmes uses cause and effect to relate the events of the simple chain.
   B   Holmes uses fast pacing to relate the events of the simple chain.
   C   Holmes uses slow pacing to relate the events of the simple chain.
   D   Holmes uses flashbacks to relate the events of the simple chain.

8   **Which summary reflects the order in which events occur in the passage?**

   A   Holmes brews something in a chemical vessel. Holmes holds up a piece of paper in the sunlight. Holmes tells Watson the six missing links of the simple chain. Mr. Hilton Cubitt rings the doorbell.

   B   Holmes brews something in a chemical vessel. Mr. Hilton Cubitt rings the doorbell. Holmes tells Watson the six missing links of the simple chain. Holmes holds up a piece of paper in the sunlight.

   C   Holmes brews something in a chemical vessel. Holmes tells Watson the six missing links of the simple chain. Holmes holds up a piece of paper in the sunlight. Mr. Hilton Cubitt rings the doorbell.

   D   Holmes brews something in a chemical vessel. Holmes tells Watson the six missing links of the simple chain. Mr. Hilton Cubitt rings the doorbell. Holmes holds up a piece of paper in the sunlight.

> **Test-Taking Tip**
>
> The more you practice identifying the text structure of a passage, the more confident you will be as a reader. By noticing words that are specific to particular text structures, like *first* and *as a result*, you will understand what kind of passage you are reading. Looking for words like this when you are reading a passage on a test will help you understand the text and the questions that follow.

Writing Practice

Using transition words that are specific to a text structure helps writers develop their ideas. Texts that are organized by sequence might use words such as *yesterday, after that,* and *later.* Texts that are organized by cause and effect might use transition words such as *so, therefore, since,* and *because.*

Use a **compare-and-contrast text structure** to write a brief paragraph in which you describe how two of your favorite family traditions are alike and how they are different. You may choose traditions that exist in your immediate family, traditions that come from your extended family, or traditions you would like to start. While writing this piece, make sure that you use words that are specific to the compare-and-contrast text structure.

This lesson will help you practice identifying text structure and understand how text structure impacts key ideas. Use it with *Core Lesson 4.2 Analyze How Structure Impacts Key Ideas* to reinforce and apply your knowledge.

Key Concept

Authors structure what they write to communicate and reinforce key ideas.

Identifying Text Structures

Writers organize their work to help readers understand their ideas. They often use one of the five most common structures—sequence, compare and contrast, cause and effect, description, and problem and solution.

A text with a sequence text structure places events in time order. Another type of sequence is order of importance in which the most important point is presented first or at the end of the text. In texts that use compare-and-contrast structure, a writer compares, contrasts, or compares and contrasts ideas. Cause-and-effect texts describe how events cause other events. An event can have multiple causes or multiple effects. Texts that have the description text structure use the five senses to paint a vivid picture. Finally, problem-and-solution texts offer one or more solutions to a problem.

Many states are implementing graduated driver licensing systems to decrease the number of accidents caused by teen drivers. This passage explains how graduated driver licensing systems work.

GDL [Graduated Driver Licensing] is a novice driver licensing system that is proven effective at reducing teen drivers' high crash risk by 20–40%. States with stronger, comprehensive GDL systems see a higher reduction in teen crashes. GDL reduces teen driver exposure to high crash risk situations, such as nighttime driving and teen passengers.

5   GDL systems have three stages of licensure:

1. A learner's permit that allows driving only while supervised by a fully licensed driver.

2. An intermediate (sometimes called provisional) license that allows unsupervised driving under certain restrictions including nighttime and passenger limits.

3. A full license.

10   All new drivers can make wrong decisions behind the wheel. However teens are the most at jeopardy. They bring to the road a unique mix of inexperience, distraction, peer pressure and a tendency to underestimate risk. . . .

Most Americans typically learn to drive during the teen years, when the brain is not fully mature yet. Recent research is beginning to give us insight into why many teens have difficulty regulating risk-
15   taking behavior:

• The area of the brain that weighs consequences, suppresses impulses and organizes thoughts does not fully mature until about age 25.

• Hormones are more active in teens, which influence the brain's neurochemicals that regulate excitability and mood. The result can be thrill-seeking behavior and experiences that create
20   intense feelings.

(continued)

Learning to regulate driving behavior comes with time and practice. Defensive Driving Course-Alive at 25® offers a balanced approach to help teens not only regulate their own driving behavior, but also help them deal with the actual issues that can influence their driving behavior.

25 Driver education programs play a role in preparing teens to drive, but should not be viewed as the end of the learning-to-drive process. In order to develop safe driving skills, inexperienced drivers need opportunities to improve through gradual exposure to increasingly challenging driving tasks. Teens become safer drivers with more driving experience.

In some states, the completion of driver education qualifies a teen for full driving privileges. The National Safety Council believes this is not a wise approach. Research shows that significant hours of
30 behind-the-wheel experience are necessary to reduce crash risk. Parent involvement and Graduated Driver Licensing play important roles in developing skills.

DriveitHOME is a new program offering specially created resources to help parents keep their teens safer on the roads, especially after a teen gets a driver's license. Designed by parents for parents, the unique program includes an interactive website featuring engaging videos, practice tips and other
35 critical resources. Parents can sign up to receive weekly practice tips and suggestions via email, and are encouraged to share their own teaching techniques and experiences.

Excerpt from "Graduated Drivers" by the National Safety Council

1 Which text structure best describes the way the ideas in lines 5–9 are organized?

A Compare and contrast

B Cause and effect

C Problem and solution

D Sequence

2 Which quotation from the passage offers one solution to the problem of teen drivers' high crash risk?

A "All new drivers can make wrong decisions behind the wheel."

B "However teens are the most at jeopardy."

C "They bring to the road a unique mix of inexperience, distraction, peer pressure and a tendency to underestimate risk."

D "Teens become safer drivers with more driving experience."

3 Which quotation from the passage presents a cause for why teens have a hard time managing risky behavior behind the wheel?

A "All new drivers can make wrong decisions behind the wheel. However teens are the most at jeopardy."

B "Recent research is beginning to give us insight into why many teens have difficulty regulating risk-taking behavior."

C "Hormones are more active in teens, which influence the brain's neurochemicals that regulate excitability and mood."

D "Research shows that significant hours of behind-the-wheel experience are necessary to reduce crash risk."

4 Which sentence from the passage describes an effect of the GDL?

A "States with stronger, comprehensive GDL systems see a higher reduction in teen crashes."

B "Learning to regulate driving behavior comes with time and practice."

C "In some states, the completion of driver education qualifies a teen for full driving privileges."

D "Designed by parents for parents, the unique program includes an interactive website featuring engaging videos, practice tips and other critical resources."

Text Structure and Key Ideas

Understanding where writers place important information can help readers identify the significant ideas in a text. Often a writer emphasizes an idea by placing it at the beginning or the end of a text.

Charles Fort is well known for his research into mysterious events. This passage describes his research related to unusual frog and toad sightings.

A tremendous number of little toads, one or two months old, fell from a great thick cloud that appeared suddenly in a clear sky, in August 1804, near Toulouse, France, according to a letter from Prof. Pontus to M. Arago. (*Comptes Rendus, 3-54.*)

5　An issue of *Scientific American* magazine, dated July 12, 1873, reported that "A shower of frogs which darkened the air and covered the ground for a long distance is the reported result of a recent rainstorm at Kansas City, MO."

Some experts claim that small frogs and toads have never fallen from the sky, but in every purported case were "on the ground in the first place," or that there have been such falls "up from one place in a whirlwind, and down in another."

10　See, for instance, *Leisure Hours*, 3-779 for accounts of small frogs, or toads, said to have been seen to fall from the sky. The writer says that all observers were mistaken and that the frogs or toads must have fallen from trees or other places overhead.

There are, it must be said, cases where the possibility of fallen frogs having "been there in the first place" is quite remote:

15　Little frogs were found in London, after a heavy storm (July 30, 1838, *Notes and Queries*, 8-7-437).

Little toads were found in a desert, after a rainfall (*Notes and Queries*, 8-8-493).

At the same time, I do not completely dismiss the conventional explanation of whirlwinds as the [reason for] falling frogs. I think that there have likely been such occurrences. In the London *Times*, July 4, 1883, there is an account of a shower of twigs and leaves and tiny toads in a storm upon the 20　slopes of the Apennines. This may have indeed been the work of a whirlwind.

That is one specific case, however. In others, while it is easy to say that small frogs that have fallen from the sky had been scooped up by a whirlwind, this gives no regard for mud, debris from the bottom of a pond, floating vegetation, or loose things from the shores. To accept a whirlwind as the cause, one would need to accept that a whirlwind somehow, very precisely, picked up frogs alone.

25　There is also the fact that, of all instances I have studied that attribute the fall of small frogs or toads to whirlwinds, only one actually identifies or places the whirlwind. Also, it seems to me that a pond going up would be quite as interesting as frogs coming down, and that anybody who had lost a pond would be heard from. Yet in Symons' *Meteorological Magazine*, a fall of small frogs, near Birmingham, England, June 30, 1892, is attributed to a specific whirlwind, without a word as to any 30　special pond that had contributed. And something else that strikes my attention here is that these frogs are described as almost white.

I am afraid there is no escape for us: we shall have to accept that upon this earth exist some still-unknown locations: places with white frogs in them.

Adapted from the writings and observations of Charles Fort

5 Why does the author begin the passage with the observations of frog and toad sightings?

A To reveal instances of frog and toad sightings before exploring what may have happened to cause the events

B To show the problem that frog and toad sightings posed in London and France

C To contrast the effects of frog and toad sightings in London with the effects of frog and toad sightings in the United States

D To present a solution for the problem of frogs and toads falling in France

6 Which lines from the passage reveals the author's skepticism about a possible cause of frog and toad sightings?

A Lines 4–6

B Lines 7–9

C Lines 17–20

D Lines 25–31

7 Which of the following meanings associated with the word "remote" seems most intended in line 14?

A Unfriendly

B Unlikely

C Distant

D Device

8 Which sentence from the passage reveals a possible cause of frogs and toads falling from the sky?

A "Little frogs were found in London, after a heavy storm."

B "Little toads were found in a desert, after a rainfall."

C "[A] shower of twigs and leaves and tiny toads [fell] . . . upon the slopes of the Apennines."

D "This may have indeed been the work of a whirlwind."

✔ Test-Taking Tip

When you are approaching a test question that requires an extended response, identify the text structure that will best fit your response. For example, if you are asked to write about the causes and effects of a natural disaster, you might want to write the causes first and then write about the effects. Knowing different types of text structures will help you decide how to organize your extended response and how to determine the best place to write your ideas within each paragraph.

Writing Practice

All friends have some similarities, and that is what makes them friends. Even though they have similarities, they are not the same. All friends also have differences.

Write two paragraphs that **compare and contrast** two of your friends or acquaintances. You might decide to compare your friends in one paragraph and to contrast your friends in the other paragraph, or you might decide to compare and contrast them point by point. While you are writing, use **descriptions** along with comparisons and contrasts to make the similarities and differences clear to the reader.

This lesson will help you practice analyzing the effects of transitional and signal words in two texts. Use it with Core Lesson 4.3 *Analyze the Effect of Transitional and Signal Words* to reinforce and apply your knowledge.

Key Concept

Writers use certain words and phrases to link ideas within sentences and between sentences.

Locating Transitions

Transitions are shifts in the text that show that the writer has moved from one idea to the next. Transitions can happen between paragraphs or within paragraphs. The best way to locate transitions is to look for signal words or phrases. Signal words and phrases express the following relationships: addition, time order, relative location, relative importance, cause and effect, comparison, contrast, example, and conclusion.

"The Fable of the Animals" is a myth from the Karuk people, who are native to California. It describes how "Man" distributed specific powers and abilities to all other animals.

A great many hundred snows ago, Kareya, sitting on the Sacred Stool, created the world. First, he made the fishes in the Big Water, then the animals on the green land, and last of all, Man! But at first the animals were all alike in power. No one knew which animals should be food for others, and which should be food for man. Then Kareya ordered them all to meet in one place, that Man might give each
5   his rank and his power. So the animals all met together one evening, when the sun was set, to wait overnight for the coming of Man on the next morning. Kareya also commanded Man to make bows and arrows, as many as there were animals, and to give the longest one to the animal which was to have the most power, and the shortest to the one which should have least power. So he did, and after nine sleeps his work was ended, and the bows and arrows which he had made were very many.

10   Now the animals, being all together, went to sleep, so they might be ready to meet Man on the next morning. But Coyote was exceedingly cunning—he was cunning above all the beasts. Coyote wanted the longest bow and the greatest power, so he could have all the other animals for his meat. He decided to stay awake all night, so that he would be first to meet Man in the morning. So he laughed to himself and stretched his nose out on his paw and pretended to sleep. About midnight he began to be sleepy.
15   He had to walk around the camp and scratch his eyes to keep them open. He grew more sleepy, so that he had to skip and jump about to keep awake. But he made so much noise, he awakened some of the other animals. When the morning star came up, he was too sleepy to keep his eyes open any longer. [As a result of his fatigue,] he took two little sticks, and sharpened them at the ends, and propped open his eyelids. Then he felt safe. He watched the morning star, with his nose stretched along his paws, and
20   fell asleep. The sharp sticks pinned his eyelids fast together.

The [next morning, the] morning star rose rapidly into the sky. The birds began to sing. The animals woke up and stretched themselves, but still Coyote lay fast asleep. When the sun rose, the animals went to meet Man. He gave the longest bow to Cougar, so he had greatest power; the second longest he gave to Bear; others he gave to the other animals, giving all but the last to Frog. But the
25   shortest one was left. Man cried out, "What animal have I missed?" Then the animals began to look about and found Coyote fast asleep, with his eyelids pinned together. All the animals began to laugh, and they jumped upon Coyote and danced upon him. Then they led him to Man, still blinded, and Man pulled out the sharp sticks and gave him the shortest bow of all. It would hardly shoot an arrow farther than a foot. All the animals laughed.

(continued)

30   But Man took pity on Coyote, because he was now weaker even than Frog. So at [Coyote's] request, Kareya gave him cunning, ten times more than before, so that he was cunning above all the animals of the wood. Therefore Coyote was friendly to Man and his children, and did many things for them.

Excerpt from "The Fable of the Animals" edited by Katharine Berry Judson in Myths and Legends of California and the Old Southwest

1 **Which signal word in lines 1–9 shows when Kareya created the fishes?**

A First

B Then

C Last

D So

2 **What does the signal word "next" in line 21 reveal about the shift in ideas from the second paragraph (lines 10–20) to the third paragraph (lines 21–29)?**

A It shows that the third paragraph provides a conclusion to the ideas in the second paragraph.

B It shows that the third paragraph contrasts information in the second paragraph.

C It shows that the third paragraph presents a shift in time from the second paragraph.

D It shows that the third paragraph gives an example of an idea suggested in the second paragraph.

3 **What relationship does the signal word "therefore" in line 32 indicate?**

A It contrasts Coyote's kind actions to Man with his meanness toward other animals.

B It compares Coyote's friendliness to Man with his friendliness to Man's children.

C It provides additional information about why Coyote was so friendly to Man and his children.

D It shows that Coyote's kind actions to Man are the effect of Man's making Coyote cunning.

4 **What does the signal word "but" in line 11 show about Coyote and the other beasts?**

A It compares Coyote's cunning to the other beasts' cunning.

B It contrasts Coyote's cunning with the other beasts' cunning.

C It shows a relative location of Coyote's cunning and the other beasts' cunning.

D It shows that Coyote's cunning is a result of the other beasts' cunning.

5 **Which type of transition does the signal phrase "as a result" in line 18 show?**

A It shows an example of how Coyote is crafty with sticks.

B It reveals the relative location where Coyote was when he sharpened sticks.

C It shows that sharpening sticks to stay awake was an effect of Coyote's fatigue.

D It shows the most important thing that Coyote could do with sticks.

✓ Test-Taking Tip

Signal words help you link ideas. When writing an extended response on a test, choose the appropriate signal words and phrases to transition between ideas within paragraphs and between paragraphs. For example, if you are writing an extended response in which you are placing your ideas in the order of importance, you should use the signal words such as *first, more important, most important,* and *primarily.*

Analyzing Transitions

Transitions, whether they come between sentences or between paragraphs, tell the reader to slow down and to focus on how the ideas have shifted. If signal words have not been used, you can infer transitions by paying attention to the relationship between ideas.

NASA is responsible for some of the most important space exploration of the 20th century. This passage examines NASA's history and provides reasons why it should be funded.

The Space Age began in 1957, with the Soviet Union's successful launch of the unmanned *Sputnik 1*. The first manned space mission came a mere four years later, in 1961, when Soviet cosmonaut Yuri Gagarin became the first human being to orbit Earth. During the five decades since, human beings have explored outer space in the same way that Europeans explored the hitherto

5 unfamiliar expanses of the Americas during the Age of Exploration—by physically going there. Impressive accomplishments—sending humans to the Moon, manually placing the Hubble telescope in Earth's orbit—can be credited to the US National Aeronautics and Space Administration (NASA). Yet, despite NASA's extraordinary history, there has been continual discussion as to whether its continued existence is justified. Today we can state that the answer is "By all means, yes."

10 Let's begin our analysis of this assertion by addressing the primary objection to it: the United States cannot afford the expense. Space exploration costs a great deal of money. However, it is a mistake to think of NASA's budget as a waste of money that would be better spent on Earth. It *is* spent on Earth. When President Eisenhower created the agency in 1958, he said that one purpose for it was the development of new technologies adaptable for everyday use. NASA has excelled in this regard. To

15 date, the organization has secured more than 6,000 patents, many of which have driven innovation in other fields. Thousands of inventions, such as cordless tools, water filters, smoke detectors, medical devices, cell phones, and home entertainment systems, can trace their technological lineage to one or more of NASA's patents.

Moreover, this pioneering of knowledge points to related advantages to space exploration—it

20 answers questions about the material world and how it works, and it also leads to new questions that, when answered, uncover still further knowledge. Surely this potential for learning is as expansive as space itself. Who knows what remains to be discovered about the universe and our place in it? Perhaps we'll stumble upon new supplies of needed natural resources, new clues about the origins of life, or even new forms of life itself—some of which, it isn't far-fetched to consider, might have much in

25 common with us and perhaps a thing or two to teach us.

As we think about all of this, we should also look at our world's likely future. There is no guarantee that humankind must forever survive and develop. Some claim that there is an increasing amount of evidence that the opposite outcome is likely. The world's population is growing at an ever-faster rate, but we have limited natural resources. There are at present more than 7 billion human beings on Earth,

30 many already living in poverty. The US Census Bureau estimates that there will be more than 9 billion humans by 2050. It seems unwise, therefore, not to put some effort toward finding new places for humans to live. This idea might seem like science fiction at present, but one decade's sci-fi is the next decade's science fact.

Finally, let's ponder a proposition that few people would dispute. Whatever the cause, a spirit of

35 curiosity and adventure is part of what it means to be a human being. To state that this inquisitiveness must be limited to the world in which we find ourselves ignores the fact that we would know little about our world if not for that spirit of adventure. To squelch our natural urge to explore space is to deny our very humanity.

6 Which shift in ideas occurs between the first paragraph (lines 1–9) and the second paragraph (lines 10–18)?

A The first paragraph presents the problems of space exploration, and the second paragraph provides a solution to that problem.

B The first paragraph discusses the beginning of space exploration, and the second paragraph reveals a shift in time order.

C The first paragraph provides NASA's history, and the second paragraph provides examples of NASA's new technologies.

D The first paragraph presents some of NASA's accomplishments, and the second paragraph concludes that NASA should not be funded anymore.

7 What does "assertion" in line 10 mean?

A Question

B Declaration

C Command

D Request

8 Which signal phrase could be placed at the beginning of this sentence in lines 16–18? "Thousands of inventions, such as cordless tools, water filters, smoke detectors, medical devices, cell phones, and home entertainment systems, can trace their technological lineage to one or more of NASA's patents."

A In brief

B By contrast

C In conclusion

D For instance

9 Which type of transition does the word "moreover" in line 19 signal?

A Cause

B Effect

C Conclusion

D Addition

10 What does the signal word at the beginning of line 34 reveal about the shift in ideas in lines 34–38?

A The signal word "finally" shows that lines 34–38 are a conclusion of ideas presented in the passage.

B The signal word "whatever" shows that lines 34–38 contrast with the other ideas in the passage.

C The signal word "finally" shows that lines 34–38 contain the relative location of ideas from the passage.

D The signal word "whatever" shows that lines 34–38 reveal a cause of events that is presented in the rest of the passage.

✅ Test-Taking Tip

When you are responding to a writing prompt in a test, reread your sentences to make sure your signal words and phrases make sense in context. Signal words or phrases that have similar meanings cannot necessarily be used interchangeably. Suppose you wanted to write a sentence that contrasted apples and oranges, for example: "Unlike oranges, apples have an edible, thin peel." You might remember that *in spite of* is another signal phrase that shows contrast. Even so, you would not be able to substitute "in spite of" for "unlike" in this sentence. Rereading each sentence that contains a signal word or phrase should help you decide whether you used the right signal word or phrase.

Writing Practice

Everyone has a variety of skills or talents. Some people are talented artists, but they might also be able to solve complex math problems. Other people are track stars who can also read music.

Write two paragraphs in which you describe two of your skills or talents. Think about the **text structure** that best fits the content of your paragraphs. Then use the correct **signal words or phrases** to **transition** between ideas within and between paragraphs. Each paragraph should focus on a different skill or talent.

_____

_____

_____

_____

_____

_____

_____

_____

_____

_____

_____

_____

_____

_____

_____

_____

_____

_____

_____

_____

_____

_____

_____

_____

_____

_____

_____

This lesson will help you practice analyzing an author's purpose and point of view in two texts. Use it with Core Lesson 5.1 *Determine Author's Purpose and Point of View* to reinforce and apply your knowledge.

Key Concept

Authors have a reason for writing, and they often have an opinion about the topic of their writing.

Identifying Author's Purpose

An author writes a text for a specific purpose. A text may be written to inform you about a topic, to persuade you to think a certain way, or to entertain you.

"Crossing the Bar" was written by Lord Alfred Tennyson in 1889. It appears in many collections of Tennyson's works, as it was his request that this poem be placed at the end of each collection of his poetry.

    Sunset and evening star,
    And one clear call for me!
    And may there be no moaning of the bar,
    When I put out to sea,

5   But such a tide as moving seems asleep,
    Too full for sound and foam,
    When that which drew from out the boundless deep
    Turns again home.

    Twilight and evening bell,
10   And after that the dark!
    And may there be no sadness of farewell,
    When I embark;

    For though from out our bourne of Time and Place
    The flood may bear me far,
15   I hope to see my Pilot face to face
    When I have crossed the bar.

      "Crossing the Bar" by Alfred Lord Tennyson

1 **Which best describes the poet's purpose for this passage?**

    A To inform

    B To explain

    C To entertain

    D To persuade

2 **Which line in the poem contributes to the author's purpose of showing the passage of time?**

    A Line 2

    B Line 4

    C Line 9

    D Line 12

3 **Which statement explains how the author's style adds to the purpose of the text?**

A The speaker uses the natural movement of the ocean to show that he accepts his coming death.

B The speaker describes the sounds and darkness at the shore to show that he is sad about leaving his family.

C The speaker describes the sound and foam of the sea to show that he is worried about a possible flood.

D The speaker tells of crossing over the waters to show that he is excited about a coming voyage.

4 **Which of the following meanings associated with the word "bar" seems most intended in lines 3 and 16?**

A A straight piece or block of material

B A bank of sand that runs near the shore

C A location where food and drinks are served

D A vertical line before the beginning of a measure

Recognizing an Author's Point of View

Point of view is the author's attitude toward a topic. A point of view may be positive, negative, or neutral. It may be expressed directly or implied.

In this speech, President George W. Bush introduces the American people to the ideas behind a proposed educational initiative known as "No Child Left Behind."

Both parties have been talking about education reform for quite a while. It's time to come together to get it done so that we can truthfully say in America, "No child will be left behind—not one single child."

We share a moment of exceptional promise—a new administration, a newly sworn-in Congress, and we have a chance to think anew and act anew.

5   All of us are impatient with the old lines of division. . . . All in this room, as well as across the country, know things must change.

We must confront the scandal of illiteracy in America, seen most clearly in high-poverty schools, where nearly 70 percent of fourth graders are unable to read at a basic level. We must address the low standing of [American] test scores amongst industrialized nations in math and science, the very
10   subjects most likely to affect our future competitiveness. We must focus the spending of federal tax dollars on things that work. . . .

Change will not come by disdaining or dismantling the federal role of education. I believe strongly in local control of schools. I trust local folks to chart the path to excellence. But educational excellence for all is a national issue, and at this moment is a presidential priority. . . .

15   And real education reform reflects four basic commitments. First, children must be tested every year in reading and math. . . . Without yearly testing, we don't know who is falling behind and who needs help. . . .

Secondly, the agents of reform must be schools and school districts, not bureaucracies. . . . One size does not fit all when it comes to educating the children in America. School districts, school officials,
20   educational entrepreneurs should not be hindered by excessive rules and red tape and regulation.

. . . If local schools do not have the freedom to change, they cannot be held accountable for failing to change. Authority and accountability must be aligned at the local level, or schools will have a convenient excuse for failure. "I would have done it this way, but some central office or Washington, D.C., caused me to do it another way."

(continued)

25   . . . Third, many of our schools, particularly low-income schools, will need help in the transition to higher standards. When a state sets standards, we must help schools achieve those standards.

We must measure, we must know; and if a school or school district falls short, we must understand that help should be applied. . . . Once failing schools are identified, we will help them improve. . . .

Fourth, American children must not be left in persistently dangerous or failing schools. When
30   schools do not teach and will not change, parents and students must have other meaningful options. . . .

Parents and children who have only bad options must eventually get good options, if we are to succeed all across the country. . . .

These four principles are the guides to our education reform package. . . . I'm sending a series of specific proposals to the United States Congress; my own blueprint for reform. . . .

35   We've got one thing in mind: an education system that's responsive to the children, an education system that educates every child, an education system that I'm confident can exist; one that's based upon sound fundamental curriculum, one that starts teaching children to read early in life, one that focuses on systems that do work, one that heralds our teachers and makes sure they've got the necessary tools to teach, but one that says every child can learn. And in this great land called America,
40   no child will be left behind.

Excerpt from *Selected Speeches of George W. Bush 2001–2008*

5 **Which statement best expresses the author's point of view?**

A   High standards leave some children behind.

B   Parents and children have too many choices in education.

C   The education system is not working and needs to be changed.

D   Education in the United States allows everyone to be successful.

6 **Which word best describes the author's point of view about the education system in the United States at the time of the speech?**

A   Positive

B   Negative

C   Neutral

D   Optimistic

7 **Which best describes the author's purpose for this passage?**

A   To persuade

B   To entertain

C   To inform

D   To explain

8 **According to the author's point of view, what is most needed in the US educational system?**

A   Reform

B   Money

C   Leaders

D   Diversity

9 **Which is not a suggestion that the author states to support his point of view?**

A   Test children every year in math and reading.

B   Allow children to leave dangerous or failing schools.

C   Create a uniform model for all children.

D   Help children transition to higher standards.

✓ **Test-Taking Tip**

When you are reading test questions, note key words that help you understand what the question is asking. For example, you might note the words *point of view* or *author's purpose*.

Writing Practice

Many schools want to increase student access to technology, but they have limited funds to purchase or to upgrade their technology. One solution that has been proposed is to allow students to bring their own devices, such as tablets and smart phones, to school to use in class. Some people argue that allowing students to bring their own devices to school will create new problems.

Write a speech in which you give your **opinion** about this issue. State your **point of view** clearly. Remember that your purpose is to **persuade** the listener to agree with your opinion. Use persuasive language, and provide reasons to support your opinion.

_____

_____

_____

_____

_____

_____

_____

_____

_____

_____

_____

_____

_____

_____

_____

_____

_____

_____

_____

_____

_____

_____

_____

_____

This lesson will help you practice using two texts to analyze how an author's purpose determines the text structure. Use it with Core Lesson 5.2 *Analyze How Author's Purpose Determines Structure* to reinforce and apply your knowledge.

Key Concept

Authors choose specific text structures to clarify what they want to say. The text structures engage the reader and help authors achieve a purpose.

Text Structure in Informational Texts

All authors have a purpose for writing. The most common purposes are to inform, to persuade, and to entertain. An author of an informational text chooses an organization, or structure, that supports the purpose for writing. Common text structures include sequence, compare and contrast, cause and effect, description, and problem and solution.

Earth Science is the study of the planet Earth. It is helpful to understand how the planet operates as a system in space. This passage presents an overview of some key concepts in Earth and space science.

Earth Science: The Study of Earth

Earth science is the study of Earth's origins and the forces at work that are constantly changing the surface of the planet. Earth science differs from the life sciences in that Earth science focuses on nonliving things rather than living things. It is a very broad field that covers the subjects of astronomy,
5 geology, meteorology, paleontology, and oceanography.

Astronomy: The Study of Space

One of the oldest fields of study in science deals with how Earth was created and how this planet fits into the design of the universe. **Astronomy** is the study of the size, movements, and composition of the planets, stars, and other deep-space objects. By observing objects in space, astronomers hope to
10 understand how our planet was created and how it evolved. A number of important theories have been advanced to explain the beginning of Earth and its universe.

The Beginning of the Universe

According to the leading theory, known as the **big bang theory**, a "cosmic egg" made up of dust and gas containing all the matter in the universe exploded. This explosion occurred 15 to 20 billion
15 years ago, creating the basic atoms of our lightest gases from which the stars formed. The big bang theory accounts for the measured expansion of the universe and the background radiation found in all directions in outer space. According to the **open universe theory**, the universe will either continue the expansion indefinitely or begin a collapse. A different theory, called the **closed universe theory**, predicts that the total mass of the universe is large enough to gather up all matter into a concentrated
20 central point and then gravitationally collapse at some point in the distant future. This collapse is referred to as the "big crunch."

The most distant (but unknown) objects detected by science are known as **quasars** (quasi-stellar radio sources). The light and energy that has arrived from these objects is about 16 billion years old. It is likely that the energy that we receive now came from these objects during their formation. Every
25 time scientists investigate deep-space objects, they must remember that information we receive now took time to get to Earth. Even the light from the sun takes eight minutes to reach Earth. The nearest star to the sun is Alpha Centauri, which is more than four light years away.

1 What is the author's main purpose for writing this piece?

A To inform

B To entertain

C To persuade

D To express emotions

2 Which best describes the overall structure of this passage?

A Sequence

B Description

C Cause and effect

D Compare and contrast

3 How does the overall structure help the author achieve his or her purpose for writing?

A It helps the reader compare Earth science and life sciences.

B It helps the reader understand which topics are included in Earth science.

C It helps the reader understand how lack of funding causes limits on astronomy research.

D It helps the reader understand the order in which astronomy theories were developed.

4 Which best describes the structure of the third paragraph (lines 13–21)?

A Sequence

B Description

C Cause and effect

D Compare and contrast

✅ Test-Taking Tip

When you are taking a multiple-choice test, read each question and formulate an answer in your head. Then read the answer choices. Choose the answer that is most similar to your answer. Following these steps will help you eliminate answer choices that are definitely incorrect.

Text Structure in Literary Texts

Like authors of informational texts, literary writers also choose text structures that convey their purposes. These text structures are similar to those used by informational writers. Sometimes literary writers enhance the text structure with special techniques. These techniques include alternating viewpoints, flashback, and parallel plots.

"The Masque of the Red Death" is a short story that was written in 1845 by Edgar Allan Poe. It takes place at a masquerade ball, where guests wear costumes and masks. The story's underlying message is that trying to avoid death is pointless.

[T]hese other apartments were densely crowded, and in them beat feverishly the heart of life. And the revel went whirlingly on, until at length there commenced the sounding of midnight upon the clock. And then the music ceased, as I have told; and the evolutions of the waltzers were quieted; and there was an uneasy cessation of all things as before. But now there were twelve strokes to be sounded by
5   the bell of the clock. . . . [B]efore the last echoes of the last chime had utterly sunk into silence, there were many individuals in the crowd who had found leisure to become aware of the presence of a masked figure which had arrested the attention of no single individual before. And the rumor of this new presence having spread itself whisperingly around, there arose at length from the whole company a buzz, or murmur, expressive of disapprobation and surprise—then, finally, of terror, of horror, and of
10   disgust.

In an assembly of phantasms such as I have painted, it may well be supposed that no ordinary appearance could have excited such sensation. In truth the masquerade license of the night was nearly unlimited; but the figure in question had out-Heroded Herod, and gone beyond the bounds of even the prince's indefinite decorum. There are chords in the hearts of the most reckless which cannot be
15   touched without emotion. Even with the utterly lost, to whom life and death are equally jests, there are matters of which no jest can be made. The whole company, indeed, seemed now deeply to feel that in the costume and bearing of the stranger neither wit nor propriety existed.

The figure was tall and gaunt, and shrouded from head to foot in the habiliments of the grave. The mask which concealed the visage was made so nearly to resemble the countenance of a stiffened
20   corpse that the closest scrutiny must have had difficulty in detecting the cheat. And yet all this might have been endured, if not approved, by the mad revellers around. But the mummer had gone so far as to assume the type of the Red Death. His vesture was dabbled in blood—and his broad brow, with all the features of the face, was besprinkled with the scarlet horror.

When the eyes of Prince Prospero fell upon this spectral image (which with a slow and solemn
25   movement, as if more fully to sustain its role, stalked to and fro among the waltzers) he was seen to be convulsed, in the first moment with a strong shudder either of terror or distaste; but, in the next, his brow reddened with rage.

Excerpt from "The Masque of the Red Death" by Edgar Allan Poe

5 What is the author's purpose for writing this piece?

A   To inform

B   To entertain

C   To persuade

D   To express emotions

6 Which term best describes the overall text structure of this passage?

A   Sequence

B   Flashback

C   Parallel plots

D   Problem and solution

7 How does the text structure help achieve the author's purpose for writing?

A   It helps the reader follow the events that occur during the masked ball.

B   It helps the reader see the events at the masked ball from various perspectives.

C   It helps the reader understand how earlier events influenced the masked character's current actions.

D   It helps the reader compare the feelings and actions of several characters at the masked ball.

8 Which technique does the author use to help tell the story?

A   Flashbacks

B   Parallel plots

C   Time-order words

D   Alternating viewpoints

9 Which of the following meanings associated with the word "sustain" seems most intended in lines 24–25?

A   Nourish

B   Keep up

C   Undergo

D   Withstand

10 Read these story events, and then choose the correct sequence.

i.   People were disturbed by the way the masked character was dressed.

ii. The prince became angry.

iii. People began to notice a masked character.

iv. The music stopped at midnight, and the party got quiet.

Which list shows the correct sequence of events?

A   i, ii, iii, iv

B   ii, iv, iii, i

C   iii, iv, ii, i

D   iv, iii, i, ii

✓ Test-Taking Tip

When possible, use your life experiences as the basis for your extended responses on a test. If you are writing about something you know well, you will feel more confident and engaged. In addition, you will have a ready supply of real-life examples to use as evidence to support your ideas.

Writing Practice

News articles are structured in a variety of ways, depending on the author's purpose. For example, an article written to inform citizens about a mayor's response to graffiti on public buildings might describe the problem and then offer several proposed solutions. However, a news article written to explain the history of a conflict between two nations might relate events in the order in which they happened.

Write a one-paragraph newspaper article about a current event that interests you. Think about your **purpose** for writing. Then select a **text structure**—such as sequence, problem and solution, cause and effect, or description—that will help you present your information in a logical way.

This lesson will help you practice inferring an author's purpose in two informational texts. Use it with Core Lesson 5.3 *Infer Author's Purpose* to reinforce and apply your knowledge.

Key Concept

When an author does not explicitly state his or her purpose for writing a text, readers can use their prior knowledge and details from the text to infer the author's purpose.

Inferring the Author's Purpose

Authors write with a specific purpose in mind. They might want to inform you about a topic, to persuade you to think a certain way, or to entertain you. They might even have more than one purpose. However, authors do not always state the purpose explicitly. Sometimes you have to infer it by using context, details, and your knowledge of the topic.

This memo was written by a human resource manager. It was distributed to employees of a hospital.

MEMO

Date: October 15

To: All Medical Staff

From: Wendy Lockwood, Human Resources Manager

5   **Subject:** Hand-washing guidelines

    This memo is a follow-up to the recent training about workplace hygiene and safety. We would like to outline the key points addressed in the training about clean hands in the workplace. These guidelines are crucial for all medical staff to follow. However, they also serve as common-sense hygiene tips for everyone in a workplace setting.

10   To ensure that all germs and bacteria are released, be sure to follow these steps:

1. Place hands together under warm water. Using antibacterial soap, rub your hands together for at least 20 seconds.
2. Thoroughly wash both sides of the hands, the wrists, and under the fingernails.
3. Rinse well.
15
4. Completely dry your hands using a clean towel, which helps remove the germs. If using a disposable towel, be sure to throw it in the trash.

    If water is not available, use an alcohol-based hand sanitizer. Place a small dollop of the product on the palm of one hand, and then rub it all over your hands and fingers until it dries.

20   Frequent hand-washing can help you and others avoid illness. You should wash your hands

- after using the bathroom.
- before and after eating or preparing food (especially raw meat).
- after sneezing, coughing, or blowing your nose.
25
- before and after tending to a wound.

(continued)

- after handling trash and/or hazardous materials.
- after touching objects contaminated by floodwater or sewage.
- after handling animals or their waste.
- when your hands are visibly dirty.

30   This information and a recording of last week's training presentation are available on our company's intranet. We strongly encourage all medical staff to review the information. Please help us adhere to the highest standards possible, ensuring the health and safety of our cohorts and patients.

Source: Centers for Disease Control and Prevention: www.cdc.gov/handwashing/

1 **Wendy Lockwood's purposes for writing the memo are to persuade and to**

A   describe situations.

B   entertain students.

C   express emotions.

D   inform readers.

2 **The main reason for including the bullet points is to convey that**

A   hands are susceptible to getting dirty.

B   people who are sick can spread disease.

C   animals should not be present in the workplace.

D   hands can become contaminated in many ways.

3 **In line 26, the word "hazardous" most nearly means**

A   dangerous.

B   dirty.

C   slippery.

D   unpleasant.

4 **Which phrase states the implied purpose of the text?**

A   To reduce training costs for the hospital

B   To prevent the spread of disease in the hospital

C   To highlight the work of researchers in the hospital

D   To address complaints from patients about the hospital

5 **Which word could most logically be added to this memo?**

A   Comfortable

B   Crucial

C   Cordial

D   Creative

Using Context to Infer Implicit Purpose

When authors do not state why they are writing, you can use your knowledge and the details in the text to infer the purpose. It is also helpful to consider the author and the context.

This passage is a speech given by President Gerald Ford toward the end of US involvement in the Vietnam War.

Instead of my addressing the image of America, I prefer to consider the reality of America. It is true that we have launched our bicentennial celebration without having achieved human perfection, but we have attained a very remarkable self-governed society that possesses the flexibility and the dynamism to grow and undertake an entirely new agenda, an agenda for America's third century.

5   So, I ask you to join me in helping to write that agenda. I am as determined as a president can be to seek national rediscovery of the belief in ourselves that characterized the most creative periods in our nation's history. The greatest challenge of creativity, as I see it, lies ahead.

We, of course, are saddened indeed by the events in Indochina. But these events, tragic as they are, portend neither the end of the world nor of America's leadership in the world.

10   Let me put it this way, if I might. Some tend to feel that if we do not succeed in everything everywhere, then we have succeeded in nothing anywhere. I reject categorically such polarized thinking. We can and we should help others to help themselves. But the fate of responsible men and women everywhere, in the final decision, rests in their own hands, not in ours.

America's future depends upon Americans—especially your generation, which is now equipping 15   itself to assume the challenges of the future, to help write the agenda for America.

Earlier today, in this great community, I spoke about the need to maintain our defenses. Tonight, I would like to talk about another kind of strength, the true source of American power that transcends all of the deterrent powers for peace of our armed forces. I am speaking here of our belief in ourselves and our belief in our nation.

20   Abraham Lincoln asked, in his own words, and I quote, "What constitutes the bulwark of our own liberty and independence?" And he answered, "It is not our frowning battlements or bristling seacoasts, our army or our navy. Our defense is in the spirit which prized liberty as the heritage of all men, in all lands everywhere."

It is in this spirit that we must now move beyond the discords of the past decade. It is in this spirit 25   that I ask you to join me in writing an agenda for the future.

Excerpt from "A War That Is Finished" by President Gerald R. Ford, April 23, 1975

6 The speaker was the president of the United States. Which statement about the presidency is most relevant in determining the purpose of Ford's speech?

    A The president is elected every four years.

    B The president leads his or her political party.

    C The president guides the nation and the military.

    D The president signs legislation written by Congress.

7 Which contextual information is most relevant in determining the purpose of Ford's speech?

    A Some Americans were discouraged by the Vietnam War.

    B The speech was made at Tulane University in Louisiana.

    C President Ford served in the US Navy during World War II.

    D Many celebrations were held to celebrate the US bicentennial.

8 Which sentence from the speech best conveys Ford's overall purpose?

    A "Instead of my addressing the image of America, I prefer to consider the reality of America."

    B "We, of course, are saddened indeed by the events in Indochina."

    C "I am speaking here of our belief in ourselves and our belief in our nation."

    D "I ask you to join me in writing an agenda for the future."

9 What was President Ford's main purpose for delivering this speech?

    A To explain ideas

    B To express emotion

    C To inform students

    D To persuade people

✔ Test-Taking Tip

If you are unsure of the answer to a question, note the question number and move on. Continuing with the remaining questions might help you figure out the answer to a difficult question. At the end of the test, if you have time, you can return to the questions you noted but didn't answer.

Writing Practice

Think about your favorite advertisement. It probably doesn't come right out and ask you to purchase the product. Instead, it tries to persuade you to want the product or service by listing features and by using persuasive words to entice you.

Write a paragraph in which you convey your feelings about a product or service you enjoy without explicitly stating your purpose: to **persuade** the reader to agree with your opinion. Use persuasive language and provide details that will make your purpose clear.

_____
_____
_____
_____
_____
_____
_____
_____
_____
_____
_____
_____
_____
_____
_____
_____
_____
_____
_____
_____
_____
_____

This lesson will help you practice analyzing how authors differentiate and support their positions. Use it with Core Lesson 5.4 *Analyze How Authors Differentiate Their Positions* to reinforce and apply your knowledge.

Key Concept

Authors can strengthen their positions by acknowledging viewpoints that differ from theirs and by using evidence or reasoning to refute them.

Identifying an Author's Position

To support their positions, or opinions, on a topic, authors often introduce differing viewpoints. These viewpoints can be complementary or conflicting. Writers can then strengthen their position in one of two ways. They can show how the complementary viewpoints support their position, or they can disprove, or refute, conflicting viewpoints or show that those viewpoints are unreasonable.

Scientists and educators are intrigued by the topic of intelligence. This article explores research about child prodigies. It considers the question of whether the intelligence of highly gifted individuals is biological or the result of their environment.

Does the brain of a prodigy or a genius differ from the average human brain? Research in various fields of science has provided evidence to answer this question. It suggests that the brains of child prodigies function differently than the brains of average children. A recent theory also states that the ability of a prodigy results from a certain combination of clearly identifiable factors. First, a child's
5 own personality and temperament are important elements. Second, environment and parents are significant considerations. Finally, the repetition of a specific activity contributes to the nurture of the incredible talents of prodigies.

A prodigy is an exceptionally talented child or young person. At a very young age—typically by the age of ten—the child demonstrates expertise in a particular field. This field is one that is normally
10 associated with and mastered by adults. All prodigies have seemingly inborn talents. Although no single underlying cause is behind their precocity in music, mathematics, or some other sphere, prodigies do share some common characteristics.

A prodigy's special talent usually manifests itself early in life. One example is the Austrian composer Wolfgang Amadeus Mozart, who was composing at the age of five. Another is the British
15 philosopher John Stuart Mill, who was reading Greek and Latin by age eight and philosophy by age ten.

Some experts believe that a prodigy is born with naturally exceptional talent. The inherent talent of a child prodigy is reinforced by a strong drive to excel. A prodigy possesses a single-minded focus on sharpening skills through virtually continuous practice. This dedication is often nurtured and developed by parents or teachers, especially those who have similar talents and abilities.

20 For example, Wolfgang Amadeus Mozart was the son of violinist and composer Leopold Mozart. Leopold instructed his daughter and Wolfgang in music. A man of ambition, Leopold imposed the discipline required for his children to succeed as pianists and composers. John Stuart Mill's father, James Mill, was the only teacher the young philosophy prodigy ever had. Mozart and Mill spent many hours daily practicing and perfecting their special talents. Both seemed to have been born to the right
25 parents, lived in favorable environments, and possessed the proper temperaments to emerge as child prodigies. As a result, each went on to make significant contributions to his respective field.

(continued)

Some researchers claim that deliberate practice alone sets prodigies off from their average peers. However, research has indicated that child prodigies have inherent skills. In fact, brain studies involving child prodigies has indicated that the right frontal lobes in the brains of prodigies receive six
30 or seven times the normal blood flow measured in children of average ability. The right frontal lobe of the brain controls skills directly related to music and mathematics. Neuroscientists use imaging procedures like the PET scan or the MRI scan to study brain structure and function.

Scientists have also determined that a prodigy seems to alternate easily between the right and left hemispheres of the brain, as measured by activities specific to each hemisphere. Many gifted
35 children even appear to be ambidextrous. This means they use their right and left hands equally well. Undoubtedly new research will enhance our understanding of the brain. Results should illuminate differences in brain function between gifted and ordinary human beings.

1 Which of the following statements best reflects the author's position?

  A Prodigies' success is solely the result of the way their brains function.

  B Prodigies are the result of an environment that nurtures their development.

  C More research must be conducted to understand why prodigies excel.

  D A combination of nature and environment contribute to prodigies' success.

2 An opposing viewpoint cited by the author is that prodigies

  A acquire their skills solely through deliberate practice.

  B may manifest their talent later in life.

  C are born with naturally exceptional talent.

  D have similar brain structures to ordinary humans.

3 Read the following statement.

"In fact, brain studies involving child prodigies has indicated that the right frontal lobes in the brains of prodigies receive six or seven times the normal blood flow measured in children of average ability."

The author uses this statement to

  A explain the assertion that it is only environment that makes prodigies excel.

  B support the assertion that prodigies' brains function differently than ordinary people.

  C refute the assertion that prodigies' brains are similar to those of ordinary people.

  D provide evidence for the assertion that environment doesn't play a role in making prodigies.

4 Which of the following meanings associated with the word "field" seems most intended in lines 2, 9, and 26?

  A A large area without trees

  B The area you can see through a lens

  C To catch and throw a ball to a teammate

  D An area of activity or study

✅ Test-Taking Tip

Before writing a test essay, take a few minutes to plan your response. You might want to use a graphic organizer to organize your thoughts. Consider using a flowchart to explain steps in a process or a Venn diagram to compare and contrast ideas. A diagram that is used to visually represent causes and effects can also work for problems and solutions. Finally, concept webs are helpful for showing relationships among ideas.

Analyzing Support for an Author's Position

To make their persuasive texts effective, authors provide evidence to support their position. They also offer evidence to refute opposing viewpoints. Without evidence, readers are not likely to be convinced that they should agree with the author or disagree with the opposing position.

This passage is an excerpt from a speech delivered to Congress by President Lyndon B. Johnson in March 1965.

Wednesday I will send to Congress a law designed to eliminate illegal barriers to the right to vote. . . . This bill will establish a simple, uniform standard which cannot be used, however ingenious the effort, to flout our Constitution.

5 It will provide for citizens to be registered by officials of the United States government if the state officials refuse to register them.

It will eliminate tedious, unnecessary lawsuits which delay the right to vote.

Finally, this legislation will ensure that properly registered individuals are not prohibited from voting.

I will welcome the suggestions from all the members of Congress—I have no doubt that I will get
10 some—on ways and means to strengthen this law and to make it effective. But experience has plainly shown that this is the only path to carry out the command of the Constitution.

To those who seek to avoid action by their national government in their own communities, who want to and who seek to maintain purely local control over elections, the answer is simple:

Open your polling places to all your people. Allow men and women to register and vote whatever
15 the color of their skin. Extend the rights of citizenship to every citizen of this land. . . .

There is no constitutional issue here. The command of the Constitution is plain.

There is no moral issue. It is wrong—deadly wrong—to deny any of your fellow Americans the right to vote in this country.

There is no issue of states' rights or national rights. There is only the struggle for human rights. . . .

20 The last time a president sent a civil rights bill to the Congress it contained a provision to protect voting rights in federal elections. That civil rights bill was passed after eight long months of debate. And when that bill came to my desk from the Congress for my signature, the heart of the voting provision had been eliminated.

This time, on this issue, there must be no delay, no hesitation and no compromise with our purpose.
25 We cannot, we must not, refuse to protect the right of every American to vote in every election that he may desire to participate in. And we ought not and we cannot and we must not wait another eight months before we get a bill. We have already waited a hundred years and more, and the time for waiting is gone.

So I ask you to join me in working long hours—nights and weekends, if necessary—to pass this
30 bill. And I don't make that request lightly. For from the window where I sit with the problems of our country I recognize that outside this chamber is the outraged conscience of a nation, the grave concern of many nations, and the harsh judgment of history on our acts. . . .

(continued)

But even if we pass this bill, the battle will not be over. What happened in Selma* is part of a far larger movement which reaches into every section and state of America. It is the effort of [African Americans] to secure for themselves the full blessings of American life.

35

Their cause must be our cause too. Because it is not just [African Americans], but really it is all of us, who must overcome the crippling legacy of bigotry and injustice.

And we shall overcome.

_____

* Police in Selma, Alabama, physically attacked hundreds of civil-rights marchers.

Excerpt from the "We Shall Overcome" speech by Lyndon B. Johnson

5 What is Lyndon Johnson's position?

A Congress must work harder.

B Congress must draft a new bill.

C Congress must guarantee states' rights.

D Congress must pass the voting rights bill.

6 What is the opposing position that Johnson refutes in line 19?

A The national government should determine election laws.

B States' rights take precedence over national rights.

C All people should have the right to vote in elections.

D The entire country agrees that change should be made.

7 How does Johnson strengthen his position?

A By refuting opposing viewpoints

B By creating opposing viewpoints

C By ignoring opposing viewpoints

D By supporting opposing viewpoints

8 Some opponents of Johnson in Congress felt that they should have an opportunity to revise his voting rights bill. In which part of the speech does Johnson provide evidence that discredits these opponents?

A Lines 9–11

B Lines 17–18

C Lines 20–23

D Lines 36–37

Writing Practice

Some schools have added service learning to their programs. This component requires students to complete volunteer hours as a part of their coursework or as a graduation requirement. Often these volunteer programs are incorporated into the curriculum. For example, a history class studying World War II might volunteer at a local veterans' hospital.

Write an essay stating your opinion about whether service learning belongs in schools. Develop a logical **argument** in which you clearly state your opinion and introduce an **opposing viewpoint**. Indicate that you understand that position and explain how it is different from yours. Cite evidence to support your position and to refute the opposing position.

This lesson will help you practice analyzing an author's intention and effect in two texts. Use it with Core Lesson 5.5 *Analyze Author's Intention and Effect* to reinforce and apply your knowledge.

Key Concept

Authors use several types of rhetorical devices to communicate their position and to achieve their goals for writing.

Identifying Rhetorical Devices

Authors write with goals, or intentions, in mind. Among the many techniques they use are rhetorical devices, which help authors create the desired effects on their audiences. Some common rhetorical devices are analogy, asking questions, enumeration, juxtaposition of opposites, qualification statements, repetition, and parallelism.

Konrad Bercovici was born in Romania in 1882. He was a journalist who also wrote fictional short stories. The setting of "Ghitza" comes from Bercovici's memories of his early childhood on the banks of the Danube River.

That winter had been a very severe one in Romania. The Danube froze solid a week before Christmas and remained tight for five months. It was as if the blue waters were suddenly turned into steel. From across the river, from the Dobrudja, on sleds pulled by long-horned oxen, the Tartars brought barrels of frozen honey, quarters of killed lambs, poultry and game, and returned heavily
5   laden with bags of flour and rolls of sole leather. The whole day long the crack of whips and the curses of the drivers rent the icy atmosphere. Whatever their destination, the carters were in a hurry to reach human habitation before nightfall—before the dreaded time when packs of wolves came out to prey for food.

In cold, clear nights, when even the wind was frozen still, the lugubrious howling of the wolf
10   permitted no sleep. The indoor people spent the night praying for the lives and souls of the travellers.

All through the winter there was not one morning but some man or animal was found torn or eaten in our neighbourhood. The people of the village at first built fires on the shores to scare the beasts away, but they had to give it up because the thatched roofs of the huts in the village were set on fire in windy nights by flying sparks. The cold cowed the fiercest dogs. The wolves, crazed by hunger, grew
15   more daring from day to day. They showed their heads even in daylight. When Baba Hana, the old . . . fortune-teller, ran into the school-house one morning and cried, "Wolf, wolf in the yard," the teacher was inclined to attribute her scare to a long drink the night before. But that very night, Stan, the horseshoer, who had returned late from the inn and had evidently not closed the door as he entered the smithy, was eaten up by the beasts. And the smithy stood in the centre of the village! A stone's throw
20   from the inn, and the thatch-roofed school, and the red painted church!

Excerpt from "Ghitza" by Konrad Bercovici

1 Which type of rhetorical device is the author using in the sentence, "It was as if the blue waters were suddenly turned into steel"?

A Enumeration

B Repetition

C Parallelism

D Analogy

2 Which type of rhetorical device is used in the sentence, "Whatever their destination, the carters were in a hurry to reach human habitation before nightfall—before the dreaded time when packs of wolves came out to prey for food"?

A Qualifying statement

B Analogy

C Enumeration

D Juxtaposition of opposites

3 Which of the following sentences is an example of enumeration?

A "The Danube froze solid a week before Christmas and remained tight for five months."

B "In cold, clear nights, when even the wind was frozen still, the lugubrious howling of the wolf permitted no sleep."

C "A stone's throw from the inn, and the thatch-roofed school, and the red painted church!"

D "The wolves, crazed by hunger, grew more daring from day to day."

4 In line 4, the word "quarters" most nearly means

A coins worth twenty-five cents.

B one-fourth portions of slaughtered animals.

C lodgings for soldiers or crew members.

D at close range or nearly in contact.

Identifying an Author's Intention and Effect

Authors write for a purpose—to entertain, to inform, or to persuade. Authors also write with an intention, which combines purpose and point of view. The author's intention is what he or she hopes to accomplish with the written work. The author uses rhetorical devices to produce the desired effect.

Frederick Douglass was born into slavery in the early 1800s. He learned how to read and write, and he escaped to freedom in 1838. Douglass became a highly respected abolitionist, writer, orator, and statesman.

There were no beds given the slaves, unless one coarse blanket be considered such, and none but the men and women had these. This, however, is not considered a very great privation. They find less difficulty from the want of beds, than from the want of time to sleep; for when their day's work in the field is done, the most of them having their washing, mending, and cooking to do, and having

5 few or none of the ordinary facilities for doing either of these, very many of their sleeping hours are consumed in preparing for the field the coming day; and when this is done, old and young, male and female, married and single, drop down side by side, on one common bed,—the cold, damp floor,—each covering himself or herself with their miserable blankets; and here they sleep till they are summoned to the field by the driver's horn. At the sound of this, all must rise, and be off to the field.

10 There must be no halting; every one must be at his or her post; and woe betides them who hear not this morning summons to the field; for if they are not awakened by the sense of hearing, they are by the sense of feeling: no age nor sex finds any favor. Mr. Severe, the overseer, used to stand by the door of the quarter, armed with a large hickory stick and heavy cowskin, ready to whip any one who was so unfortunate as not to hear, or, from any other cause, was prevented from being ready to start for the

15 field at the sound of the horn.

(continued)

Mr. Severe was rightly named: he was a cruel man. I have seen him whip a woman, causing the blood to run half an hour at the time; and this, too, in the midst of her crying children, pleading for their mother's release. He seemed to take pleasure in manifesting his fiendish barbarity. Added to his cruelty, he was a profane swearer. It was enough to chill the blood and stiffen the hair of an ordinary man to

20   hear him talk. Scarce a sentence escaped him but that was commenced or concluded by some horrid oath. The field was the place to witness his cruelty and profanity. His presence made it both the field of blood and of blasphemy. From the rising till the going down of the sun, he was cursing, raving, cutting, and slashing among the slaves of the field, in the most frightful manner. His career was short. He died very soon after I went to Colonel Lloyd's; and he died as he lived, uttering, with his dying groans, bitter

25   curses and horrid oaths. His death was regarded by the slaves as the result of a merciful providence.

Excerpt from "Narrative of the Life of Frederick Douglass an American Slave" by Frederick Douglass

5 **Judging from the rhetorical devices he uses, Frederick Douglass's intention was likely**

   A to convince readers that Mr. Severe's death was deserved.

   B to convey how unfairly he and other slaves were treated.

   C to clarify what it is like to work on a farm.

   D to entertain readers with a tale from his childhood.

6 **Which sentence best describes the effect of rhetoric in the narrative?**

   A It prompts people to be skeptical about the experiences of slaves.

   B It stimulates a discussion about life in the rural south in the 1800s.

   C It inspires people to make changes in their daily lives.

   D It evokes an emotional response to the treatment of slaves.

7 **In the excerpt ". . . and when this is done, old and young, male and female, married and single, drop down side by side . . . ," the author uses the rhetorical device of**

   A analogy.

   B asking questions.

   C enumeration.

   D qualifying statement.

8 **Which of the following excerpts from the text does not convey the author's intention?**

   A "His career was short."

   B "There were no beds given the slaves . . ."

   C ". . . the cold, damp floor . . ."

   D ". . . ready to whip any one . . ."

Language Practice

A participle is a verb that acts as an adjective. It modifies nouns and pronouns and comes in two forms: present, ending with -*ing*, and past, ending with -*ed*. Not all verbs with these endings are participles. When you use participles, make sure you use the correct form.

Read quickly through the draft feature article in the box below. Then go to the spread-out version, and consider the suggestions for revision.

---

1   Officer Chavez watched as the howl winds snapped trees and ripped shingles off of rooftops. She had been monitoring the National Weather Service's alerts over the last week. And since this wasn't her first tropical storm, she knew what was coming. Soon the dreading storm surge followed.

2   Rain and seawater flooded the streets and washed sand off the beaches. The seawall helped buffer the damage from the crashing waves, but it couldn't hold back the rise sea levels. The homes built on pilings and stilts would escape the damage from floodwaters, but homes built at street level and cars throughout the city would suffer severe water damage.

---

1   Officer Chavez watched as the <u>howl</u>
<u> </u>
      1

winds snapped trees and ripped shingles off

of rooftops. She had been monitoring the

National Weather Service's alerts over the last

week. And since this wasn't her first tropical

storm, she knew what was coming. Soon the

<u>dreading</u> storm surge followed.
  2

2   Rain and seawater flooded the streets

and washed sand off the beaches. The seawall

helped buffer the damage from the <u>crashing</u>
               3

waves, but it couldn't hold back the <u>rise sea</u>
              4

levels. The homes built on pilings and stilts

would escape the damage from floodwaters,

but homes built at street level and cars

throughout the city would suffer severe

water damage.

1   **A** *(No change)*
    B howls
    C howling
    D howled

2   **A** *(No change)*
    B dreaded
    C dreading
    D dreads

3   **A** *(No change)*
    B crash
    C crashes
    D crashed

4   **A** *(No change)*
    B rises
    C rose
    D rising

✓ Test-Taking Tip

To familiarize yourself with the specifics of a test, consider using a test-taking tutorial. Tutorials often provide information on how to navigate through the test, types of questions, and test-taking strategies. You will also learn how to keep track of the remaining time and how to monitor your progress.

Writing Practice

Have you ever read something that had a dramatic effect on you? Perhaps it helped you see an issue in a new way, or maybe it included descriptions that evoked an emotional response. A writer's intention and use of rhetorical devices might create these effects. When you are reading, it is helpful to think critically about the devices that the writer uses to achieve his or her goals.

Analyze one of the reading passages in this lesson. Summarize the excerpt, and **explain the author's intention and effect**. Describe at least two rhetorical devices the writer uses, and explain how those devices helped the writer achieve his goals. Support your ideas with details and examples.

_____

_____

_____

_____

_____

_____

_____

_____

_____

_____

_____

_____

_____

_____

_____

_____

_____

_____

_____

_____

_____

_____

_____

_____

_____

This lesson will help you practice identifying argument development in two texts. Use it with Core Lesson 6.1 *Identify Argument Development* to reinforce and apply your knowledge.

Key Concept

The purpose of an argument is to persuade the reader that a claim is reasonable. A well-developed argument includes reasons and evidence that support the writer's claim.

Developing an Argument

An argument starts with a claim, or a statement of the author's opinion or position on a topic. The author wants to persuade readers to believe or to act on the claim. In a good argument, claims are supported by evidence such as reasons, facts, and examples. The conclusion of an argument may restate the author's claim, summarize the evidence, or call upon the reader to take action.

In "Common Sense," published in January 1776, Thomas Paine urges American colonists to declare their independence from British rule. The pamphlet influenced revolutionary leaders such as George Washington. The peers referred to in the passage are nobility, who inherited their positions, but people in the commons were elected.

I offer a few remarks on the so much boasted constitution of England. That it was noble for the dark and slavish times in which it was erected, is granted. When the world was overrun with tyranny the least remove therefrom was a glorious rescue. But that it is imperfect, subject to convulsions, and incapable of producing what it seems to promise, is easily demonstrated. . . .

5   I know it is difficult to get over local or long standing prejudices, yet if we will suffer ourselves to examine the component parts of the English constitution, we shall find them to be the base remains of two ancient tyrannies, compounded with some new republican materials.

FIRST—The remains of monarchial tyranny in the person of the king.

SECONDLY—The remains of aristocratical tyranny in the persons of the peers.

10   THIRDLY— The new republican materials in the persons of the commons, on whose virtue depends the freedom of England.

The two first, by being hereditary, are independent of the people; wherefore in a CONSTITUTIONAL SENSE they contribute nothing towards the freedom of the state.

To say that the constitution of England is a UNION of three powers reciprocally CHECKING each 15   other, is farcical, either the words have no meaning, or they are flat contradictions.

To say that the commons is a check upon the king, presupposes two things:

FIRST—That the king is not to be trusted without being looked after, or in other words, that a thirst for absolute power is the natural disease of monarchy.

SECONDLY—That the commons, by being appointed for that purpose, are either wiser or more 20   worthy of confidence than the crown.

But as the same constitution which gives the commons a power to check the king by withholding the supplies, gives afterwards the king a power to check the commons, by empowering him to reject their other bills; it again supposes that the king is wiser than those whom it has already supposed to be wiser than him. A mere absurdity!

Excerpt from "Common Sense" by Thomas Paine

1 **Which statement best expresses one of Thomas Paine's main claims in this passage?**

A   The king can reject bills that the commons passes.

B   Members of the peers are part of the old tyranny.

C   Members of the commons are elected by the people.

D   England's constitution does not encourage liberty.

2 **Which is the best meaning for the word "check" as it is used in lines 16, 21, and 22?**

A   Investigate something

B   Hold accountable

C   Compare to an original source

D   Inspect for satisfactory conditions

3 **Which phrase best describes the quality of the evidence that Paine presents to support his argument?**

A   Contradictory to the claim

B   Insufficient to support the claim

C   Irrelevant to the claim

D   Relevant to the claim

4 **Which statement related to the claim that the constitution of England is absurd is a fact?**

A   The king has the power to reject the commons' bills.

B   The king is not to be trusted and should be looked after by the commons.

C   The members of the commons are wiser and more reliable than the king.

D   The members of the peers and the king are part of an ancient tyranny.

5 **Which type of conclusion does Paine use to the end this passage?**

A   Restatement of ideas

B   Call to action

C   Ideas that extend the argument

D   One new idea

Analyzing Argument Development

Whether an author's claim is unstated or clearly laid out in the text, you can gain a better understanding of the author's claim when you analyze the author's argument. When an argument is well structured, the relationship between ideas is clear and readers can easily understand the author's point of view.

Raphael Palma was a Filipino politician, writer, and educator. In *The Woman and the Right to Vote*, published in 1919, Palma explains why he supports the inclusion of women in all aspects of public life in the Philippines. Women won the right to vote in the Philippines in 1937.

Female suffrage is a reform demanded by the social conditions of our times, by the high culture of woman, and by the aspiration of all classes of society to organize and work for the interests they have in common. . . .

5 It is an interesting phenomenon that whenever an attempt is made to introduce a social reform . . . there is never a lack of opposition. . . . As was to be expected, the eternal calamity howlers and false prophets of evil raise their fatidical [prophetic] voices . . . in protest against female suffrage. [They] invoke the sanctity of the home and the necessity of perpetuating customs that have been observed for many years.

10 Frankly speaking, I have no patience with people who voice such objections. . . . I remember very well that in the past, not so very long ago, the same apprehension and fears were felt with regard to higher education for our women. . . . We are now able to observe the results. If these results are found to be detrimental to the social and political welfare of the country, it is our duty to undo what we have done and to return to where we were before.

15 Fortunately, nobody would think of such a thing. . . . Education has not atrophied or impaired any of the fundamental faculties of woman; on the contrary, it has enhanced and enriched them. . . . Thank God, people are no longer ready to cast ridicule upon what some used to consider the foolish presumption of women to know as much as the men. This is doubtless due to the fact that the disastrous results predicted by the calamity howlers, the terrible prophets of failure, have not materialized.

20 Very well; if you allow the instruction and education of woman in all the branches of science, you must allow woman to take on her place not only in domestic life, but also in social and public life. Instruction and education have a twofold purpose; individually, they redeem the human intellect from the perils of ignorance, and socially they prepare man and woman for the proper performance of their duties of citizenship. A person is not educated exclusively for his or her own good, but . . . to utilize the 25 knowledge [he or she] has acquired for the benefit and improvement of the society in which [he or she] is living.

In societies, therefore, where woman is admitted to all the professions and where no source of knowledge is barred to her, woman must necessarily and logically be allowed to take a part in the public life, otherwise, her education would be incomplete or society would commit an injustice towards 30 her, giving her the means to educate herself and then depriving her of the necessary power to use that education for the benefit of society and collective progress.

Excerpt from *The Woman and the Right to Vote* by Rafael Palma

6 **What is the claim made in this passage?**

    A Women are entitled to the right to vote.

    B Women participate in all aspects of education.

    C Women are admitted to all the professions.

    D Women participate in many aspects of public life.

7 **How does the author feel about people who protest against women's right to vote?**

    A He thinks that they are correct.

    B He thinks that they are doing their duty.

    C He thinks that they have no reason to protest.

    D He thinks that they should be better educated.

8 **What type of evidence does the author cite to support his claim about the success of women in education?**

    A A fact about women's suffrage

    B An example of women's success in public life

    C An expert opinion about women's intelligence

    D A personal opinion about women

9 **Which statement best describes how Palma builds his argument?**

    A He states his claim and supports it with facts, reasons, and examples.

    B He states his claim and supports it with his opinion on the topic.

    C He states his claim and supports it with expert opinions on the topic.

    D He states his claim and supports it with examples of ways to gain the vote.

10 **Which sentence best describes the way the author connects his ideas in this passage?**

    A He connects his ideas chronologically.

    B He connects his ideas logically.

    C He connects his ideas in the form of a question and answer.

    D He connects his ideas through comparison and contrast.

11 **Which sentence best describes the author's conclusion?**

    A A woman has access to all sources of knowledge and all professions.

    B A woman is not educated solely for her own good.

    C It is not necessary to perpetuate customs that have been observed for many years.

    D It is logical and necessary for women to participate in public life by voting.

✔ Test-Taking Tip

When you need to answer test questions based on a reading passage, you need to eliminate information that is not necessary for answering the questions. One way to do this is to read through the passage, taking notes of important information, then reviewing the questions to see what information is covered and what is not.

Writing Practice

People have many reasons to develop arguments. Maybe you have strong feelings about a proposed law. Maybe you are trying to convince your employer that you are the best candidate for an open position. When you develop an argument, be sure to state your claim clearly and support your claim with facts and evidence.

Write a paragraph making a **claim** that an action you support is the right action. It can be something you advocate for your personal life or an action that is community-based. Provide facts, reasons, and examples as **evidence** to support your claim. Finally, write a **conclusion** that summarizes your supporting evidence and reiterates your claim.

This lesson will help you practice identifying supporting evidence in two texts. Use it with Core Lesson 6.2 *Identify Supporting Evidence* to reinforce and apply your knowledge.

Key Concept

Authors use various types of reasoning in developing an argument. Some types of reasoning are useful, but others are ineffective.

Supporting Evidence

Authors making a claim in an argument must support that claim with evidence such as facts, reasons, and examples. Authors use this supporting evidence to back up their claim and to persuade you, the reader, that the claim is reasonable. The evidence presented must be logical, and it must be connected to the claim. Emotional appeals and faulty logic do not qualify as supporting evidence.

In 1860 the mayor of New York City outlined the limits of his power and the limits of his responsibility to correct corrupt behavior in city government. This editorial was written in response to the mayor's statement.

Mayor Wood, in his eagerness to impress the public with the belief that he cannot justly be held responsible for defects or malfeasances in the city government, overlooks or misrepresents one point of considerable importance. He states that there is no general supervision confided to the mayor; — these are his words:

5 "While the Common Council, with the mayor, can enact an ordinance, the administrative authority is not thus defined. This is diffused and uncertain. It is disseminated among several independent departments. There is no general head; there is no chief executive. Instead of one, there are eight coordinate executives, separate and independent of each other, the mayor having no supervisory control. These departments constitute the whole administrative municipal government of the
10 corporation."

This is an entire mistake. The charter makes the heads of nearly all the departments directly responsible to the mayor. The comptroller and corporation counsel are, it is true, elected by the people, and are not accountable to the executive; but the Croton Aqueduct board, the street commissioner, the city inspector, and the four superintendents of bureaux under him, are all appointed by the mayor and
15 aldermen, and may at any time be removed by the mayor and board for cause. Any malfeasance or neglect of duty on the part of either of those officers, entitles the mayor instantly to supersede them. What more does Mayor Wood desire? . . . In speaking of the street inspector the mayor says:

"The mayor, being without power, should not be held accountable by the public. If nuisances abound and the streets remain filthy, it will be unjust to lay the responsibility at his door. Until he has
20 power to appoint and remove the subordinates upon whom it is incumbent to perform these duties, he should be relieved from any censure which attaches to the neglect. It is well for the public and myself to have an understanding upon the subject at the commencement of my administration."

"The public and myself" should have an accurate understanding of the subject, if they have any at all: —yet the mayor's words convey an impression in regard to the matter which is not correct. In the
25 same paragraph the mayor says: "The city inspector and the superintendents under him are appointed and removed in the same manner as the street commissioner"; and in regard to that officer, he says:

(continued)

"Like the officers of the Croton board, he derives his appointment, in the first instance, from the mayor and aldermen, but with a tenure of two years, unless sooner removed for cause, which removal requires the sanction of a majority of all the members elected to the Board of Aldermen."

30   His own admissions thus completely contradict his assertion that the mayor is without power, and should therefore be without responsibility. He has power in every case of misconduct to remove the offender from office, and to demand the concurrence of the Board of Aldermen. Does he doubt the disposition of that board to second promptly any effort he may make to remedy evils or punish mal-practices on the part of city officers? If so, he can very easily throw upon them the responsibility

35   which he deprecates so much. Let him remove an officer for misconduct, and show clear cause for the proceeding, and he will be sustained by the public, whether the board second his action or not. But the fact that he is not arbitrary and absolute, —that others share the power of punishment which is placed in his hands, cannot relieve him from the just responsibility which belongs to his office.

Excerpt from "The One Man Power," New York Times, January 5, 1860

1 Which claim does the author make in this passage about the mayor?

   A The mayor is shirking his responsibilities.

   B The mayor is taking on too much responsibility.

   C The mayor has no real power over city employees.

   D The mayor is not responsible for removing officers.

2 How does the mayor describe his role in city government?

   A He has supervisory power over members of city government.

   B He is responsible for removing officers for misconduct.

   C He cannot ignore his duty to evaluate the work of appointed officials.

   D He is not responsible for removing officers for misconduct in city government.

3 Which statement includes logical evidence used to support the author's claim?

   A The mayor does not have the responsibility to supervise city executives.

   B The mayor has the responsibility to help the public understand how power is distributed in the city.

   C The mayor does not have power to control all city offices, so he should not be held accountable for all city services.

   D The mayor has the power to remove an offender from office and to demand that the Board of Aldermen agree with his decision to do so.

4 How would the mayor's statements be described?

   A They are false.

   B They are authoritative.

   C They are contradictory.

   D They are based on truth.

5 Which word best describes the mayor's logic in explaining his lack of responsibility?

   A Connected

   B Faulty

   C Sound

   D Supporting

Connecting Claims and Evidence

When you read an argument, use reasoning to evaluate the author's argument and to determine whether the argument is valid. You can safely say that the argument is valid and reasonable if the following conditions are met: First, the reasoning is logical; second, you can cite specific evidence that supports and connects directly to the author's claim.

In 1952 then-Senator Richard Nixon, a candidate for the vice presidency of the United States, was accused of taking money from his campaign supporters in exchange for political favors. He defended his actions in a speech that was later called "Checkers" because Nixon admitted that the family dog, Checkers, had been a gift from a political supporter.

My fellow Americans,

I come before you tonight as a candidate for the vice presidency and as a man whose honesty and integrity has been questioned. . . .

I am sure that you have read the charges, and you have heard it, that I, Senator Nixon, took $18,000
5   from a group of my supporters.

. . . [L]et me say this: Not a cent of the $18,000 or any other money of that type ever went to me for my personal use. Every penny of it was used to pay for political expenses that I did not think should be charged to the taxpayers of the United States.

It was not a secret fund. . . .

10   I just don't believe in that, and I can say that never, while I have been in the Senate of the United States, as far as the people that contributed to this fund are concerned, have I made a telephone call to an agency, nor have I gone down to an agency on their behalf.

And the records will show that, the records which are in the hands of the administration.

. . . [T]he senator gets $15,000 a year in salary. . . . [T]hen he gets an allowance to handle the people
15   that work in his office to handle his mail. . . .

It is paid directly to the individuals, that the senator puts on his pay roll, but all of these people and all of these allowances are for strictly official business. . . . But there are other expenses that are not covered by the Government. And I think I can best discuss those expenses by asking you some questions.

20   Do you think that when I or any other senator makes a political speech and has it printed, we should charge the printing of that speech and the mailing of that speech to the taxpayers?

Do you think, for example, when I or any other senator makes a trip to his home state to make a purely political speech that the cost of that trip should be charged to the taxpayers?

Do you think when a senator makes political broadcasts or political television broadcasts, radio or
25   television that the expense of those broadcasts should be charged to the taxpayers?

. . . The answer is no. The taxpayers should not be required to finance items which are not official business but which are primarily political business.

Well, then the question arises, you say, "Well, how do you pay for these and how can you do it legally?" . . .

(continued)

30   . . . I felt that the best way to handle these necessary political expenses of getting my message to the American people and the speeches I made . . . was to accept the aid which people in my home state of California, who contributed to my campaign and who continued to make these contributions after I was elected, were glad to make.

35   And let me say that I am proud of the fact that not one of them has ever asked me for a special favor. I am proud of the fact that not one of them has ever asked me to vote on a bill other than my own conscience would dictate. And I am proud of the fact that the taxpayers by subterfuge or otherwise have never paid one dime for expenses which I thought were political and should not be charged [to] the taxpayers.

Excerpt from the "Checkers" speech by Richard M. Nixon, September 23, 1952

6 **Which claim is made by Richard Nixon in this speech?**

  A He hired his wife to manage his political expenses.

  B He did not use money from supporters for personal expenses.

  C He received money from the government for political expenses.

  D He did not receive money from supporters for political expenses.

7 **Which type of evidence appears in the statement that "The taxpayers should not be required to finance items which are not official business but which are primarily political business."?**

  A Example

  B Verifiable fact

  C Emotional appeal

  D Supporting reason

8 **In line 26, what does the word "finance" most nearly mean?**

  A Manage large amounts of money

  B Provide funds for someone or for a venture

  C Raise the funds to contribute support for a project

  D Donate resources and monetary affairs of a government or organization

9 **What evidence does Nixon provide to support his claim that he used the money given to him for political expenses?**

  A Broadcasts

  B Letters

  C Records

  D Speeches

10 **The fact that Nixon does not have proof that he avoided giving special favors for contributions makes his argument**

  A faulty.

  B logical.

  C reasonable.

  D valid.

✔ Test-Taking Tip

When a test includes questions related to a passage, it is often helpful to read the questions before reading the passage. You can jot down notes and key words to help you identify the information that you'll need to look for in the passage. Then as you first read the passage, keep the questions in mind and look for the information that you need to answer them correctly.

Writing Practice

Many people have done things that others disagree with. For example, Nixon firmly believed that he had spent taxpayer money and political contributions wisely, but some people were criticizing his behavior. Recall something you have done or a decision you have made that someone disagreed with.

Build an **argument** defending something you have done in your life or a decision you have made that others disagreed with. Start with a claim, and then list **supporting evidence** connected to your claim. Study your evidence. Delete any evidence that is faulty or that is based on an emotional appeal. Write a paragraph using your evidence to support your claim.

_____

_____

_____

_____

_____

_____

_____

_____

_____

_____

_____

_____

_____

_____

_____

_____

_____

_____

_____

_____

_____

_____

_____

_____

This lesson will help you practice evaluating the relevance and sufficiency of supporting evidence in two texts. Use it with Core Lesson 6.3 *Evaluate Relevance and Sufficiency* to reinforce and apply your knowledge.

Key Concept

To create a reasonable argument, an author must provide relevant and sufficient evidence for his or her claim.

Building a Case

To build an effective argument, writers must support their claim with evidence that is relevant not only to the claim but also to the audience's interests and needs. Writers must also provide more than one piece of evidence to build a convincing argument. The validity of the argument depends on the relevancy and sufficiency of the evidence.

Corporations must balance the cost of employee health care with the need to be profitable. In this memo, company leaders describe a proposed sick-leave law in New York City and explain its impact on the company's financial state.

Corporate Memo on Sick-Leave Legislation

In response to the current influenza outbreak, the New York City Council is fast-tracking a piece of legislation. If passed, this would place statutory standards on the administration of corporate sick-leave policies. In a nutshell, it would require all
5   New York City employers to provide the following:

- 10 paid sick days a year for full-time employees, and
- 5 paid sick days a year for employees working between 20 and 32 hours per week.

We strongly encourage employees to oppose this legislation. We have always
10   acknowledged the importance of employee health. We also realize that our employees are more productive when their salary and position in the workforce are protected. Our current policy of granting sick leave on a documented, case-by-case basis is efficient and effective. It provides protection for our employees, their families, and society as a whole:

15   - It helps to maintain workplace health, in support of CDC guidelines. These guidelines suggest that people infected with influenza remain isolated for at least 24 hours after their fever breaks.
- It helps to maintain a healthy school environment for the children of our employees by allowing parents to remain home while their children are
20   contagious.

Current law does not require employers to provide sick leave, paid or unpaid, under any circumstances. If, however, a company is held to a specific number of sick days, it is likewise obliged to compensate employees for their unused sick days. This amount must be paid yearly or when an employee leaves the company.

(continued)

---

25   Our current policy, then, is a vital tool for maintaining our bottom line. This, in turn, translates into benefits and job security for you, the employee.

- According to a March 2010 Department of Labor Statistics report, the cost of sick leave to a business or agency can average 81 cents per hour per employee. We are a mid-sized company. We employ approximately 1,200 full-time and
30   part-time workers. Using the DLS report as a guide, let's consider some figures.

One full-time employee works 260 days a year. At 8 hours per workday, an individual works 2,080 hours per year. Multiply that by the number of employees (1,200), and there are 2,496,000 work hours per year in our company. Finally, multiply the number of work hours by the per-hour cost of sick leave ($.81), and you get
35    $2,021,760 per year.

This is an unacceptable level of expense. It would force overall cost reduction. This cost reduction would most likely be administered through layoffs and reduced employee salaries. As an employee, voter, and citizen, this concerns you directly. Phone your city representative to protest this intrusion into the private sector—and remind
40   him or her that you vote!

Source: Corporate Memo on Sick-Leave Legislation

1 Which statement provides evidence to support the claim that employees should oppose mandatory paid sick leave?

A   Employees should support their company's position.

B   The company cannot afford mandatory paid sick leave.

C   The New York City council is trying to pass legislation for mandatory paid sick leave.

D   The mandatory sick leave legislation is in response to the influenza outbreak.

2 Which piece of evidence supports the claim that the company has "always acknowledged the importance of employee health"?

A   The company recognizes that "employees are more productive when their salary and position in the workforce are protected."

B   "Current law does not require employers to provide sick leave," but this company does provide it.

C   A company that provides a number of paid sick days is expected to "compensate employees for their unused sick days."

D   The cost of sick leave to a business or agency can average "81 cents per hour per employee."

3 Which statement is directly relevant to the audience?

A   "We have always acknowledged the importance of employee health."

B   "Our current policy, then, is a vital tool for maintaining our bottom line."

C   "This in turn translates into benefits and job security for you, the employee."

D   "We employ approximately 1,200 full-time and part-time workers."

4 The financial information in the memo is relevant to the claim because it shows how the new law would

A   negatively affect employees' job security.

B   improve the company's health-care policy.

C   prevent the company from giving its CEO a raise.

D   ensure that employees do not lose income when they are sick.

5 Which type of evidence does the author provide to support the claim that legislated sick leave would cost the company a lot of money?

A Verifiable but faulty

B Biased and repetitive

C Relevant and sufficient

D Valid but contradictory

6 The author links the evidence to the claim at the end of the passage by stating that the

A city leaders have doubts about the proposed legislation.

B company's management is going to oppose the legislation.

C employees should oppose the legislation out of loyalty to the company.

D employees are directly affected by this legislation and should oppose it.

Evaluating Evidence in Various Texts

When you evaluate the evidence in a text, you look for appropriate evidence that supports the author's claim and that is relevant to the topic and to the audience's interests. You should also check for sufficient evidence, in strength and amount, to support the claim.

President Ronald Reagan believed that the government should support the military but that private citizens should look after people's social needs. In this speech, made during a recession, Reagan explains his intention to cut the budget.

Today marks my first State of the Union address to you. . . .

Late in 1981 we sank into the present recession, largely because continued high interest rates hurt the auto industry and construction. And there was a drop in productivity, and the already high unemployment increased.

5   This time, however, things are different. We have an economic program in place, completely different from the artificial quick fixes of the past. It calls for a reduction of the rate of increase in government spending. . . . But reduced spending alone isn't enough. We've just implemented the first and smallest phase of a three-year tax-rate reduction designed to stimulate the economy and create jobs. . . .

10   Now, the budget deficit this year will exceed our earlier expectations. The recession did that. It lowered revenues and increased costs. . . .

We must cut out more nonessential government spending and rout out more waste. . . .

The budget plan I submit to you on February 8th will realize major savings by dismantling the Departments of Energy and Education. . . . We'll continue to redirect our resources to our two highest 15 budget priorities—a strong national defense to keep America free and at peace and a reliable safety net of social programs for those who have contributed and those who are in need. . . .

Our faith in the American people is reflected in another major endeavor. Our private sector initiatives task force is seeking out successful community models of school, church, business, union, foundation, and civic programs that help community needs. Such groups are almost invariably far 20 more efficient than government in running social programs.

(continued)

We're not asking them to replace discarded and often discredited government programs dollar for dollar, service for service. We just want to help them perform the good works they choose and help others to profit by their example. . . .

25 Our foreign policy is a policy of strength, fairness, and balance. By restoring America's military credibility, by pursuing peace at the negotiating table wherever both sides are willing to sit down in good faith, and by regaining the respect of America's allies and adversaries alike, we have strengthened our country's position as a force for peace and progress in the world. . . .

We have made pledges of a new frankness in our public statements and worldwide broadcasts. In the face of a climate of falsehood and misinformation, we've promised the world a season of truth—the
30 truth of our great civilized ideas: individual liberty, representative government, the rule of law under God. We've never needed walls or minefields or barbed wire to keep our people in. Nor do we declare martial law to keep our people from voting for the kind of government they want. . . .

A hundred and twenty years ago, the greatest of all our presidents delivered his second State of the Union message in this chamber. "We cannot escape history," Abraham Lincoln warned. "We of this
35 Congress and this administration will be remembered in spite of ourselves." The "trial through which we pass will light us down, in honor or dishonor, to the latest [last] generation."

Well, that president and that Congress did not fail the American people. Together they weathered the storm and preserved the Union. Let it be said of us that we, too, did not fail; that we, too, worked together to bring America through difficult times. Let us so conduct ourselves that two centuries from
40 now, another Congress and another president, meeting in this chamber as we are meeting, will speak of us with pride, saying that we met the test and preserved for them in their day the sacred flame of liberty—this last, best hope of man on Earth.

Excerpt from "Address Before a Joint Session of the Congress Reporting on the State of the Union" by Ronald Reagan

7 **How does President Reagan use Abraham Lincoln's words to support his claim that the country needs to work together to bring the United States through difficult times?**

  A As sufficient evidence

  B As relevant evidence

  C As an additional claim

  D As opposition to a claim

8 **In which sentence does President Reagan present evidence to support his claim that government programs can be cut?**

  A "[Volunteer] groups are almost invariably far more efficient than government in running social programs."

  B "We just want to help [private sector groups] perform the good works they choose and help others to profit by their example."

  C "[W]e have strengthened our country's position as a force for peace and progress in the world."

  D "[We do not] declare martial law to keep our people from voting for the kind of government they want."

9 Which of the following meanings associated with the word "dismantling" seems most intended in line 13?

A   Rebuilding

B   Restructuring

C   Improving

D   Eliminating

10 Which statement is relevant evidence to support President Reagan's claim that the government will do its part to turn around the recession?

A   He has promised the country a season of truth.

B   He will not declare martial law to change voting.

C   He will not raise taxes to pay for the new budget.

D   He believes our foreign policy is fair, strong, and balanced.

11 President Reagan's argument is supported by several pieces of evidence related to his claim, but the lack of specific examples makes the evidence

A   relevant.

B   sufficient.

C   irrelevant.

D   insufficient.

12 Which phrase best describes the evidence that the recession caused the budget deficit?

A   Interesting but biased

B   Connected but faulty

C   Relevant but not sufficient

D   Factual but not verifiable

✔ Test-Taking Tip

When you take a test that involves reading a text, scan the text for features such as headings and lists. As you scan, look in the text features and the text for words that are associated with the topic and words that are frequently repeated. These steps will help activate your prior knowledge about the topic and make it easier for you to answer questions about it.

Writing Practice

People write arguments for a number of reasons. They might be trying to convince others to invest in a project, or they could be writing a letter to the editor of a local newspaper to convince voters to support a certain political candidate.

Write a paragraph about a social program in your community that interests you, such as foster care or mental health services. In your paragraph, make a **claim** for the usefulness of this program, and provide evidence to support your claim. Make sure that the **evidence** is **relevant** to your claim and that it is of interest to your audience. Be sure to provide more than one piece of evidence so your claim is **sufficiently supported**.

_____

_____

_____

_____

_____

_____

_____

_____

_____

_____

_____

_____

_____

_____

_____

_____

_____

_____

_____

_____

_____

_____

_____

This lesson will help you practice evaluating the validity and reasoning used in two arguments. Use it with Core Lesson 6.4 *Evaluate Validity and Reasoning* to reinforce and apply your knowledge.

Key Concept

Readers can use logical tests to determine whether the reasoning that authors use in their arguments is valid.

Understanding Validity and Reasoning

An argument's validity depends on whether the argument is logical and factually reliable. An argument is valid when it is supported with sound, or sensible, evidence. An argument is reasonable when each piece of evidence is connected in a logical way to the claim and to other pieces of evidence. An argument is invalid if the author exhibits bias or presents contradictory evidence.

In the late 19th and early 20th centuries, women fought for suffrage. State by state, they gained suffrage until the federal government added the 19th Amendment to the US Constitution in 1920. This passage was written in 1911 by an opponent of women's suffrage.

Suffrage is not a right. It is a privilege that may or may not be granted. Politics is no place for a woman, consequently the privilege should not be granted to her. The mother's influence is needed in the home. . . . Let her teach her daughters that modesty, patience and gentleness are the charms of woman. Let her teach her sons that an honest conscience is every man's first political law; that no

5   splendor can rob him nor no force justify the surrender of the simplest right of a free and independent citizen. The mothers of this country can shape the destinies of the nation by keeping in their places and attending to those duties that God Almighty intended for them. The kindly, gentle influence of the mother in the home and the dignified influence of the teacher in the school will far outweigh all the influence of all the mannish female politicians on earth.

10   The courageous, chivalrous, and manly men and the womanly women . . . are opposed to this innovation in American political life. There was a bill (the Sanford bill) before the last legislature which proposed to leave the equal suffrage question to women to decide first before the men should vote on it. This bill was defeated by the suffragettes because they knew that the women would vote down the amendment by a vote of ten to one. Do women have to vote in order to receive the protection

15   of men? Why, men have gone to war, endured every privation, and death itself in defense of woman. To man, woman is the dearest creature on earth, and there is no extreme to which he would not go for his mother or sister. . . . Woman does not have to vote to secure her rights. Man will go to any extreme to protect and elevate her now. As long as woman is woman and keeps her place she will get more protection and more consideration than man gets. When she abdicates her throne she throws down the

20   scepter of her power and loses her influence.

Woman suffrage has been proven a failure in states that have tried it. It is wrong. California should profit by the mistakes of other states. Not one reform has equal suffrage effected.

Excerpt from *An Argument Against Women's Suffrage* by J. B. Sanford, Chairman of California Democratic Caucus

1 What is the author's claim in this passage?

A Women's suffrage should not be allowed.

B Women are gentle creatures and should be revered.

C Women's suffrage has been a failure in other states.

D Women belong in the home and in schools as teachers.

2 What does "suffrage" (lines 1, 12, and 21) mean?

A The right to vote

B The right to go to war

C The securing of rights

D The right to be a citizen

3 Which idea from this passage is a verifiable fact?

A Women should keep their place in the home.

B Women do not have to vote to secure their rights.

C The Sanford bill was defeated by the suffragettes.

D Men can protect women if women keep their exalted position.

4 The evidence used by the author to support his claim is

A reasonable and logically sound.

B unreasonable but logically sound.

C reasonable but not logically sound.

D unreasonable and not logically sound.

5 Which words best describe the author's argument as a whole?

A Biased but logical

B Biased and invalid

C Reasonable and valid

D Logical but unreasonable

Evaluating Validity and Reasoning in Texts

To evaluate the validity of an argument, check whether the evidence is accurate and is connected to the claim. To evaluate an argument's reasoning, make sure the evidence relates to the claim and is linked to other evidence in a logical way. The argument's reasoning is not sound if the evidence does not support the claim.

In 2012 Barack Obama ran for a second term as president of the United States. His opponent was Mitt Romney, a Republican who proposed tax cuts for the wealthiest Americans and blamed Obama for the economic difficulties that the nation was experiencing.

We are here to build an economy where work pays off so that no matter what you look like or where you come from, you can make it here if you try. . . .

We've got the best workers in the world. . . . [N]o matter what the naysayers may say, . . . there's not another country on Earth that wouldn't gladly trade places with the United States of America. . . .

5   What's standing in our way is . . . the uncompromising view that says we should be going back to the old, top-down economics that got us into this mess in the first place. . . .

(continued)

And I don't exaggerate when it comes to how my opponent and his allies in Congress view this economy. They believe . . . that if we give more tax breaks to some of the wealthiest Americans, and we get rid of regulations . . . that somehow prosperity will rain down on everybody. . . .

10   So you're talking about each year, a tax cut that's equivalent of our defense budget for the next 10 years. . . . [T]his policy center . . . ran the numbers . . . And they determined that Governor Romney's plan would effectively raise taxes on middle-class families with children by an average of $2,000—to pay for this tax cut. . . . He'd ask the middle class to pay more in taxes so that he could give another $250,000 tax cut to people making more than $3 million a year. . . . It's like Robin Hood in reverse. . . .

15   They have tried to sell us this trickle-down, tax cut fairy dust before. . . . It didn't work then; it won't work now. It's not a plan to create jobs. It's not a plan to reduce our deficit. And it is not a plan to move our economy forward. . . .

We need tax cuts for working Americans. We need tax cuts for families who are trying to raise kids, and keep them healthy, and send them to college, and keep a roof over their heads.

20   So that's the choice in this election. That's what this is about. That's why I'm running for a second term as president of the United States. . . .

Four years ago, I promised to cut middle-class taxes—that's exactly what I've done, by a total of about $3,600 for the typical family. . . .

    [W]hen a construction worker has got some money in his pocket, he goes out and buys a new
25 car. . . . [W]hen the middle class is doing well, then business is doing well, and those at the top do well. Everybody does well. That's what we believe in—an economy that grows from the middle class out and the bottom up. That's the choice in this election. . . .

And over the course of the next three months, the other side is going to spend more money than we have ever seen on ads that basically say the same thing you've been hearing for months. They know
30 their economics theory won't sell, so their ads are going to say the same thing over and over again, which is: The economy is not where it needs to be and it's Obama's fault. . . .

    Their strategists admit it. They say . . . we're not going to put out any plans. We're just going to see if this works. . . .

    They don't have that plan. I do. . . .

35   And if you still believe in me, and you're willing to stand with me, . . . we will finish what we started in 2008, and we will show the world why the United States of America is the greatest nation on Earth.

Excerpt from "Remarks by the President at Campaign Event—Stamford, CT" by Barack Obama

6 **Which evidence is a verifiable fact?**

A Obama cut taxes by about $3,600 for the typical middle-class family.

B The United States has the best workers in the world.

C Every country in the world would want to trade places with the United States.

D The United States is the best country on Earth.

7 **Obama gives Romney's tax plan as an example to**

A support the idea that trickle-down economics always works.

B refute the idea that trickle-down economics doesn't always work.

C support the idea that trickle-down economics doesn't work at all.

D support the idea that trickle-down economics can sometimes work.

8 **The evidence about middle-class families helping the economy when they have more income is logically related to the idea that**

A giving the rich a tax cut will help the economy.

B raising taxes on everyone will help the economy.

C raising taxes on the middle class will not help the economy.

D lowering taxes on the middle class will not help the economy.

9 **Which phrase best describes the evidence presented to support Obama's claim?**

A Faulty reasoning but valid evidence

B Sound reasoning and valid evidence

C Sound reasoning but invalid evidence

D Faulty reasoning and invalid evidence

10 **Which of the following sentences most strongly supports Obama's claim?**

A The opponent wants to cut taxes to stimulate the economy.

B The opponent says problems with the economy are Obama's fault.

C The opponent doesn't have a solid economic plan, but Obama does.

D The opponent spends money on ads that repeat the same message.

✅ Test-Taking Tip

When you take a test, first answer questions that are easy for you. This approach increases your chances of completing the greatest number of items. Avoid getting stuck on a question. If you can't answer it quickly, move on. Then go back to the more challenging questions if you have time.

Writing Practice

To get elected to a position, politicians and other community leaders give campaign speeches. These carefully crafted speeches are designed to convince the audience that the speaker is the best person for the job.

Write a short campaign **speech** describing why you (or someone else) should be elected to a position. This can be a position in your town, in a school community, or in a larger political body. Provide facts and reasons as evidence for your claim that you (or your candidate) should be elected. Finally, write a few sentences evaluating the **validity** and **reasoning** of your claim. Explain how you logically connected your evidence to your claim and gave sound reasons for your claim.

_____

_____

_____

_____

_____

_____

_____

_____

_____

_____

_____

_____

_____

_____

_____

_____

_____

_____

_____

_____

_____

_____

This lesson will help you practice evaluating logic and identifying hidden assumptions in two texts. Use it with Core Lesson 6.5 *Evaluate Logic and Identify Hidden Assumptions* to reinforce and apply your knowledge.

Key Concept

Authors may support their claims with arguments based on logical reasoning.

Evaluating Arguments Founded on Logical Reasoning

When supporting evidence, such as facts, examples, and expert opinions, is not available or appropriate, writers need to base their arguments on logical reasoning instead. In this type of argument, writers start by making an assumption. Then they build their argument, using the assumption as the basis for a series of deductions.

The author of the following article discusses the widespread phenomenon of obesity.

Doctors say that obesity causes or aggravates diseases such as diabetes, high blood pressure, and heart disease. In fact, about 90 percent of the type II diabetes cases worldwide are caused by excessive weight. The causes of obesity are too varied for doctors to be able to suggest a simple solution to the problem.

5   According to the US Centers for Disease Control and Prevention, "Overweight and obesity are both labels for ranges of weight that are greater than what is generally considered healthy for a given height." In medical terms, obesity means having a body-mass index (BMI) of 30 or higher. BMI is an estimate of total body fat. It is based on a calculation using a person's height and weight.

Despite the many negative effects of obesity, about 34 percent of adults and 17 percent of children 10   2–19 years old in the United States are obese. Obesity is also a problem in most other industrialized countries.

Some studies support an explanation of body weight called the "set-point theory." According to this theory, a person's genes determine his or her preferred weight. The brain adjusts a person's metabolism and eating behavior to maintain weight at this genetically determined level. No one has proved the 15   set-point theory. However, doctors have observed that most people's bodies resist a weight that is lower than the "normal" weight for that person.

Some people believe that the set-point theory helps explain why people find it difficult to maintain weight loss. These people are fighting against their bodies' set points. To weigh less than their set points, they must constantly exercise and limit food intake.

20   There is evidence that environmental factors have a strong influence on weight gain and obesity. Researchers have found that obesity affects people in wealthier industrial countries more than people in poorer countries. Because there is a large food supply in industrial nations, the people there tend to eat more high-calorie, processed foods. Because they have access to transportation and perform less manual labor, they have lower levels of physical activity.

25   Doctors believe that many weight-loss programs are mostly ineffective. As many as 95 percent of people who lose weight on a specific program will gain it back within five years. Because body weight is the result of genes, environment, metabolism, behavior, and socioeconomic status, there is no one solution for weight loss.

1 **What is the claim in this passage?**

A That 95 percent of people who lose weight on a diet will gain it back

B That a person's BMI determines whether or not that person is obese

C That people in wealthy countries have a higher risk for being obese

D That the causes of obesity are too varied to suggest a simple solution

2 **Which statement is an assumption made in the passage?**

A That a person's genes determine his or her preferred weight

B That obesity is a medical problem that needs to be solved

C That the BMI is based on a calculation using height and weight

D That people in industrialized countries have lower levels of physical activity

3 **What purpose does the explanation of the set-point theory serve in this passage?**

A It is a claim.

B It is a deduction.

C It is an assumption.

D It is a fact.

4 **What does "intake" (line 19) mean?**

A A quantity of something taken in

B An opening through which fluid flows

C A contraction or narrowing of fabric

D A shaft that serves to ventilate

5 **To support the claim, the author of this passage gives information about studies on obesity and**

A criticizes methods used by the studies.

B expresses disagreements about the results.

C lists specific plans for further studies.

D formulates deductions from the results.

Evaluating Arguments Based on Hidden Assumptions

Sometimes the assumption on which a writer bases an argument is unstated, or "hidden." If the reasoning in the argument depends on the reader accepting an idea that is not explicitly stated, this idea is the hidden assumption. The validity of this supposition affects the validity of the argument as a whole. It can be challenging to find this assumption.

Thomas Bowdler (1754–1825) was an English doctor and philanthropist. He is famous for creating a version of the most popular works of William Shakespeare, removing language he found offensive. His actions gave rise to the term "bowdlerize," to censor literature or, later, films.

[T]he works of the poet may be considered in a very different light from those of the painter and the statuary. Shak[e]speare, inimitable Shak[e]speare, will remain the subject of admiration as long as taste and literature shall exist. . . . [H]is writings will be handed down to posterity in their native beauty, although the present attempt to add to his fame should prove entirely abortive. Here, then, is
5   the great difference. If the endeavor to improve the picture or the statue should be unsuccessful, the beauty of the original would be destroyed, and the injury be irreparable. In such a case, let the artist refrain from using the chisel or the pencil. [But] with the works of the poet no such danger occurs. . . . [T]he critic need not be afraid of employing his pen, for the original will continue unimpaired. . . .

(continued)

10 　That Shak[e]speare is the first of dramatic writers will be denied by few. I doubt whether it will be denied by any who have really studied his works, and compared the beauties which they contain with the very finest productions either of our own or of former ages. It must, however, be acknowledged, by his warmest admirers, that some defects are to be found in the writings of our immortal bard. The language is not always faultless. Many words and expressions occur which are of so indecent a nature as to render it highly desirable that they should be erased. Of these, the greater part are evidently

15 　introduced to gratify the bad taste of the age in which he lived. [T]he rest may perhaps be ascribed to his own unbridled fancy. But neither the vicious taste of the age, nor the brilliant effusions of wit, can afford an excuse for profaneness or obscenity. . . . [I]f these could be obliterated, the transcendent genius of the poet would undoubtedly shine with more unclouded lustre. To banish every thing of this nature from the writings of Shak[e]speare is the object of the present undertaking. My earnest wish is

20 　to render his plays unsullied by any scene, by any speech, or if possible, by any word that can give pain to the most chaste, or offence to the most religious of his readers.

Excerpt from *The Family Shakespeare* by Thomas Bowdler

6 What is the author's claim in this passage?

A Families should read Shakespeare's plays.

B Shakespeare is a widely admired dramatic writer.

C Shakespeare wrote for the tastes and language of his age.

D The language in Shakespeare's works should be cleaned up.

7 What is the hidden assumption in this passage?

A Shakespeare's plays compare favorably with modern plays.

B Words that may offend readers lower the artistic quality of literature.

C Shakespeare's works would be more beautiful without obscene words.

D Critics can change words in a passage and not damage the original work.

8 Which assumption do you have to accept to evaluate the author's argument as valid?

A Changing a painting or a sculpture damages the work.

B Changing a painting or a sculpture does not damage the work.

C Changing the words in a work of literature damages the work.

D Changing the words in a work of literature does not damage the work.

9 Which statement is based on an invalid assumption?

A Shakespeare's works should be read by everyone who loves literature.

B Shakespeare's words fit with the language of his times and his culture.

C Shakespeare's genius would shine more if his works were censored.

D Shakespeare's plays are among the finest in dramatic literature.

10 The idea that Shakespeare's use of obscene language is a defect in his writing is

A the author's personal opinion.

B factual evidence presented to support the claim.

C a common observation among writers.

D an expert opinion that the author quotes as evidence.

✅ Test-Taking Tip

When you are taking a test, before you move on to another question, reread the question and your answer together. Make sure you have correctly understood the question and answer choices and have selected the answer that you intended to select.

Language Practice

Verbs may be active or passive. If the subject of the sentence performs the action, the verb is active. If the subject receives the action, the verb is passive. A passive verb includes a form of the verb *be* and the past participle of the main verb.

Read quickly through the draft passage in the box below. Then go to the spread-out version and consider the suggestions for revision.

---

1   The library is hardly ever visited by my niece, Yasmin. When I was a kid, I practically *lived* there. Books were brought home by the armful. My parents rarely bought me any. Yasmin reads on her tablet computer or buys books online.

2   As I got older, I performed research at the library. I can still remember pulling open the long drawers of the card catalog and searching for the right card. I was quite familiar with the Dewey Decimal System. I would head to the stacks and be immersed in the thousands of books, volumes of encyclopedias, and dozens of periodicals.

3   My niece does almost all her research on her laptop computer. If she has to get a library book, Yasmin reserves it online. When she arrives at the library, someone at the circulation desk hands her the book. After checking it out, Yasmin promptly leaves. I'm afraid my niece will never know the pleasure of spending a long afternoon at the library.

Choose the version of the sentence or phrase from the passage that contains an active verb. If the sentence or phrase in the passage already contains an active verb, choose (*No change*).

1   <u>The library is hardly ever visited by my</u>

              ₁

<u>niece, Yasmin.</u> When I was a kid, I practically

  ₁

lived there. <u>Books were brought home by the</u>

                     ₂

<u>armful.</u> My parents rarely bought me any.

 ₂

Yasmin reads on her tablet computer or buys

books online.

2   As I got older, I performed research

at the library. I can still remember pulling

open the long drawers of the card catalog

and searching for the right card. I was quite

familiar with the Dewey Decimal System.

<u>I would head to the stacks and be immersed</u>

                              ₃

<u>in the thousands of books,</u> volumes of

         ₃

encyclopedias, and dozens of periodicals.

1 A (*No change*)

   B My niece, Yasmin, hardly ever visits the library.

   C The library is hardly ever a place visited by my niece, Yasmin.

   D Hardly ever is there a visit to the library by my niece, Yasmin.

2 A (*No change*)

   B Home is where books were brought by the armful.

   C I brought home books by the armful.

   D An armful of books were brought home by me.

3 A (*No change*)

   B To the stacks I would head and be immersed in the thousands of books . . .

   C The stacks were where I would be immersed in the thousands of books . . .

   D I would head to the stacks and immerse myself in the thousands of books . . .

3 My niece does almost all her research on her laptop computer. If she has to get a library book, Yasmin reserves it online. When she arrives at the library, <u>someone at the</u>
4
<u>circulation desk hands her the book.</u> After
4
checking it out, Yasmin promptly leaves. I'm afraid my niece will never know the pleasure of spending a long afternoon at the library.

4 A (*No change*)

B . . . she is handed the book by someone at the circulation desk . . .

C . . . at the circulation desk she is handed the book . . .

D . . . the book is handed to her by someone at the circulation desk . . .

Writing Practice

Many arguments rest on hidden assumptions. This often happens when the writer or speaker believes that the audience understands and agrees with the assumption. Think about political campaign speeches. Candidates often talk about how their policies will not involve raising taxes. The underlying, unstated assumption is that no one wants to pay higher taxes.

Think of a way of behaving that most people believe is appropriate. Then write a short paragraph suggesting that people follow a rule at work based on this assumption, but do not state the assumption. Be sure to support your claim with logical reasoning. Then state your **hidden assumption** in a separate sentence.

This lesson will help you practice comparing the formats of two similar texts. Use it with Core Lesson 7.1 *Compare Similar Topics in Different Formats* to reinforce and apply your knowledge.

Key Concept

Different writers can present similar information in different formats. Each format fits the message that the writer wants to convey.

Comparing Texts on Similar Topics

Two texts about the same topic can be presented in different ways. The texts might have different formats; for example, a scientific article and an advertisement could present facts about a new medication. The texts could be influenced by the context, or the circumstances in which the author wrote. A description of an event written at the time when the event occurred would probably differ from a description written later for a history book. Format and context affect a reader's understanding of a text.

The following passages are about Mammoth Cave, located in south central Kentucky.

Some idea of the impression which Mammoth Cave makes upon the senses, irrespective even of sight, may be had from the fact that blind people go there to see it, and are greatly struck with it. . . . The blind seem as much impressed by it as those who have their sight. When the guide pauses at the more interesting points, or lights the scene up with a great torch . . . and points out the more striking
5 features, the blind exclaim, "How wonderful! How beautiful!" They can feel it, if they cannot see it. They get some idea of the spaciousness when words are uttered. The voice goes forth in these colossal chambers like a bird. When no word is spoken, the silence is of a kind never experienced on the surface of the earth. . . . This, and the absolute darkness, to a person with eyes makes him feel as if he were face to face with the primordial nothingness. . . .

10 Here in the loose soil are ruts worn by cart-wheels in 1812, when, during the war with Great Britain, the earth was searched to make saltpetre. The guide kicks corn-cobs out of the dust where the oxen were fed at noon, and they look nearly as fresh as ever they did. In those frail corn-cobs and in those wheel-tracks, as if the carts had but just gone along, one seemed to come very near to the youth of the century, almost to overtake it.

15 Probably the prettiest thing they have to show you in Mammoth Cave is the "Star Chamber." . . . The guide takes your lantern from you and leaves you seated upon a bench by the wayside, in the profound cosmic darkness. He retreats down a side alley that seems to go down to a lower level, and at a certain point shades his lamp with his hat, so that the light falls upon the ceiling over your head. You look up, and the first thought is that there is an opening just there that permits you to look forth upon
20 the midnight skies. You see the darker horizon line where the sky ends and the mountains begin. The sky is blue-black and is thickly studded with stars—rather small stars, but apparently genuine. At one point a long luminous streak simulates exactly the form and effect of a comet.

(continued)

As you gaze, the guide slowly moves his hat, and a black cloud gradually creeps over the sky, and all is blackness again. Then you hear footsteps retreating and dying away in the distance. Presently
25 all is still, save the ringing in your own ears. Then after a few moments, during which you have sat in silence like that of the interstellar spaces, you hear over your left shoulder a distant flapping of wings, followed by the crowing of a cock. You turn your head in that direction and behold a faint dawn breaking on the horizon. It slowly increases till you hear footsteps approaching, and your dusky companion, playing the part of Apollo with lamp in hand, ushers in the light of day. It is rather
30 theatrical, but a very pleasant diversion nevertheless.

Excerpt from "In Mammoth Cave" by John Burroughs

Mammoth Cave National Park was established in 1941. It preserves and protects the world's longest known cave system, along with a portion of the Green River valley and much of south central Kentucky. More than 400 miles of its caves have been explored to date.

Study has shown the park to be far more complex than first imagined, and not simply because of
5 its labyrinthine underground. The area sustains a broad diversity of plant and animal life, in myriad specialized and interconnected ecosystems. More than 70 threatened, endangered, or state-listed species make their homes there. The Federal Endangered Species Act of 1973 gives park officials the means to ensure the survival of these species.

The cave system ecosystem ranks among the most diverse in the world, hosting more than 130
10 varieties of animal. These species are almost equally divided among the three classes of cave life: troglobites, which need a cave environment to survive; troglophiles, which can survive in or out of caves; and trogloxenes, which use caves primarily for refuge.

Even if one does not consider the abundance of life underground, the Mammoth Cave area merits its National Park status due solely to the extraordinary density and variety of its plant life. While . . .
15 Great Smoky Mountains National Park, has approximately 1,500 flowering species in its more than 500,000 acres, Mammoth Cave National Park supports more than 1,300 species within only one-tenth of that acreage.

The park is open to visitors year-round. Most of its resources and facilities are available free of charge. The following fees are charged for cave tours, camping, and selected picnic shelters.

Adapted from "Mammoth Cave National Park" by the National Park Service

Cave Tour Fees			
Cave Tour	Adults	Youth*	Seniors
Mammoth Passage Tour	$5.00	$3.50	$2.50
Historic Tour	$12.00	$8.00	$6.00
Grand Avenue Tour	$24.00	$18.00	$12.00
Great Onyx Tour	$15.00	$11.00	$7.50
Violet City Lantern Tour	$15.00	$11.00	$7.50
River Styx Tour	$13.00	$9.00	$6.50
Star Chamber Tour	$12.00	$8.00	$6.00
Wild Cave Tour	$48.00	n/a	$24.00
Introduction to Caving	$23.00	$18.00	$11.50
Trog	n/a	$14.00	n/a
*Youth is 6–12 years of age.			

Campground and Picnic Shelter Fees	
Campsite/ Picnic Area	Fee *Senior discounts in ( )*
Mammoth Cave Campground	$17.00 *($8.50)*
Maple Springs Group Camp	$30.00
Houchins Ferry Campground	$12.00 *($6.00)*
Open-Air Picnic Shelter	$25.00/day; limited availability
Enclosed Picnic Shelter	$50.00/day; one shelter, available Sat/Sun March 1– Memorial Day; daily Memorial Day–Labor Day; Sat/Sun Labor Day–November 30

1 Which of the following statements is true about both passages?

A   The genre is the same.

B   The format is the same.

C   The narrator is the same.

D   The topic is the same.

2 Which fact about the context of passage 1 most affects your understanding of the passage?

A   It is an excerpt from a longer work.

B   It was written in the late 19th century.

C   It is a work of nonfiction.

D   It was written by a nature essayist.

3 Who is the intended audience for passage 2?

A   Park visitors

B   Historians

C   Families

D   Conservationists

4 How do the main purposes of the two passages differ?

A   Passage 1 was written to inform; passage 2 was written to entertain.

B   Passage 1 was written to persuade; passage 2 was written to entertain.

C   Passage 1 was written to entertain; passage 2 was written to inform.

D   Passage 1 was written to entertain; passage 2 was written to persuade.

Comparing Fiction and Nonfiction

It is not always easy to distinguish fiction from nonfiction. A fictional tale may be rooted in fact, and a nonfiction text may describe an amazing event that is difficult to believe. By studying a text's characteristics, you can identify it as fiction or nonfiction. Pay particular attention to the text's context, purpose, and tone.

The Spanish Inquisition was a religious court established in 1478. Its main purpose was to find and punish people who did not agree with the Catholic faith. Today many of the methods used as punishment would be considered torture. The following passages are about the Spanish Inquisition.

There were three sorts of persons distinguished by the Tribunal as suspected of heresy [belief disagreeing with a particular religion, in this case Catholicism]: those who were lightly suspected, those who were seriously suspected, and those who were violently suspected.

5   There were three methods of torture; the cord, fire, and water. In the first method, they tied the hands behind the back of the patient by means of a cord which passed through a pulley attached to the roof, and the executioners drew him up as high as possible. After suspending him for some time, the cord was loosened, and he fell within six inches of the ground. This terrible shock dislocated all the joints and cut the flesh even to the sinews. The process was renewed every hour and left the patient without strength or motion. It was not until after the physician had declared that the sufferer could no
10   longer endure the torture without dying, that the Inquisitors sent him back to prison.

(continued)

The second was performed by means of water. The executioners stretched the victim over a wooden instrument like a spout . . . without any bottom but a stick passing across it. The body falling backwards came to such a position that the feet were higher than the head. In this cruel position the executioners passed into the throat a piece of fine linen, wet, a part of which covered the nostrils.

15 They then turned water into the mouth and nose and left it to filter so slowly that one hour at least was consumed before the sufferer had swallowed a drop, although it trickled without interruption. Thus the patient found no interval for respiration.

If by this second torment they could obtain no confession, the inquisitors resorted to fire. For this purpose the executioners tied the hands and feet in such a manner that the sufferer could not change

20 his position. They then rubbed the feet with oil and lard, and other penetrating matter, and placed them before the fire, until the flesh was so roasted that the bones and sinews appeared in every part.

Excerpt from *Records of the Spanish Inquisition*, translated by Andrew Dickson White

Unreal!—Even while I breathed there came to my nostrils the breath of the vapour of heated iron! A suffocating odour pervaded the prison! A deeper glow settled each moment in the eyes that glared at my agonies! A richer tint of crimson diffused itself over the pictured horrors of blood. . . . I gasped for breath! There could be no doubt of the design of my tormentors—oh! . . . most demoniac of men! Yet,

5 for a wild moment, did my spirit refuse to comprehend the meaning of what I saw. At length it forced— it wrestled its way into my soul—it burned itself in upon my shuddering reason.—Oh! for a voice to speak!—oh! horror!—oh! any horror but this! With a shriek, I rushed from the margin, and buried my face in my hands—weeping bitterly. . . .

"Death," I said, "any death but that of the pit!" Fool! Might I have not known that into the pit it

10 was the object of the burning iron to urge me? Could I . . . withstand its pressure? And now, flatter and flatter grew the lozenge. . . . Its centre, and of course, its greatest width, came just over the yawning gulf. I shrank back—but the closing walls pressed me resistlessly onward. At length for my seared and writhing body there was no longer an inch of foothold on the firm floor of the prison. I struggled no more, but the agony of my soul found vent in one loud, long, and final scream of despair. I felt that I

15 tottered upon the brink—I averted my eyes—

There was a discordant hum of human voices! There was a loud blast as of many trumpets! There was a harsh grating as of a thousand thunders! The fiery walls rushed back! An outstretched arm caught my own as I fell, fainting, into the abyss. It was that of General Lasalle. The French army had entered Toledo. The Inquisition was in the hands of its enemies.

Excerpt from "The Pit and the Pendulum" by Edgar Allan Poe

5 What is the topic of both passages?

  A The key players in the creation of the Spanish Inquisition

  B The purposes behind the formation of the Spanish Inquisition

  C The methods of torture used during the Spanish Inquisition

  D The events that led to the end of the Spanish Inquisition

6 How do the authors' approaches to the subject differ?

  A White criticizes the methods used by the inquisitors; Poe shows sympathy for the accused.

  B White gives a factual account of torture methods; Poe focuses on the terror felt by a prisoner.

  C White details the torture experienced by one man; Poe writes about the experiences of many.

  D White writes from the point of view of the inquisitor; Poe writes from the point of view of the accused.

7 What is the main purpose of passage 1?

  A To help

  B To persuade

  C To entertain

  D To inform

8 In line 12 of passage 1, the word "instrument" most nearly means

  A device used to produce music.

  B means of getting something done.

  C measuring device.

  D tool or an implement.

9 What is the genre of "The Pit and the Pendulum"?

  A Essay

  B Fiction

  C Memoir

  D Nonfiction

✅ Test-Taking Tip

If you are not happy with your score in one or more subtests, consider retaking those tests. You can retake each subtest twice in a 12-month period. You will be at an advantage the second time because you can focus your studying and you'll be familiar with the test's format.

Writing Practice

One of the first decisions authors make is how they will address a topic. For example, will the writer tell a fictional story about the topic or write a nonfiction article? A nonfiction writer must determine whether to state facts, express opinions, or do both. Writers must also select the format that will best convey their message to the audience.

Write two accounts of a significant event in your life, such as meeting a future spouse or partner, getting your first job, or learning how to drive a car. The first account should be an **informational text**. Provide facts and details about the event. Write the second account as a **fictional story** or a **persuasive essay**. Use language that conveys your purpose.

_____

_____

_____

_____

_____

_____

_____

_____

_____

_____

_____

_____

_____

_____

_____

_____

_____

_____

_____

_____

_____

_____

This lesson will help you practice comparing two texts from similar genres. Use it with Core Lesson 7.2 *Compare Similar Genres* to reinforce and apply your knowledge.

Key Concept

Authors may use similar genres to address common themes or ideas.

Identifying Genre

A genre is a category of writing that has specific characteristics. Identifying the differences in genres helps the reader understand the differences in the authors' purposes for writing.

These two passages are about Japanese culture. One passage describes the importance of a particular part of Japanese culture. The other is about the life of Japanese Americans in the late 19th century.

Tea began as a medicine and grew into a beverage. In China, in the eighth century, it entered the realm of poetry as one of the polite amusements. The fifteenth century saw Japan ennoble it into a religion of aestheticism—Teaism. Teaism is a cult founded on the adoration of the beautiful among the sordid facts of everyday existence. It inculcates purity and harmony, the mystery of mutual charity,
5   the romanticism of the social order. It is essentially a worship of the Imperfect, as it is a tender attempt to accomplish something possible in this impossible thing we know as life. . . .

The long isolation of Japan from the rest of the world, so conducive to introspection, has been highly favorable to the development of Teaism. Our home and habits, costume and cuisine, porcelain, lacquer, painting—our very literature—all have been subject to its influence. No student of Japanese
10   culture could ever ignore its presence. It has permeated the elegance of noble boudoirs, and entered the abode of the humble. Our peasants have learned to arrange flowers, our meanest laborer to offer his salutation to the rocks and waters. In our common parlance we speak of the man "with no tea" in him, when he is insusceptible to the serio-comic interests of the personal drama. Again we stigmatize the untamed aesthete who, regardless of the mundane tragedy, runs riot in the springtide of emancipated
15   emotions, as one "with too much tea" in him.

The outsider may indeed wonder at this seeming much ado about nothing. What a tempest in a tea-cup! he will say. But when we consider how small after all the cup of human enjoyment is, how soon overflowed with tears, how easily drained to the dregs in our quenchless thirst for infinity, we shall not blame ourselves for making so much of the tea-cup. Mankind has done worse. . . .

20   Those who cannot feel the littleness of great things in themselves are apt to overlook the greatness of little things in others. The average Westerner, in his sleek complacency, will see in the tea ceremony but another instance of the thousand and one oddities which constitute the quaintness and childishness of the East to him. He was wont to regard Japan as barbarous while she indulged in the gentle arts of peace: he calls her civilized since she began to commit wholesale slaughter on Manchurian battlefields.
25   Much comment has been given lately to the Code of the Samurai—the Art of Death which makes our soldiers exult in self-sacrifice; but scarcely any attention has been drawn to Teaism, which represents so much of our Art of Life.

Excerpt from *The Book of Tea* by Kakuzo Okakura

One of the first groups of settlers that came from Japan to the United States, the Wakamatsu Tea and Silk Farm Colony under the leadership of John Schnell, arrived at Cold Hill, El Dorado County, in June 1869. Additional colonists arrived in the fall of 1869. These first immigrants brought mulberry trees, silk cocoons, tea plants, bamboo roots, and other agricultural products. The U.S. Census of 1870
5   showed 55 Japanese in the United States; 33 were in California, with 22 living at Gold Hill. Within a few years of the colony's founding, the colonists had dispersed, their agricultural venture a failure.

The 1880 Census showed 86 Japanese in California, with a total of 148 in the United States. Possibly these were students, or Japanese who had illegally left their country, since Japanese laborers were not allowed to leave their country until after 1884 when an agreement was signed between the Japanese
10   government and Hawaiian sugar plantations to allow labor immigration. From Hawaii, many Japanese continued on to the United States mainland. . . .

Laborers for the Hawaiian sugar plantations were carefully chosen. . . . [A] systematic method of recruiting workers from specific regions in Japan was established. Natives from Hiroshima, Kumamoto, Yamaguchi, and Fukushima were sought for their supposed expertise in agriculture, for
15   their hard work, and for their willingness to travel. . . .

Except for a temporary suspension of immigration to Hawaii in 1900, the flow of immigration from Japan remained relatively unaffected until 1907–08, when agitation from white supremacist organizations, labor unions, and politicians resulted in the "Gentlemen's Agreement," curtailing further immigration of laborers from Japan. A provision in the Gentlemen's Agreement, however, permitted
20   wives and children of laborers, as well as laborers who had already been in the United States, to continue to enter the country. Until that time, Japanese immigrants had been primarily male. The 1900 Census indicates that only 410 of 24,326 Japanese were female. From 1908 to 1924, Japanese women continued to immigrate to the United States, some as "picture brides."

In Japan . . . go-betweens arranged marriages between compatible males and females. . . .
25   [A]n exchange of photographs became a first step in this long process. Entering the bride's name in the groom's family registry legally constituted marriage. Those Japanese males who could afford the cost of traveling to Japan returned there to be married. Others resorted to long-distance . . . marriages. . . . [T]he bride would immigrate to the United States as the wife of a laborer. . . . For wives who entered after 1910, the first glimpse of the United States was the Detention Barracks at Angel Island in San
30   Francisco Bay. New immigrants were processed there, and given medical exams. As a result, this was the place where most "picture brides" saw their new husbands for the first time.

Excerpt from "A History of Japanese Americans in California" by the National Park Service

1 Which genres are used in the two passages?

  A Passage 1 is biography; Passage 2 is historical fiction.

  B Passage 1 is autobiography; Passage 2 is biography.

  C Passage 1 is an essay; Passage 2 is a historical article.

  D Passage 1 is a folktale; Passage 2 is an essay.

2 What is the main purpose of both passages?

  A To inform readers about Japanese culture

  B To entertain readers with Japanese literature

  C To persuade readers to meet Japanese people

  D To support readers learning Japanese

3 What is the main difference in literary technique between the two passages?

  A Passage 1 includes vivid descriptions; Passage 2 relies on facts and figures.

  B Passage 1 begins in the 8th century; Passage 2 begins in the 19th century.

  C Passage 1 is about Teaism in Japan; Passage 2 is about immigrants.

  D Passage 1 contains a plot; Passage 2 contains only facts and figures.

4 How does the portrayal of the Japanese differ in these two passages?

  A Passage 1 depicts the Japanese as hard working; Passage 2 depicts the Japanese as lazy.

  B Passage 1 shows the refinement of Japanese culture; Passage 2 shows the plight of Japanese laborers in America.

  C Passage 1 emphasizes the woman's place in Japan; Passage 2 highlights the lack of Japanese women in America at the turn of the 20th century.

  D Passage 1 depicts Japanese culture as more advanced than other cultures; Passage 2 depicts Japanese culture as less advanced than American culture.

✅ Test-Taking Tip

Unlike multiple-choice questions on a test, an essay is graded by a human. Therefore, keep your reader in mind as you write. Engage the reader with clear explanations, lively descriptions, and specific details. Reread your essay to check for correct grammar and punctuation. Practice the rules of grammar and punctuation ahead of time so you and your reader can focus on the content of your essay.

Comparing Texts from Similar Genres

Some nonfiction texts—such as memoirs, biographies, or letters—are narratives. They tell the story of a person, event, time, or place. As you compare narrative texts of similar genres, pay attention to text features, literary techniques, tone, and the author's attitude toward the topic.

These two passages are about life in the western United States in the late 19th and early 20th centuries. In the first passage, the author describes a trip down the Yellowstone River. In the second passage, the author describes an experience in Yosemite Valley.

As we edged our way out to a better position, the sun rose and threw a series of three rainbows in the mist clouds as they floated up out of the shadowed depths. The lowest and clearest of these semicircles of irised spray seemed to spring from a patch of bright saffron sand, where it was laid bare by the melting snow. Now I know where the story of the gold at the end of the rainbow came from.

5   Carr and I tried to come through from the canyon by moonlight last night and had rather a bad time of it. First a fog obscured the moon. Then we tried to take a shortcut by following the telephone line, got lost in the dark, and stayed lost till the moon set and made it darker still. In cutting across the hills to get back into Hayden Valley, Carr fell over a snow bank and landed right in the middle of the road. . . .

10   After a while we were lost again, this time in a level space bounded on four sides by a winding creek. I know it was on four sides of the place, for we carefully walked off toward each point of the compass in rotation, and each time landed in the creek. We finally escaped by wading. How we got in without wading will always be a mystery. . . .

We passed the famous and only Mud Geyser an hour before daybreak. Things were in a bad way
15   with him, judging from the noise. . . . Carr said it reminded him of something between a mad bull buffalo and a boatload of seasick tourists when the summer wind stirs up the lake. But Carr was too tired and disgusted to be elegant. Indeed, we were both pretty well played out. Personally, I felt just about like the Mud Geyser sounded.

Excerpt from *Down the Yellowstone* by Lewis R. Freeman

November 1st [1868]

I was extremely glad to receive yet one more of your ever welcome letters. . . . I am not surprised to hear of your leaving Madison and am anxious to know where your lot will be cast. . . . If you make your home in California, I know from experience how keenly you will feel the absence of the special
5   flowers you love. . . . [However,] I think that you will find in California just what you desire in climate and scenery, for both are so varied.

March is the springtime of the plains, April the summer, and May the autumn. The other months are dry and wet winter. . . . I rode across the seasons in going to the Yosemite last spring. I started from the Joaquin in the last week of May. All the plain flowers, so lately fresh in the power of full beauty, were
10   dead. Their parched leaves crisped and fell to powder. . . .

After riding for two days in this autumn I found summer again in the higher foothills. Flower petals were spread confidingly open, the grasses waved their branches all bright and gay in the colors of healthy prime, and the winds and streams were cool. Forty or fifty miles further into the mountains, I came to spring. The leaves on the oak were small and drooping, and they still retained
15   their first tintings of crimson and purple, and the wrinkles of their bud folds were distinct as if newly opened. . . .

(continued)

A few miles farther "onward and upward" I found the edge of winter. Scarce a grass could be seen. . . . Soon my horse was plunging in snow ten feet in depth, the sky became darker and more terrible, many-voiced mountain winds swept the pines, speaking the dread language of the cold
20   north. . . .

Descending these higher mountains towards the Yosemite, the snow gradually disappeared from the pines and the sky . . . and violets appeared again, and I once more found spring in the grand valley. Thus meet and blend the seasons of these mountains and plains, beautiful in their joinings as those of lake and land or of the bands of the rainbow. . . .

25   Ever yours most cordially,

                                                                                                    J.M.

Excerpt from *Letters to a Friend*; written to Mrs. Ezra S. Carr, 1866–1879 by John Muir

5 **The genre of Passage 2 is a letter. What is the genre of the Passage 1?**

  A Biography

  B Memoir

  C Persuasive essay

  D Historical fiction

6 **How do the attitudes of the authors differ?**

  A Lewis is amused; Muir is amazed.

  B Lewis is disgusted; Muir is fearful.

  C Lewis is awestruck; Muir is amused.

  D Lewis is surprised; Muir is awestruck.

7 **In Passage 2, what does "keenly" in line 3 mean?**

  A Cleverly

  B Sharply

  C Sensitively

  D Intensely

8 **Which characteristics do the two texts share?**

  A Both passages convey a serious tone.

  B Both passages include a date and signature.

  C Both passages are told in the first person.

  D Both passages directly address readers.

Writing Practice

> Biographies are about the life of a person other than the author. Autobiographies are about the life of the author. These genres are related, but each has distinct qualities, which are influenced by the author's purpose and point of view.
>
> Write two paragraphs about yourself: the first as a **biography** and the second as an **autobiography**. The biography should be written in the third person; its point of view should be objective. The autobiography should be written in the first person; it should be subjective, since you are telling about events from your viewpoint.

This lesson will help you practice analyzing opposing arguments expressed in two texts. Use it with Core Lesson 7.3 *Analyze Two Arguments* to reinforce and apply your knowledge.

Key Concept

In order to choose which side of an argument to support, a reader must evaluate the evidence and logic used by each side.

Comparing and Contrasting Two Arguments

For every argument in favor of an opinion, there is likely an argument that disputes that opinion, or argues against it. When reading an argument, begin by identifying the claim. Then analyze the evidence to determine whether the claim is valid and well supported.

Charles Darwin's theory of evolution was hotly contested in the early 1900s. The strongest opponents of the theory were those who believed God created all life on Earth. Darwin believed that only the strongest members of a species survive. He believed desirable traits are transferred to the next generation. That generation's best traits are transferred to the next generation, and so on. He called this process *natural selection*. The two passages that follow discuss Darwin's theory of evolution.

Not very long before birth the human embryo is strikingly similar to the embryo of the ape. Still earlier, it presents an appearance very like that of the embryos of other mammals lower in the scale, like the cat and the rabbit. . . . Indeed, as we trace back the still earlier history, more and more characters are found which are the common properties of wider and wider arrays of organisms.
5   [A]t one time the embryo exhibits gill-slits in the sides of its throat which in all essential respects are just like those of the embryos of birds and reptiles and amphibian. . . . Can we reasonably regard these resemblances as indications of anything else but a community of ancestry of the forms that exhibit them?

Yet a still more wonderful fact is revealed by the study of the very earliest stages of individual
10   development. The human embryo begins its very existence as a single cell,—nothing more and nothing less. . . . I do not think we could ask nature for more complete proof that human beings have evolved from one-cell ancestors as simple as modern protozoa. . . . They at least are real and not the logical deductions of reason. . . .

And now . . . we may look to nature for fossil evidence regarding the ancestry of our species. Much
15   is known about the remains of many kinds of men who lived in prehistoric times, but we need consider here only one form which lived long before the glacial period in the so-called Tertiary times. In 1894 a scientist named Dubois discovered in Java some of the remains of an animal which was partly ape and partly man. So well did these remains exhibit the characters of Haeckel's hypothetical ape-man, *Pithecanthropus*, that the name fitted the creature like a glove. Specifically, the cranium presents
20   an arch which is intermediate between that of the average ape and of the lowest human beings. It possessed protruding brows like those of the gorilla. The estimated brain capacity was about one thousand cubic centimeters, four hundred more than that of any known ape, and much less than the [human average]. Even without other characters, these would indicate that the animal was actually a "missing link" in the scientific sense,—that is, a form which is near the common progenitors of the
25   modern species of apes and of man. . . . So *Pithecanthropus* is a part of the chain leading to man, not far from the place where the human line sprang from a lower primate ancestor. . . .

(continued)

The foregoing facts illustrate the conclusive evidence brought forward by science that human evolution in physical respects is true. Even if we wished to do so, we cannot do away with the facts of structure and development and fossil history, nor is there any other explanation more reasonable than
30 evolution for these facts.

Excerpt from *The Doctrine of Evolution: Its Basis and Its Scope* by Henry Edward Crampton

[I]t would be indeed strange, if no honest man could be found to tell . . . the truth regarding Darwinism. This has occurred sooner than I dared to hope. This chapter can announce the glad tidings that even in "social-democratic science" Darwinism is doomed to decay. Much printer's ink will, of course, be yet wasted before it will be so entirely dead as to be no longer available as a weapon against
5 Christianity; but a beginning at least has been made.

In the December [issue] of the ninth year of the *Sozialistische Monatshefte*, a social-democratic writer, Curt Grottewitz, undertakes to bring out an article on "Darwinian Myths." It is stated there that Darwin had a few eminent followers, but that the educated world took no notice of their work; that now, however, they seemed to be attracting more attention. "There is no doubt that a number of
10 Darwinian views, which are still prevalent to-day, have sunk to the level of untenable myths. . . ." . . .

Grottewitz very frankly continues: "The difficulty with the Darwinian doctrines consists in the fact that they are incapable of being strictly and irrefutably demonstrated. The origin of one species from another, the conservation of useful forms, the existence of countless intermediary links, are all assumptions, which could never be supported by concrete cases found in actual experience." Some
15 are said to be well established indirectly by proofs drawn from probabilities, while others are proved to be absolutely untenable. Among the latter Grottewitz includes "[natural] selection," which is indeed a monstrous figment of the imagination. There was moreover really no reason for adhering to it so long. It is eminently untrue, that the biological research of the last few years proved for the *first* time the untenableness of this doctrine, as Grottewitz seems to think. Clear thinkers recognized its
20 untenableness long ago. . . .

It is certainly a very peculiar phenomenon; for decades we behold a doctrine reverently re-echoed; thoughtful investigators expose its folly, but still the worship continues.

Excerpt from *At the Deathbed of Darwinism* by Eberhard Dennert

1 What is the claim of Crampton's argument?

A Human embryos are similar to ape embryos.

B Humans are physically similar to other types of primates.

C Fossils show the evolution of humans over time.

D Humans have evolved over the centuries.

2 Crampton's argument about evolution is credible because the evidence is based on

A opinion.

B hearsay.

C facts.

D logic.

3 What does "scale" (line 3 of Crampton's argument) mean?

A An indication of distance on a map

B A thin plate covering the skin of a fish

C A series of tests used to rate performance

D A graduated series

4 Which additional claim would Crampton be most likely to make?

A Humans were created in God's image.

B Unused traits disappear as a species evolves.

C Fossils are not sufficient proof of evolution.

D There is no relationship between humans and monkeys.

5 **What is the claim of Dennert's argument?**

    A Evolution cannot be proved.

    B Darwinism damages Christianity.

    C Darwinism is not widely accepted.

    D Natural selection is impossible.

6 **Which statement describes Dennert's view of the theory of evolution?**

    A He supports it.

    B He disputes it.

    C He understands it.

    D He questions it.

Analyzing Evidence in Two Arguments

When readers compare opposing arguments, they must carefully evaluate the evidence provided by each author and decide whether that evidence is relevant, accurate, sufficient, credible, and logical so the claim is well supported.

7 **How does the Pithecanthropus support Crampton's argument?**

    A It shows that other well-regarded scientists supported Darwin's theory of evolution.

    B It proves that humans are more highly evolved than other primates.

    C It supports the claim of a physiological relationship between humans and apes.

    D It indicates that the Pithecanthropus is not the "missing link."

8 **Which type of evidence does Crampton use to support his argument?**

    A Scientific research and analysis

    B Opinion

    C Heresay

    D Witness statements

9 **Which type of evidence does Dennert use to support his argument?**

    A Scientific research

    B Opinion

    C Logic

    D Record of events

10 **Which evidence in Crampton's argument contradicts the claim of Dennert's argument?**

    A Cats and rabbits are on the lower end of the evolutionary scale.

    B Humans and apes are primates with similar structures.

    C A "missing link" between ape and human once existed.

    D Amphibians, reptiles, and birds have similar embryonic structures.

✔ Test-Taking Tip

How much should you write in an essay for a writing test? As much as you need to clearly respond to the prompt and to provide supporting evidence. If you do not have much to say about the topic, do not try to stretch your material. Adding extraneous or irrelevant information just to make your essay longer can actually harm your overall score.

Writing Practice

You need to compare and contrast opposing arguments to determine which argument you agree with. To make an informed decision, compare the arguments and evaluate the evidence for accuracy, relevance, and sufficiency. Once you have analyzed the two arguments, you can decide whether to support either side.

Briefly **compare and contrast** two sides of an argument that you've recently read or heard, such as a debate between two politicians or a disagreement between friends about which movie to see. Which **argument** was stronger? Why? Did you agree with either argument? Explain why or why not. Support your viewpoint with evidence.

_____

_____

_____

_____

_____

_____

_____

_____

_____

_____

_____

_____

_____

_____

_____

_____

_____

_____

_____

_____

_____

_____

This lesson will help you practice evaluating the impact of genre and format. Use it with Core Lesson 7.4 *Evaluate the Impact of Genre and Format* to reinforce and apply your knowledge.

Key Concept

By comparing genres that present similar ideas, readers can identify differences in scope, impact, purpose, and intended audience.

Comparing Textual and Visual Genres

The genre and the format that writers choose depend in part on their purpose. Writers, as well as visual artists, consider the impact, or effect, that they want to have on their audience. The same topic presented as text or in a visual format can affect readers in different ways.

The following passages are a newspaper article, a poem, and a time line. The "Captain" in the poem refers to President Abraham Lincoln.

If any evidence were needed of the love of the people for Abraham Lincoln and their confidence in him, it is furnished by the remarkable spectacle of the last few days. Never did a conqueror . . . receive such proof of the devotion of a nation, as that which has been accorded to the remains of the martyred president on their way to be deposited in their last resting place.

5   Amid the magnificent pageants which have been witnessed in their progress from city to city, one thing has been prominent—and that is, the profound feeling which has touched all hearts. The decorations which have been witnessed as the sorrowful procession advanced from place to place, have been unparalleled in the history of this country. . . . The whole nation has risen up to do homage to his memory.

10   If the feelings of sorrow on the part of the people have been deep and real, elsewhere, they have been even more so in our late president's state and home. Here his virtues were appreciated and the struggles by which he so worthily arose to such distinction . . . were fully understood. Here were those who never lost faith in the pilot at the helm, even when the storm of civil war beat most violently about the "ship of state." Here he always received sympathy and encouragement from those who knew him
15   best.

The events of yesterday and to-day in this community are full of the most impressive significance. From our midst, a little more than four years ago, President Lincoln was called to the highest office in the gift of the people. Yesterday, all that is mortal of him returned to us wrapped in the habiliments of the grave. Thousands who loved the man for his virtues and the cause for which he was the noble
20   champion, wept at the ruin for which the assassin has wrought. . . . Illinois receives her murdered son again to her bosom, no less loving than when she sent him forth to the most distinguished honor. To-day we lay him reverently to rest amid the scenes he loved so well. Millions will drop a tear to his memory, and future generations will make pilgrimages to the tomb. Peace to his ashes.

Excerpt from "How They Loved Him," *Springfield Daily State Journal*

O Captain! my Captain! our fearful trip is done,

The ship has weather'd every rack, the prize we sought is won,

The port is near, the bells I hear, the people all exulting,

While follow eyes the steady keel, the vessel grim and daring;

5   But O heart! heart! heart!

        O the bleeding drops of red,

            Where on the deck my Captain lies,

                Fallen cold and dead.

O Captain! my Captain! rise up and hear the bells;

10   Rise up—for you the flag is flung—for you the bugle trills,

For you bouquets and ribbon'd wreaths—for you the shores a-crowding,

For you they call, the swaying mass, their eager faces turning;

        Here Captain! dear father!

            This arm beneath your head!

15   It is some dream that on the deck,

                You've fallen cold and dead.

My Captain does not answer, his lips are pale and still,

My father does not feel my arm, he has no pulse nor will,

The ship is anchor'd safe and sound, its voyage closed and done,

20   From fearful trip the victor ship comes in with object won;

        Exult O shores, and ring O bells!

            But I with mournful tread,

                Walk the deck my Captain lies,

                    Fallen cold and dead.

"O Captain! My Captain!" by Walt Whitman

1865

Lincoln shot	Lincoln funeral held at White House	Lincoln's body laid to rest in Springfield, IL
April 14	**April 19**	**May 4**

April 15
Lincoln dies

April 21
Lincoln funeral train leaves Washington, D.C.

1. "How They Loved Him," "O Captain! My Captain!," and the time line share the same

   A topic.
   B format.
   C genre.
   D narrator.

2. Which of the following meanings associated with the word "devotion" seems most intended in line 3 of "How They Loved Him"?

   A Prayer or worship
   B Use of time, energy, and money
   C Deep religiousness
   D Love or loyalty

3. Which statement best describes the impact of "O Captain! My Captain!" on readers?

   A Readers learn facts about Lincoln's assassination.
   B Readers understand the despair people felt after Lincoln's death.
   C Readers analyze how Lincoln's death could have been prevented.
   D Readers agree that Lincoln was our greatest president.

4. Which statement best describes how the time line compares to the article and poem?

   A The time line visually communicates information about the events that occurred after Lincoln was shot; the other two texts convey the emotional toll of his assassination.
   B The time line provides interesting facts about events prior to Lincoln's death; the other two texts describe what happened after his death.
   C The time line organizes the events leading up to Lincoln's death in a visual way; the other two texts rely on text to convey the same information.
   D The time line visually organizes information about the weeks after Lincoln's death; the other two texts describe those events in detail.

Evaluating Differences between Textual Genres

When they are considering differences between genres, readers can compare the unique characteristics of each genre. They can also determine the intended audience of a piece of writing. Finally, they can identify the scope of the information that is presented; some texts cover a broad range of information about a topic, and other texts limit the range to one specific event or idea.

The following two passages are nonfiction articles about natural disasters.

Evacuations are more common than many people realize. Fires and floods cause evacuations most frequently across the U.S. and almost every year, people along coastlines evacuate as hurricanes approach. . . .

5. In some circumstances, local officials . . . require mandatory evacuations. In others, evacuations are advised or households decide to evacuate to avoid situations they believe are potentially dangerous. When community evacuations become necessary local officials provide information to the public through the media. In some circumstances, other warning methods, such as sirens, text alerts, emails or telephone calls are used. . . .

(continued)

10 If the event is a weather condition, such as a hurricane, you might have a day or two to get ready. However, many disasters allow no time for people to gather even the most basic necessities, which is why planning ahead is essential.

Plan how you will assemble your family and supplies and anticipate where you will go for different situations. Choose several destinations in different directions so you have options in an emergency and know the evacuation routes to get to those destinations. Follow these guidelines for evacuation:

15 • Plan places where your family will meet, both within and outside of your immediate neighborhood. . . .

• If you have a car, keep a full tank of gas in it if an evacuation seems likely. . . . Gas stations may be closed during emergencies and unable to pump gas during power outages. Plan to take one car per family to reduce congestion and delay.

20 • Become familiar with alternate routes . . . out of your area. . . .

• Leave early enough to avoid being trapped by severe weather.

• Follow recommended evacuation routes. Do not take shortcuts; they may be blocked.

• Be alert for road hazards such as washed-out roads . . . and downed power lines. . . .

• Take your emergency supply kit unless . . . it has been contaminated.

25 • Listen to a battery-powered radio and follow local evacuation instructions.

• Take your pets with you, but understand that only service animals may be permitted in public shelters. Plan how you will care for your pets in an emergency.

Excerpt from "Evacuating Yourself and Your Family" by the Federal Emergency Management Agency

The earthquake in San Francisco shook down hundreds of thousands of dollars' worth of walls and chimneys. But the conflagration that followed burned up hundreds of millions of dollars' worth of property. There is no estimating within hundreds of millions the actual damage wrought.

Not in history has a modern imperial city been so completely destroyed. San Francisco is gone.
5 Nothing remains of it but memories and a fringe of dwelling houses on its outskirts. Its industrial section is wiped out. Its business section is wiped out. Its social and residential section is wiped out. The factories and warehouses, the great stores and newspaper buildings, the hotels and the palaces . . . are all gone. . . . Within an hour after the earthquake shock, the smoke of San Francisco's burning was a lurid tower visible a hundred miles away. And for three days and nights this lurid tower swayed in the
10 sky, reddening the sun, darkening the day, and filling the land with smoke.

On Wednesday morning at a quarter past five came the earthquake. A minute later the flames were leaping upward. In a dozen different quarters south of Market Street, in the working-class ghetto, and in the factories, fires started. There was no opposing the flames. There was no organization, no communication. All the cunning adjustments of a twentieth-century city had been smashed by
15 the earthquake. The streets were humped into ridges and depressions and piled with the debris of fallen walls. The steel rails were twisted into perpendicular and horizontal angles. The telephone and telegraph systems were disrupted. And the great water mains had burst.

(continued)

By Wednesday afternoon . . . half the heart of the city was gone. . . . East, west, north, and south,
strong winds were blowing upon the doomed city. The heated air rising made an enormous suck. Thus
20 did the fire of itself build its own colossal chimney through the atmosphere. . . .

San Francisco . . . is like the crater of a volcano, around which are camped tens of thousands of
refugees. . . . All the surrounding cities and towns are jammed with the homeless ones, where they
are being cared for by the relief committees. The refugees were carried free by the railroads to any
point they wished to go, and it is estimated that over one hundred thousand people have left. . . . The
25 government has the situation in hand, and, thanks to the immediate relief given by the whole United
States, there is not the slightest possibility of a famine. The bankers and business men have already set
about making preparations to rebuild San Francisco.

Excerpt from "The Story of an Eye-Witness" by Jack London

5 **Which characteristic applies only to
passage 2?**

A   Practical advice

B   Information

C   Vivid descriptions

D   Third-person narration

6 **Which conclusion could the reader draw
about the intended audience of passage 1?**

A   The audience is people who might need to
prepare for a natural disaster.

B   The audience is people who have
experienced a natural disaster.

C   The audience is people who want to learn
about the weather.

D   The audience is people who work for the
Federal Emergency Management Agency.

7 **How does the genre support the author's
purpose in writing "The Story of an Eye-
Witness"?**

A   It allows the reader to understand key
concepts about earthquakes.

B   It allows the reader to keep track of the
sequence of events.

C   It allows the author to include rich details
that appeal to the reader's emotions.

D   It allows the author to persuade readers to
prepare for earthquakes.

8 **When comparing the two passages, the
scope of passage 1 is**

A   narrower than the scope of passage 2.

B   broader than the scope of passage 2.

C   equal to the scope of passage 2.

D   superior to the scope of passage 2.

✔ Test-Taking Tip

As you plan to write an essay for a test, ask yourself, "What is my purpose
for writing?" and "Who is my intended audience?" The purpose and the
audience will influence your choice of genre and format.

Writing Practice

Many people enjoy playing sports or participating in a performing art such as singing or dancing. Knowing the rules or understanding the skills helps you play or perform, and it can enhance your viewing of games or performances.

Write two paragraphs, each in a different **format**. In the first paragraph, use bullet points or numbered lists to provide information about the rules of a sport or skills needed to perform a certain song, dance, and so on. In the second paragraph, use descriptive details to write a narrative account of a game or a performance.

_____

_____

_____

_____

_____

_____

_____

_____

_____

_____

_____

_____

_____

_____

_____

_____

_____

_____

_____

_____

_____

_____

_____

_____

Lesson 1.1

Main Idea in Informational Text, p. 2

1 **B** The headings above each section explains what the section is about. This helps you identify the main idea of the section. The passage title provides information about what the entire passage is about but does not focus on specific sections. The first and last sentences provide details, not the main idea of the sections.

2 **B** Answer B is the only detail that is about starting the work.

3 **C** Answer C tells the main idea of the section. The other sentences are not related to rates.

4 **D** The "Change orders" section explains how change orders need to be used when the scope of work changes. This includes adding work to the project. The other sections are about other aspects of the PT system.

5 **D** The main idea tells what the passage is about. The paragraphs in the memo outline the various procedures that employees must implement when using the new purchasing system.

6 **A** The topic sentence is presented at the start of the passage so employees will know what the text is about. The topic sentence is not the least important information. Reading the topic sentence does not eliminate the need to read the details in the rest of the passage.

Main Idea in Literary Text, p. 4

7 **A** Answer A explains the main idea of the excerpt. The other sentences do not reflect the details in the passage.

8 **B** The lack of imagination makes the man ill-equipped for the harsh environment. The other details are not about his shortcomings.

9 **D** Answer D explains the main idea of the paragraph. The other sentences are details or untrue statements.

10 **A** The excerpt is about how instinct is more important than knowledge in severe cold.

11 **B**

12 **D** There is no topic sentence in this passage. However, the author uses details to imply the main idea.

Language Practice, p. 5

1 **B**

2 **C**

3 **B**

4 **D**

Writing Practice, p. 6

Make sure your paragraph has a main idea that is expressed by a topic sentence or implied by the supporting details. All your supporting details should support the main idea.

> Answers will vary. Sample answer: Bruce Springsteen was called "The Boss" long before he was a famous singer. He earned the name from the musicians he paid to back him up in his early days. After they performed at a club, the club manager or owner would pay Bruce because he was the person they had hired. Then Bruce would give the musicians their share of the earnings. The musicians would tease him by calling him "The Boss."

Lesson 1.2

Identifying Supporting Details, p. 8

1 **C** Supporting details may include facts, examples, reasons, and descriptions. The information about mythology and the calendar are facts that help support the main idea that Greeks and Romans contributed to other cultures.

2 A Answer A supports the main idea that Greeks and Romans contributed to the culture of surrounding areas. It provides examples—traditions and technology—of what they contributed to other cultures. The other answers give information about Greeks and Romans, but they do not link this information to the surrounding cultures.

3 C The main idea of paragraph 4 is that mythology had an important role in Greek and Roman culture. Answer C is the only detail that supports this main idea. The other answers give details about the Romans and culture, but they do not mention mythology or the Greek or Roman gods.

4 B Paragraph 2 contains details about cultural development in ancient Greece. This includes supporting details about citizen participation in the Greek government.

5 C Answer C is a supporting detail describing government structure. The other answers do not relate to the structure of Roman society. Answer A is a detail about myths, answer B is about athletics, and answer D is about the Roman calendar.

Using Details to Make Generalizations, p. 10

6 A Answer A is supported by the detail: "Arrows, and missiles of every kind, were seen in the midst of the flocks." Answer B is incorrect because the passage says that the birds were left on the ground. Answer C is incorrect because no mention is made of health threats to the community. Answer D is incorrect because the people are killing the birds, not protecting them.

7 D The narrator sees the mass shooting as wasteful and unjust. Answers A and B describe the narrator's feelings toward the pigeons rather than the shooting. Answer C describes the shooting of firearms.

8 A Answer A provides a villager's viewpoint of why the mass killing of the pigeons is justified—the pigeons are a nuisance because they eat the crops. Answers C and D describe how the narrator kills a single pigeon when he wants food. Answer B is unrelated.

9 B

Language Practice, p. 11

1 A

2 B

3 D

4 C

Writing Practice, p. 12

Make sure your paragraph has a generalization and at least three types of supporting details. Your supporting details may include descriptions, examples, reasons, and facts.

> Answers will vary. Sample answer: As Hurricane Ida prepares to hit the island of Galveston, people are preparing for the worst. Hurricanes are often disastrous for people who do not fully prepare. The mayor ordered an emergency evacuation of all residents Thursday morning. Before leaving, many people boarded up windows and secured valuable items, causing the city to look like a ghost town. People in the surrounding area are encouraged to prepare for the storm by assembling emergency kits that include water, dry food, flashlights, a battery-operated radio, blankets, and a first-aid kit. As the storm approaches, people can expect heavy winds, increased rainfall, and a possible storm surge. People are warned to seek shelter indoors, away from windows and possible flying debris.

Lesson 1.3

Direct and Implied Main Ideas, p. 14

1 A Because the writer does not directly state the main idea, the reader must infer the main idea by studying the details.

2 D The whole passage is about the change in US policies over time. The other answer choices are supporting details.

3 A The main idea of the first paragraph is stated explicitly in the first sentence of the paragraph. The other choices are supporting details.

4 D The implied main idea of paragraphs 7 and 8 is that the United States expanded its borders to the Pacific coast through a war with Mexico.

Implied Main Ideas and Supporting Details, p. 16

5 A Details in passages often help you determine the main idea of a story.

6 D The main idea is not directly stated. Instead, readers must identify the implied main idea by figuring out how the supporting ideas are related.

7 A The main idea of the passage is that "Things are not always the way we see them." This is suggested when the boy realizes that his own house has golden windows when he looks at it from a distance.

8 C When the girl says that the boy has mistaken the house, it supports the main idea that "Things aren't always the way we see them."

9 B

Writing Practice, p. 17

The main idea of your paragraph can be stated directly or implied. Support your main idea with facts, examples, descriptions, or other details.

> Answers will vary. Sample answer: What do a box of cereal, a fluffy red sweater, and a power drill have in common? Most likely all their packages contain bar codes. Bar codes are an amazing invention. To many people, bar codes look like a line of black and white bars with some numbers underneath. However, there is more to a bar code than meets the eye. These black and white stripes are read by computers. They contain a variety of information—from product description to price. Stores use bar codes to make sure the price of merchandise is correctly rung up. Bar codes also help track which products have been sold. This provides a record of inventory, making it easier for managers to order new merchandise. For these reasons, bar codes are an important modern invention.

Lesson 1.4

Summarizing Key Information, p. 19

1 C The passage describes the time a mother and daughter spend waiting for an overdue ship, probably with their loved one on board. Although they are factually correct, answers A and B do not restate the main idea of the poem. The poem does not describe the women sharing memories, so answer D is incorrect.

2 B The main idea of the passage is that two women wait for a ship that never returns. Answer B is the only detail that supports this main idea. Answers A and D help describe the setting, and answer C helps readers visualize the actions of the women, but these are not key to understanding the main idea of the poem.

3 D *"And heaven on the long reach home"* implies that the ship will never return. The wind and the sea spray help the reader picture the scene, but these details do not need to be included in a summary. Mention of the older woman's eyesight is not an important detail either.

4 C

Summarizing a Text, p. 20

5 B The statement retells the key points of the first paragraph. The statement does not critique or quote from the first paragraph; it does not refer to just one supporting detail.

6 C The text describes precautions that travelers should take when they are traveling during hurricane season. The other answers relate to details, but they do not paraphrase the main idea of the passage

7 D The main idea is that travelers should be prepared. Answer D is an important detail about one way to prepare for travel. The other options do not relate to being prepared while traveling during the hurricane season.

8 A   Answer A summarizes all the details in the paragraph. The other choices contain information that is not included in the passage or relate to only one detail.

9 A   This passage includes the boldfaced headings "Travel Alert" and "Hurricane Season." These headings point out important information that should be included in a summary. The passage does not contain italicized text. The date of the alert and paragraph breaks do not need to be included in a summary.

10 B   The main idea is "During hurricane season, travelers should be prepared for emergencies." This statement should be at the beginning of the summary. Statements ii, iv, v, and vi are important details in the passage that should be part of the summary. Statement iii is not accurate information, and statement vii is not an important detail.

Writing Practice, p. 22

Make sure your paragraph concisely states the main idea and supporting details. When you summarize a book or movie, details about the characters, setting, main events, and conflict should be included. A summary might tell how the conflict is resolved—but not all summaries reveal the end of the story.

> Answers will vary. Sample answer: *The Kane Prophecy*, written by Oliver Scott, is set many years in the future, after current civilizations collapse due to an outbreak of a deadly virus. A group of people led by a boy named Hunter begin to suspect they are not alone in the world, and they follow signs to another group of survivors. At first they are hesitant to join the group because they are worried that those people might be infected. As the story progresses, the two groups join forces and discover that the world is not what they once believed. Together, the two groups build a new colony and fight off an army that seeks to keep them out of a fortified city of survivors. In the end, they realize that they have become immune to the virus and that the immunity holds the promise of a healthy future for all of society.

Lesson 1.5

Using Fictional Elements to Determine Theme, p. 24

1 A   The theme is the central message of the passage. The slow and steady work of the Measuring-Worm expresses the story's theme that perseverance leads to success.

2 C   In the story, the Measuring-Worm slowly creeps up the cliff over the course of a year and is the only one who is successful in rescuing the boys. The passage is about persistence, not about working together, judging appearances, or being strong.

3 D   The perseverance of the Measuring-Worm is an important detail in identifying the theme. The other sentences describe different things that happen in the story, but they do not directly relate to the central theme.

4 D

Synthesizing Multiple Main Ideas to Determine Theme, p. 25

5 D   The story is told from the narrator's point of view, allowing the reader to understand the lessons that both characters learn. When these lessons are synthesized, they reveal the theme. The story is not told from the perspective of the king, patriot, or Great Head Factotum.

6 B   The story is a satire, which uses irony to help the reader understand a situation. The use of the term *patriot* highlights the man's dishonesty and disloyalty. The other sentences provide details about the main character but do not help identify the theme.

7 C   In the short story, the patriot is dishonest in his words and actions. These actions reveal the theme. The other statements do not describe the theme.

8 C   The theme of the story is implied and can be found by synthesizing the information from the characterization of the king and the patriot, the language used in the dialog, and the outcome of the interaction between the characters.

Writing Practice, p. 26

Make sure your short story has a theme that is stated or implied. You may reveal your theme through characterization, point of view, setting, plot, language, conflict, or a combination of these elements.

Answers will vary. Sample answer: Many, many years ago there was a spider called Anansi who lived outside a village of hardworking animals. One day Anansi was hungry but too lazy to fix his own dinner. He could smell the wonderful things his neighbors were making and decided to explore. He came across Rabbit making a fine yam stew. "Mmmm . . . that smells wonderful," Anansi flattered Rabbit. "Can I have a bowl?" Rabbit replied that he could but informed Anansi that it wasn't ready yet. Anansi wanted to look for other food, but he did not want to miss out on the yam stew. Then he had an idea. "Rabbit, I will tie this yarn to my leg," Anansi said, smiling. "When the stew is ready, give it a little tug, and I'll come back." Anansi continued on his way until he met Monkey. Monkey was making a lovely bean soup but it also was not yet ready. Once again, Anansi was in too much of a hurry to wait, so he tied some yarn to another leg and bid Monkey to give it a pull when the bean soup was ready. Anansi continued his explorations around the village. Before long, he had a piece of yarn tied to each leg. "How clever I am," Anansi thought to himself. "Soon I will have eight yummy suppers, without doing any work!" Just then, Anansi felt a tug on the yarn from Rabbit. "Time for supper!" he smiled. But before he could go, he felt another and another and another tug. Each piece of yarn pulled Anansi in a different direction, and with each pull his legs got longer and thinner. Finally, Anansi was able to roll into the water, which washed away the yarn. However, to this day, Anansi the Spider has very thin, long legs.

Lesson 2.1

Sequence of Time, p. 28

1 **C** "At first" and "till" tell you that Elizabeth first felt sorry and then became angry.

2 **D** The phrase "when he ceased" tells you what happened just before the color rose in Elizabeth's cheeks.

3 **A** The word "As" could be replace with "While." The meanings would be the same.

4 **B**

5 **D** In the passage, Mr. Darcy expresses his feelings, and then Elizabeth becomes angry. Next Elizabeth expresses her feelings, and finally Mr. Darcy reacts with anger. Therefore, Elizabeth's anger is the second event.

Sequence in a Process, p. 29

6 **A** The sequence described in that section is a process. It is not a flashback, a transition, or a feature.

7 **D** Each section of the text explains a process, and in both cases they are explained in chronological order. The sections themselves are also arranged in chronological order.

8 **C** The only feature used in this passage to show the organization of the text is boldfaced headings. The two questions in these headings help the reader understand the order of events.

9 **B** The passage explains that scientists use seismic surveys to find the right places to drill wells. Then they study rock samples and take measurements. Because the process described in the section is in chronological order, this means that studying samples and taking measurements takes place after seismic surveys are completed.

Writing Practice, p. 30

Make sure that your paragraph uses past tense and includes at least four steps in a process. One step should be an out-of-sequence event. Use transition words to explain when that event occurred.

Answers will vary. Sample answer: Last week I taught Sara how to write an e-mail. I began by showing her how to get to her e-mail login page. But even before doing that, I had to show her how to open the Web browser! I showed her how to log in with her user name and password. Then I explained that "Compose" means "Write a New Message." We typed my e-mail address in the "To" field and then typed "My First E-mail" in the subject line. I told her to write me a special message in the main box. Lastly, she hit the "Send" button, and away it went. She was excited to hear my smartphone beep when I received her incoming message.

Lesson 2.2

Inferring a Writer's Meaning, p. 32

1 B From Dick Baker's speech and dress, you can figure out that he was a simple man who was not well educated. The reference to his heart being finer than gold (line 3) is a metaphor that means Baker is kindhearted. The other statements do not describe Dick Baker.

2 D The narrator seems to doubt that Tom Quartz is special. The narrator does not imply that he agrees with Dick Baker or that he thinks Jim is not as smart as the cat. Dogs are never mentioned.

3 C The actions of the cat—lying low, observing the miners, sleeping on the miners' coats—are normal actions for cats. However, the cat's owner sees the cat's behavior as "superintending" (acting like a supervisor), and he interprets the cat's behavior as humanlike. Most people would not consider these actions supernatural, impressive, or like a circus animal.

4 D Dick Baker says the cat "never *could* altogether understand that eternal sinkin' of a shaft an' never pannin' out anything." The reader can infer that the cat does not think mining underground is a worthwhile activity. There was no mention that the cat was interested in quartz or preferred digging deep.

5 B Dick Baker describes the event in a way that is entertaining. He does not express sadness, satisfaction, or fear.

Citing Evidence, p. 33

6 D The impenetrable darkness and the mist covering the hills are examples used to support the idea that this is a night when one ought to be indoors. These descriptions are not inferences made by readers. The "darkness [was] impenetrable" is an opinion, and "raw mist [was] enveloping hill and valley" is a fact about the weather.

7 A

8 C The narrator's description of his feelings is the best evidence to support the inference that he feels uneasy in the house. The other excerpts do not express discomfort or tension.

9 C Because the man leaving the house mentions that others are expected, readers can logically infer that guests have been invited. Because the house is furnished, a reader would not infer that the house has never been lived in. There was no evidence that the man was the butler. Finally, the narrator seems intrigued and has no intention of leaving immediately.

Writing Practice, p. 35

Make sure your paragraph includes at least two explicit facts, two explicit opinions, and one implied detail about your subject.

> Answers will vary. Sample answer: My cousin Reynaldo is the most impressive person I know. He is raising three kids, and he runs his own business. Now he is starting a master's degree program in business administration. Yet he is always so calm and cool, and he never seems tired. I aspire to be as successful as my cousin when I reach that stage in my life. (Note: *The implied detail is that the writer is younger than the cousin.*)

Lesson 2.3

Identifying Literary Elements, p. 37

1 B The nephew calls Scrooge dismal and morose, so Scrooge is in a bad mood. Answers C and D describe the nephew, not Scrooge. The clerk, the nephew, and the people outside are cold, but Scrooge is not described this way.

2 C The phrases describe the story's setting, specifically the weather of the place where the story takes place. The phrases do not describe the characters, the narrative, or the theme.

3 B The text does not tell us that Scrooge walked to work; he is already working when this passage begins. The text does include choices A, C, and D.

4 D Characterization is the writer's way of helping the reader visualize a character. Answer D is a description of Scrooge's nephew. The other choices do not describe characters.

Analyzing Relationships in Text, p. 38

5 D The room can be considered the setting, and the observations made about the room relate directly to the plot. The other choices do not specifically relate the setting to the overall plot of the mystery story.

6 B In the story, the tavern owner shows the rooms to Coroner Golden and the deputy sheriff, who are investigating an incident involving a young woman. Choices A and D would have happened prior to the events in the passage, and Choice C is an event that does not occur in the passage.

7 C The text explains that the tavern is old and that the owner does not want to change the tavern. Choice A is incorrect because the owner loves the place, and no information is given about changing the owner's mood or his life.

8 B The wallpaper in the room (setting), which is not the same color or pattern that a witness reported, ties the story to its plot. The gable, Jake's sleeping in room 3, and the closeness of the tavern to Danton do not tie the plot to the setting.

9 C

10 D The deputy sheriff has some suspicions, but he also makes important observations before coming to any conclusions. The other choices are ideas that are not in this story.

Writing Practice, p. 40

Make sure your paragraph describes an important event and includes details about the place where the event occurred, including why this place was important.

> Answers will vary. Sample answer: My sister's wedding was all the more memorable because of where she held it, with all the pluses and minuses of that place. She held it on the beach at sunset, so the wedding was beautiful and romantic. The wedding vows related the couple's love to the size of the ocean, which you could see behind them. The only problem for the guests was the sand: people had to go barefoot or try to walk to their seats in their dress shoes. The only problem for my sister was the wind: that ocean breeze was so strong that it almost blew her veil off her head. In most of the photos, she's trying to keep her veil from flying away.

Lesson 2.4

Interpreting Implied Relationships between Ideas, p. 42

1 D The fact that the weather in central Canada is cold and dry is implied, and it must be inferred by the reader based on explicit details. The other answer options are explicit in the text, so they do not have to be inferred.

2 B The author's use of a similar structure and contrasting words (*unstable/stable, faster than*) in the two paragraphs establish that the author is contrasting cold and warm air masses. If the author were comparing the two types of air masses, he or she would indicate what is the same, rather than different, about them. In addition, the author does not explain how one air mass transforms into another.

3 C The text does not say explicitly that cold air masses produce more rain. However, because cold air masses can produce heavy loads of precipitation and warm air masses produce drizzle, this is a reasonable inference. Drizzle is a form of rain that occurs with some warm air masses. Gusty winds are not steady, so they would not occur with warm air masses. Choice B is explicitly stated in the passage; it does not have to be inferred.

4 D The text explicitly says that the Coriolis Effect is a force that affects all wind and water currents, so a reader can infer that hurricanes as well as tornadoes have a counterclockwise spin. For that reason, choice C is incorrect. And since tornadoes take place over land in central states, choices A and B are also incorrect.

Citing Evidence of Implied Relationships, p. 44

5 D A reader can logically predict that Gwendolen's mother will interrupt the couple at any minute because it is her habit to return suddenly. A reader could not logically predict any of the other choices from Gwendolyn's statement.

6 B

7 D It is logical to infer that Algernon knows both characters because he spoke to Gwendolen and told her that he knew someone named Ernest. It is not logical to assume that Algernon dislikes Jack and Gwendolen or that Algernon is Gwendolen's cousin. Readers are aware that Jack does know Algernon, because Gwendolen says that Algernon referred to Jack (aka Ernest) as his friend.

8 C The proximity of the two statements tells readers that Jack wants to be christened, or named, Ernest so that he can be married to Gwendolen using the name Ernest. He does not want to be named Algernon, change his name after marrying, or have Gwendolen change her name before getting married.

Writing Practice, p. 45

Make sure your paragraph describes two different cities with two similarities and two differences. Also make sure it includes a detail about one city that implies that it is better or worse than the other.

> Answers may vary. Sample answer: New York and San Francisco are two of the most interesting cities in the United States, although both are very expensive to live in. New York has live music, shows, and art exhibits every day of the week. San Francisco has amazing attractions of architecture and nature inside the city and around it. New Yorkers can dine on cheap and delicious food from anywhere in the world. San Franciscans can dine in restaurants serving food straight from a nearby organic farm. But for me, the most important difference is the weather: New York's winters are too cold, and its summers are too hot. The Pacific coast it is!

Lesson 2.5

Examining Complex Literary Texts, p. 47

1 A The title and the first sentence of the last paragraph indicate that the narrator is talking about a cat. In other paragraphs, he begins by using the first person and mentions his childhood and his marriage, so the reader also knows that the author is also talking about his life. The other choices do not cover what the passage is mainly about.

2 C The following phrases support this answer: "perhaps, some intellect . . . will reduce my phantasm [fantasy/nightmare] to the commonplace [ordinary]"; "nothing more than an ordinary succession of very natural causes and effects." Because the narrator states that he is telling the story "without comment," it is unlikely he is trying to persuade readers. He also says that readers might find the events less terrifying than he does. Finally, he is not concerned whether readers understand why he has written his account—rather, he wonders whether readers will understand the events themselves.

3 C The main idea is that the narrator married someone who also loved animals, and together they adopted many different types of pets. The narrator does not say that his wife had pets before their marriage. Nor does he say that she was agreeable; he says that the pets are agreeable. In addition, he states that his wife procured (got) pets for him, not that she allowed him to do so.

4 A

Understanding Complex Informational Texts, p. 49

5 A From the introduction and the end of the second paragraph, we see that Obama is concerned with the affordability, or cost, of higher education. The other choices are not the theme of this speech.

6 D The difference between the rise in tuition costs and the rise in income is the strongest evidence that tuition is not affordable. The other choices are mentioned in the speech as problems, but do not support the idea that tuition is unaffordable.

7 D By visualizing someone sighing or grimacing as he or she writes a check to a bank for $1000 each month, a reader would understand the burden of repaying the student loan. Picturing an unemployment line would help a reader understand unemployment rates, but not the cost of tuition. The other choices would not help the reader better understand the problem.

8 B The text in this section lays out the different steps taken by the government to protect students from being exploited by lenders and to help them obtain and repay loans. The other choices mention one step or another, but not the entire process.

9 C The text tells us that Obama is glad that changes have been made but does not feel that the problem of tuition affordability has been resolved. The other choices are explicit details from the text, but they do not state the conclusion.

Language Practice, p. 50
1 C
2 A
3 D
4 A

Writing Practice, p. 51

Make sure your paragraph explains a rule or procedure and uses vocabulary that is specific to that activity.

> Answers will vary. Sample answer: In boxing, the classic one-two combo consists of a jab followed by a cross. Because the jab is thrown from the more forward side of the body, it is used to establish the appropriate distance between the striker and his or her opponent. It is immediately followed by a cross, which comes from the rear hand and requires the rotation of the torso and hips to cover the same distance. This movement of the whole body adds force to the cross, which is why it is considered a power punch. The striker can follow the jab-cross combination with a hook, an uppercut, or both.

Lesson 3.1

Identifying Connotative and Figurative Meanings, p. 53

1 B Orchestras do not really breathe, but they can play music in a halting or fitful manner. This phrase is an example of personification, which is a type of figurative language.

2 A Graphic imagery such as "A blood-red thing that writhes from out/The scenic solitude!" is meant to haunt or disturb the reader.

3 D The speaker's attitude is one of misery, or distress. The speaker uses the phrase "funeral pall" (line 35) to describe how the play of life (the "tragedy," line 39) ends.

4 C The mime, who represents humankind, is food for the worm (line 30). This worm is Poe's metaphor for death.

5 B The speaker describes humans as mimes, puppets who cannot control their own lives but who think of themselves as God.

6 C *Writhes* describes a twisting, squirming movement of the body. In this poem, it is used to show the movements of the dreaded Conqueror Worm. The other answer choices do not provide negative images.

Understanding Connotative and Figurative Meaning in Various Texts, p. 55

7 D The narrator describes Dame Van Winkle as constantly nagging Rip. This is meant to make the reader sympathetic toward him.

8 C

9 B In paragraph 2, "adherent" is used when talking about Wolf, Rip's faithful dog. In paragraph 4, "adherents" refers to a group of men. In both cases, the word could be replaced by "friend." "Adherent" is always used in a positive sense, so it cannot mean "enemy." Neither Rip Van Winkle nor Nicholas Vedder served as teachers.

10 A In the fourth paragraph (lines 23–30), the author paints a picture of the men idly chatting and Nicholas Vedder tranquilly smoking his pipe. In the fifth paragraph (lines 31-34), however, Dame Van Winkle suddenly breaks into the men's gathering, criticizes the men, and then attacks Vedder for encouraging her husband to sit idly.

11 A Dame Van Winkle dominates her husband by always nagging at him and telling him what to do. She also dominates the men of the village when she storms into the "philosopher's club."

12 C The first paragraph describes Dame Van Winkle's constant nagging. Rip is so "henpecked" that he is forced to go outside. *Henpecked* means "bullied."

Language Practice, p. 56

1 B

2 D

3 A

4 D

Writing Practice, p. 57

Your paragraph should use connotative and figurative language to accurately convey how you felt during the experience. Your word choices should also contribute to the overall mood of your text, indicating the type of reaction you would like the reader to have after reading.

> Answers will vary. Sample answer: I could see them from the wings, hundreds of people packed into the tiny theater like sardines stuffed in a tin. There were so many of them, and they just stared at the stage, dourly waiting for someone to entertain them. A burst of anxiety bubbled through my stomach and up my sternum, threatening to spill out of my mouth as an ear-piercing scream. I knew my lines. I knew my cues. But I didn't know whether I could do this.

Lesson 3.2

Identifying Author's Tone in an Informational Text p. 59

1 B The topic of the letter is a complaint, so the tone is negative. Anger and frustration are appropriate tones for letters of complaint.

2 D "Imagine my surprise" is the author's way of saying, "Can you believe this?" The other sentences explain what happened, but they do not express the writer's frustration.

3 A The author of the letter uses the word *headaches* as a metaphor to describe the problems he had at the hotel. This word has a negative connotation that helps reveal the tone of the letter.

4 B The writer uses the phrases "a number of problems" and "all of these problems" to emphasize that several things went wrong during his hotel stay. The hotel manager would probably feel embarrassed that a guest at his hotel had so many problems.

5 A The tone reveals how the author feels about a subject. Changing "As the cherry on top" to "Thankfully" would demonstrate a change in the author's feelings from irritation to appreciation. Mood describes how the reader feels while reading.

Analyzing Tone in a Literary Text, p. 61

6 C The genre of the story is mystery. The tone of a mystery is commonly suspenseful.

7 B

8 D Short, terse phrases and sentences build tension in the story. This pushes the reader to move forward to find out what happens next.

9 A The mystery itself and the short sentences contribute to the intense tone.

10 A Mr. Sedgwick's lengthy inner monologue adds tension to the story. The reader must stop and wait while Mr. Sedgwick thinks about his guests. The paragraph does not describe the butler's search, and it does not actually name Darrow as the thief. The brief description at the end is part of Mr. Sedgwick's inner thoughts.

11 B The speaker of the sentence is uncertain and possibly a little afraid. If she boldly, proudly, or loudly offered her opinion, it would change the tone of the paragraph.

Your paragraph should include connotative words, figurative language, and sentence structures that express your tone and match your purpose for writing.

> Answers will vary. Sample answer: I have so many responsibilities now that I am an adult. I have to decide when to go to bed, and if I stay up late, it's too bad! I still have to get up early so I can get to work on time. I make my breakfast and pack my lunch. I buy the groceries and cook the food. And don't get me started on laundry! If I don't do it, I won't have clean clothes to wear. No one is going to do the laundry for me. I deposit my paychecks and pay the bills. It's all so much responsibility.

Lesson 3.3

Choosing the Right Word, p. 64

1 C When Maria tells her father that she sings to ease her melancholy, she is telling him that she is sad. She is not relaxed; "leisure" refers to the time she spends reading or singing. She is not troubled by the books she reads, although her father finds the books troublesome. She is not happy; her father says that Maria *should* be merry.

2 A The word *honored* shows the esteem Maria had for her mother. She does not mention her mother's reputation, nor does she mention her feelings about her mother's death.

3 D Maria's father has a negative view about his deceased wife. He says that she henpecked him while she was alive. *Henpeck* has a negative connotation; it refers to a wife's constant nagging.

4 B The word *as* signals a comparison. Comparisons formed using the word *like* or *as* are similes.

5 B The phrase "depraved wretch" has a very negative connotation. Maria hates her fiancé; she describes him as having a "polished exterior" and no regard for the happiness of others.

Analyzing and Evaluating Word Choice in Various Texts, p. 66

6 C Anthony used persuasive language in her speech as she detailed what the preamble to the Constitution really means. Her explanations were meant to show the discrepancies between rights for men and rights for all.

7 D Anthony began her speech by addressing "friends and fellow citizens." She wanted all of the American public to rally behind the idea of voting rights for women. None of the other choices describe all the people she was trying to reach with her speech.

8 D

9 B Nothing was actually being thrown to the winds. This phrase is an example of figurative language. It provides the reader or listener with a visual image. All the other phrases are literal expressions; they mean exactly what the words say.

10 A *Mockery* has a negative connotation; it conveys the idea that talk of liberty has no meaning for people who cannot vote. *Silly* makes women's plight seem unimportant. *Difficult* does not express Anthony's scorn. *Encouraging* ignores the frustration women might feel when it is implied that those who cannot vote can enjoy "liberty."

11 B Anthony wanted other people to become angry and to take up the cause of suffrage for women. She was not describing a hopeful situation for women who wanted to vote. She did not want people to become depressed. And although her speech might have excited some people, Anthony's intention was clearly to get people angry enough to change the law.

Writing Practice, p. 67

In your paragraph, clearly state your perspective on the topic. Then choose words that align with your feelings. Use descriptive phrases, words with strong connotations, and figurative language such as metaphors and similes.

> Answers will vary. Sample answer: I think the closing of six schools in our school district is a despicable use of the school board's power. Education isn't just an issue for families with school-aged children. It's the backbone of our community; without it we are stuck in a slump. The schools that are closing are, of course, the schools needed the most— the schools where kids get their sole hot meal, the schools where teachers often play the role of parents, the schools where children are safe for a few hours each day.

Lesson 4.1

Identifying Text Structure, p. 69

1 C The passage uses sequence to narrate the events of the *Titanic's* first trip.

2 D The size of the *Titanic* is contrasted with other ships. The *Titanic* was much larger than any other ship in the harbor.

3 D The word *next* is commonly used when the text structure is sequence. It helps point out the order of events.

4 B Many people gathered at the harbor because they wanted to say farewell to their friends and relatives.

Variations in Organization, p. 71

5 A The events in the paragraph are told from start to finish. This is known as chronological order, or time order.

6 B

7 D Holmes uses flashbacks to organize the ideas in paragraph 12 (lines 18–23). He refers to events that happened "last night" and "four weeks ago."

8 D When the passage begins, Holmes is brewing something. Then Holmes describes the missing links of the simple chain of events. Next Mr. Hilton Cubitt rings the doorbell. Finally Holmes holds up a piece of paper.

Writing Practice, p. 72

Make sure your paragraph uses a compare-and-contrast text structure and highlights two family traditions. It should include words such as *both, but,* and *in contrast* to show similarities and differences.

> Answers will vary. Sample answer: My family loves to celebrate holidays with great food and lots of family time. Our biggest holiday celebration each year is our Thanksgiving feast, which is always at my Aunt Gloria's house. She cooks a turkey big enough to feed 25 hungry guests, including all 14 of my cousins and even some close family friends. Everyone brings a dish to share, and we have a contest each year for the best pie. The party is loud and boisterous. In contrast, just my immediate family gathers to celebrate New Year's Day. Although it's also a family gathering that involves food, it's different because there are just the five of us. My dad makes his famous pancakes, and my mom fries up the bacon. We drink hot chocolate and share our resolutions for the new year. My brother builds a fire, and we play card games and enjoy a peaceful afternoon together.

Lesson 4.2

Identifying Text Structures, p. 74

1 D Lines 5–9 establish the order of steps that GDL systems require teenagers to complete. These steps must be completed in order, so sequence is the way that this text structure is organized.

2 D One solution to the problem of teen drivers' high crash risk is giving teen drivers more driving experience. Research proves that this solution makes teens safer drivers.

3 C Active hormones are a cause for teens' difficulty in managing risky behavior. The other answer choices relate to risky behavior, but they do not explain possible causes.

4 A A reduction in teen crashes is a direct effect of the GDL. The other choices do not describe an effect of the GDL.

Text Structure and Key Ideas, p. 76

5 A The writer begins the passage with frog and toad sightings (effects) and introduces the possible causes for these events later.

6 D Lines 25–31 emphasizes that the author is uncertain about why frogs and toads seem to fall from the sky at times. In the other lines, the author is citing the opinions of other authors or experts.

7 B

8 D   A whirlwind is cited as a possible cause of frogs and toads falling from the sky. The other answer choices describe the effects, or results, of storms.

Writing Practice, p. 77

Make sure your paragraphs show a clear compare-and-contrast structure. You should have included descriptions of your friends to support the points you are comparing and contrasting.

> Answers will vary. Sample answer: When you meet my best friend Tanisha, the first thing that you will notice is the bright smile that is always painted on her dimpled face. When she smiles, her eyes curl at the corners and even sparkle a bit. I first met Tanisha in second grade, and she was laughing about something that I don't remember anymore. In fact, Tanisha thinks that everything is funny. Once, we were eating lunch and she laughed so hard that she couldn't catch her breath for a couple of minutes. My other friend, Amanda, is much quieter and more serious. Like Tanisha, Amanda likes to laugh, but she doesn't laugh as much as Tanisha does.

> When Amanda gets stressed, she likes to find a quiet space and listen to music. Unlike Amanda, Tanisha deals with stress by being around her friends. To relax, Tanisha and Amanda like to go to the movies or to the mall. Although they love the mall, they like to buy different things. Amanda always shops for accessories such as earrings and scarves, and Tanisha loves shoes. In fact, Tanisha has so many shoes that she once gave away a garbage bag full of shoes to a clothing drive, and she still had a mountain of shoes left in her closet. Despite their differences, Tanisha and Amanda are great friends of mine, and I hope we stay friends forever.

Lesson 4.3

Locating Transitions, p. 79

1 A   *First* is the signal word that describes when Kareya created the fishes. The other words are signal words, but they are not related to information about when Kareya created the fishes.

2 C   The signal word *next* shows what happens the morning following events in the second paragraph. This transition reveals a shift in time. It does not signal a conclusion, a contrast, or an example.

3 D   The signal word *therefore* indicates cause and effect. Because Man gave cunning to Coyote, Coyote is kind to Man. *Therefore* does not indicate a contrast, a comparison, or additional information.

4 B   The signal word *but* reveals a contrast. *But* does not reveal a comparison (similarity), a location, or a cause-and-effect relationship.

5 C   The signal phrase *as a result* shows an effect. Because Coyote was tired, he sharpened sticks to help himself keep his eyes open. *As a result* does not indicate an example, a location, or importance.

Analyzing Transitions, p. 81

6 C   The first paragraph provides important information about NASA's history. The list at the end of the second paragraph provides examples of NASA's technological inventions.

7 B

8 D   This sentence provides examples of NASA's impact on technological inventions. The signal phrase *for instance* would provide examples of this relationship. The term "in brief" is not appropriate here because the sentence does not provide a summary. "By contrast" indicates that something will be contrasted, which does not happen in these sentences. "In conclusion" would indicate that the paragraph or passage is coming to a conclusion, which is not correct.

9 D   The signal word *moreover* shows an addition. It does not signal a cause, an effect, or a conclusion.

10 A   The signal word *finally* shows that the writer is arriving at a conclusion. It does not indicate relative location. The term *whatever* is not a signal word used to reveal a shift in ideas.

Writing Practice, p. 82

Make sure each paragraph clearly focuses on one particular skill or talent and uses signal words or phrases to transition between the ideas.

> Answers will vary. Sample answer: I am a talented musician. I have been playing the trumpet since I was nine. When I was in middle school, I won a Young Musician's Award. In addition, I have entered many local competitions, and I have competed in several other states, including Michigan, Indiana, and Illinois. At family gatherings, my brothers sing, and I play the trumpet to accompany them.
>
> I am also really good at board games. My family and I play Scrabble every Saturday night, and I usually win by at least 50 points. There are other board games that I play well, including Monopoly, checkers, and chess. I am trying to learn a lot of new games; for example, I am trying to learn certain card games. I started playing hearts and bridge a couple of months ago, and I am getting better every day. I think the combination of these two talents makes me unique.

Lesson 5.1

Identifying Author's Purpose, p. 83

1 C Poetry is usually written to entertain by appealing to the emotions of the reader. In this poem, Tennyson is not trying to persuade, to inform, or to explain.

2 C The speaker uses the image of twilight and evening to show the passage of time during the day and through life. Lines 2, 4, and 12 do not relate to the passage of time.

3 A The poem describes the speaker's feeling about dying by comparing death to the movement of ocean waves. He hopes his family is not sad at his passing. The waves are part of the tide of life, not a flood or a voyage.

4 B

Recognizing an Author's Point of View, p. 85

5 C This passage outlines George W. Bush's plans for reforming education. His point of view is that there are problems with the education system that need to be changed.

6 B Bush lists a series of problems with the education system, including poorly performing schools and lack of accountability. His point of view about the US education system is negative.

7 A Bush states in the first paragraph, "It's time to come together to get it done. . . ." Bush is trying to convince the American people that No Child Left Behind should be put into law. He is not entertaining. Although he does explain and inform, his primary purpose is to convince the audience that No Child Left Behind is a good plan.

8 A Bush lists changes that need to occur in education. Therefore, his point of view is that the education system needs reform.

9 C Bush uses the transition words *first, second, third,* and *fourth* to list his four main points. Creating a uniform educational system is not one of these points.

Writing Practice, p. 86

Make sure your text has a clearly stated topic sentence that expresses your point of view. You should give reasons to support your opinion.

> Answers will vary. Sample answer: Students should be allowed to bring their own computers and other technology to school, as it has advantages for the schools, students, and teachers. First, it is expensive for schools to provide the latest technology. Allowing students to bring their own devices will increase the number of units available while saving limited financial resources. Besides the expense of purchasing technology, schools will save money by having fewer machines to maintain and update. Second, there are advantages for students. Students will be able to take e-books with them wherever they go, and they can easily share their information with others, allowing them to collaborate on projects and extend their learning beyond the walls of the classroom. By using their own devices, students will have more control over their own learning, deepening their understanding

of topics. Finally, bring-your-own-device programs are helpful to teachers. Teachers will notice that students are more engaged in their lessons because they can quickly research class topics. They can submit assignments electronically, a system that teachers will find to be efficient. Since these programs benefit schools, students, and teachers, I believe we should encourage bring-your-own-device programs in schools.

Lesson 5.2

Text Structure in Informational Texts, p. 88

1 **A** The facts, boldfaced definitions, section headings, and straightforward style are clues that this text was written to inform.

2 **B** The author defines and then describes various concepts that are important to Earth science, so the text structure is description.

3 **B** The descriptive text structure makes it easy for readers to understand which topics are studied in Earth science.

4 **C** In paragraph 3, the author explains the effects of the events that are parts of the big bang theory, the open theory, and the closed universe theory, so the structure that best describes the paragraph is cause and effect.

Text Structure in Literary Texts, p. 90

5 **B** The descriptive details of the setting and figurative language are clues that this text was written to entertain.

6 **A** The events are told in the order in which they occur, so the story has a sequence structure.

7 **A** Presenting the events in sequence allows readers to follow the story line and to focus on the details and language.

8 **C** The author's use of time-order words such as *then* and *when* helps support the organizational structure by showing the sequence of key events.

9 **B**

10 **D** The correct sequence of events is as follows: First, the party gets quiet when the music stops. Next, people notice a masked character, and then they are troubled by his appearance. Finally, the prince becomes angry.

Writing Practice, p. 91

Make sure the text structure you choose helps you present information in a way that conveys the purpose of your article.

Answers will vary. Sample answer: On October 23, the Environmental Committee of the city council recommended that the city expand its new recycling-bin program. The committee met the previous evening to discuss the recent replacement of the 19-gallon recycling bins with 34-gallon bins in the Fifth Precinct. Miguel Rostro, the committee chair, reported that because the bins are larger, the city has been able to reduce pickup of recycled materials from twice a week to once. He explained that this reduction would help compensate for the cost of the new bins. Committee member Marie Beaufort noted that the public has provided mostly positive feedback. She added that many people have commented that the new bins are easier to use, because they can be rolled. Ms. Beaufort said that most complaints have been about the difficulty of storing the larger containers in garages. Because the majority of comments from citizens have been favorable, the committee voted to recommend the expansion of the new program.

Lesson 5.3

Inferring the Author's Purpose, p. 93

1 **D** The straightforward approach and bulleted text are clues that one of the author's purpose is to inform.

2 D The bullet points indicate many times when it is appropriate to wash one's hands, implying that hands can become contaminated in many ways. It is true that people who are sick can spread disease and that hands are susceptible to getting dirty, but these are just two of the many reasons for washing one's hands. Although animals are mentioned, their presence in the workplace is not.

3 A

4 B The memo does not mention training costs, the work of researchers, or patient complaints.

5 B The text was written to inform readers about the hand-washing policy and to persuade readers to use the guidelines. The word *crucial* would stress the importance of the guidelines, and it would persuade readers that following them is important.

Using Context to Infer Implicit Purpose, p. 95

6 C Knowing it is the president's responsibility to guide the nation and the military—and thus plan for the future—is the most relevant detail. The responsibility for signing legislation, the presidential election cycle, and the leadership of political parties are not relevant to the speech.

7 A The fact that the speech was written toward the end of the Vietnam War helps you understand that Ford wanted the American people to set aside their feelings about the war and to focus instead on the future of the United States. The fact that Ford gave the speech on a college campus explains why he refers to "your generation," but it does not hint at his main purpose. Ford's service in the US Navy is not related to the purpose of his speech. The upcoming bicentennial was not directly related to Ford's main purpose.

8 D The knowledge that the president's responsibility is to set the nation's agenda helps you understand that Ford's implied purpose was to focus people on moving forward after the Vietnam War. Choices A and C are details that support Ford's purpose, but they do not convey the purpose itself. With choice B, Ford acknowledges the events in Vietnam, but feelings about Vietnam are not his focus.

9 D Ford's use of persuasive language and phrases such as "join me" and "assume the challenge" are clues that he is trying to persuade.

Writing Practice, p. 96

Your paragraph should convey your positive feelings about a product or service through the use of persuasive language and examples rather than by explicitly stating your opinion.

> Answers will vary. Sample answer: Do you enjoy going to the ballpark, watching the game while you munch on a warm, delicious hot dog? Now you can have that experience at home with the Hot-Diggety. This device cooks hot dogs to perfection. Simply place two hot dogs and two buns into the convenient slots. In seconds, out pops fresh, toasty hot dogs that you can place inside the softly grilled buns. Simply add your favorite toppings, and you can have the total ballpark experience right in your living room. This inexpensive and efficient machine is easy to store and clean and will be a hit the next time you have your friends over to enjoy the game.

Lesson 5.4

Identifying Author's Position, p. 98

1 D The author states that unique brain structure (nature) and upbringing (environment) shape the talents of prodigies. Although the author notes that new research will enhance our understanding of the brain, this is not the most important information about the author's position.

2 A The author disagrees with the viewpoint that prodigies acquire their skills solely through deliberate practice, as signaled by the word "however" following the statement "Some researchers claim that deliberate practice alone sets prodigies off from their average peers" (line 27). The fourth paragraph (lines 16–19) also indicates the author's disagreement with this viewpoint. The passage does not mention that prodigies manifest their talent later in life or that prodigies have brain structures that are similar to ordinary humans. Choice C is part of the author's argument.

3 B The statement provides scientific evidence that the brain of prodigies differs from the brain of average children. This information supports the author's statement in the first paragraph that prodigies' brains function differently than average children. The statement does not explain that it is only environment that makes prodigies excel, refute that prodigies' brains differ from ordinary people, or prove that environment doesn't play a role in the development of prodigies.

4 D

Analyzing Support for an Author's Position, p. 100

5 D Lyndon Johnson's position is that Congress should pass the voting rights bill. He says that Congress must work hard, but that is not his main point. Johnson wants Congress to pass this bill, not draft a new one. And although he refers to states' rights, that is not the primary issue here.

6 B In line 19, Johnson refutes the opposing argument that election laws are issues governed solely by the states. He claims that the freedom to vote is an issue that is far more important than states' rights versus national rights.

7 A By acknowledging and then refuting the opposing viewpoints, Johnson strengthens his position. He does not create, ignore, or support opposing viewpoints.

8 C In lines 20–23, Johnson describes what happened when Congress considered a similar bill. This previous experience explains why Johnson is insisting that Congress pass the current bill with all its provisions intact. Lines 9–11 hint at this incident but does not provide details. Johnson refutes the opposition's argument in lines 17–18 and refers to bigotry in lines 36–37, but he does not provide evidence.

Writing Practice, p. 101

Your essay should clearly state your position and support it with evidence. To strengthen your argument, your essay should acknowledge an opposing position and explain, through the use of evidence, why that position is not valid.

> Answers will vary. Sample answer: Service learning is the involvement of students in community service. Students may volunteer at their school or in the larger community. Service-learning activities offer many benefits to students, schools, and the community. They should be a part of every student's experience. Some might argue that a school's main priority should be on learning. However, there is a reason that "learning" is half of the term "service learning." These projects enhance student learning in a way that traditional classroom work cannot.
>
> For example, students who are reading novels about immigrant experiences could visit a community farm where recent refugees use their farming experience to start a new future. As students work at the farm alongside the refugees, they gain an understanding of the hard work and low pay that face refugees. Other students might organize a blanket and towel drive for an animal shelter. They create posters, write letters, and speak to a variety of groups to solicit donations. Not only does the shelter benefit, but the students gain organizational and communication skills. These examples show that service learning benefits the community, and it enriches student learning by providing authentic experiences that students cannot have in the classroom.

Lesson 5.5

Identifying Rhetorical Devices, p. 103

1 D Using an analogy, the author compares the water to steel. By comparing the water to something readers can picture, the author helps create a strong visual of the setting. Because the sentence does not list items or repeat phrases or ideas, the author has not used the rhetorical devices of enumeration, repetition, or parallelism.

2 A The second part of the sentence provides more information to convey why nightfall was so dangerous. Because the author does not make a comparison, list items, or present two opposing ideas or situations, he has not used the rhetorical devices of analogy, enumeration, or juxtaposition of opposites.

3 C This sentence lists various buildings that were close to where the mauled body was found. Therefore, the reader can understand how serious the wolf attack was to the community. None of the other sentences lists a series of examples or details.

4 B

Identifying an Author's Intention and Effect, p. 104

5 B The author uses rhetorical devices such as enumeration and juxtaposition of opposites, as well as vivid descriptions of the life of a slave, to convey how unfairly slaves were treated. The author conveys that the slaves were glad that Mr. Severe died but does not indicate that the death was deserved. Although the slaves work on a farm, the passage does not include any details about what the work was like. The passage is not a tale about his childhood but a description of what life was like for slaves.

6 D The author's use of rhetorical devices helps create an emotional response in the reader. Skepticism is not a likely response. Readers might discuss life in the rural south, but the topic is more specific than that. And the passage does not try to prompt readers to make changes in their lives.

7 C The author uses enumeration when he lists different groups of people (old and young, male and female, married and single). The author does not compare the people in an analogy, ask any questions, or provide further information in a qualifying statement.

8 A This excerpt, unlike the others, does not convey the inhumane circumstances in which the slaves lived.

Language Practice, p. 105

1 C

2 B

3 A

4 D

Writing Practice, p. 106

Make sure your paragraph discusses the author's intent and effect and mentions the use of rhetorical devices.

Answers will vary. Sample answer: In the excerpt from Konrad Bercovici's story "Ghitza," a Romanian village suffers from attacks by hungry wolves during a harsh winter. The author's intention is to entertain readers by transporting them to another place and time. He communicates this intention in two main ways. First, he creates vivid descriptions, such as "the crack of whips and the curses of the drivers rent the icy atmosphere" and "cold, clear nights, when even the wind was frozen still." The author also employs rhetorical devices. For example, he uses an analogy to compare a frozen river to steel. This analogy conveys just how cold and hard the river is. Other rhetorical devices in "Ghitza" include a qualifying statement to explain why the carters needed to get to safety by nightfall, as well as enumeration to emphasize how close to the community the wolf attacks are: "A stone's throw from the inn, and the thatch-roofed school, and the red painted church!" These rhetorical devices and the many rich details have the desired effect of helping readers feel the desperation of the villagers.

Lesson 6.1

Developing an Argument, p. 108

1 D One of Paine's main claims is that England's constitution does not encourage liberty. The fact that the king can reject bills that the commons passes and that the members of the peers are part of the old tyranny are ideas that support Paine's claim. The fact that members of the commons are elected is a statement that does not support his claim.

2 B

3 D The evidence that Paine presents is relevant to his claim. All the information in the passage relates directly to his call for liberty.

4 A The constitution of England allowed the king to reject bills passed by the commons. This is a fact that can be checked in historical references. All the other statements are opinions. They contain biased words such as "not to be trusted," "wiser," and "ancient tyranny." Loaded vocabulary is often a sign that an opinion is being expressed.

5 A Paine's conclusion is a restatement of the ideas he has presented. He does not add new information or call colonists to action.

Analyzing Argument Development, p. 110

6 A Answer A explains the claim made in the passage. The other sentences express reasons and facts provided as evidence.

7 C Palma says that he has no patience for people who protest this right. The other sentences are untrue, or they do not accurately express the author's opinion.

8 B Palma provides an example of women's success in public life as proof that women belong in public life. A fact about women's suffrage, an expert opinion about women's intelligence, and a personal opinion about women are not part of his argument.

9 A Palma states his claim and supports it with facts, reasons, and examples. Answers B and C describe ways that an argument could be supported, but the author does not use these methods. Answer D describes a solution to a problem. This is not what Palma does in this passage.

10 B Palma connects his ideas logically. He does not present ideas chronologically, in the form of questions and answers, or through comparison and contrast.

11 D Palma concludes that it is only logical for women, who are allowed to participate in every other aspect of life, to be allowed to participate fully in public life. This includes voting. The other statements are summaries of evidence.

Writing Practice, p. 111

Make sure your paragraph clearly states your claim. Provide facts, reasons, and examples as evidence to back up your claim. Conclude by restating your opinion and summarizing the evidence that backs up your claim.

> Answers will vary. Sample answer: Shopping for food at farmers' markets and local farms boosts your local economy and improves your diet. The food at farmers' markets is as fresh as possible because it has not been shipped from far away. Also, if your local farms grow organic food, the food is free of pesticides, hormones, and other chemicals that can harm your health. Communities that support their local farms benefit from the healthier food these farms produce, and the farmers benefit financially from the community support. That's a win-win situation for everyone!

Lesson 6.2

Supporting Evidence, p. 113

1 A The author claims that the mayor is avoiding his responsibility. The other statements are claims made by the mayor himself.

2 D The mayor claims that he cannot remove people from government positions for misconduct. The other statements are claims that the author is making about the mayor's powers and responsibilities.

3 D The mayor can remove offenders, with the approval of the board. Answers A and C are arguments that the mayor gives for not being held responsible for misconduct. Answer B does not relate to the author's claim that the mayor is responsible for what happens in the city.

4 C The mayor states that he has no power, but then he says that he can remove people from their positions if he has the approval of the Board of Aldermen. This is an example of how the mayor's statements are contradictory. The other answer options do not describe the mayor's statements accurately.

5 B The mayor's logic is faulty, because he contradicts himself. The other answer choices would describe sensible arguments.

Connecting Claims and Evidence, p. 115

6 B Nixon admitted that he received $18,000, but he claimed that he used the money for political, not personal, expenses. The other answer choices are false.

7 D Nixon offered this reason for why politicians need contributions from supporters. He believed that the government should not finance political business. The statement is not an example of political expenses. It is not a fact, and it does not make a strong emotional appeal.

8 B

9 C Nixon said that the records, which were then in the hands of the government, showed how he spent the money. The other answer options do not offer support for how he spent the money.

10 A Nixon had no proof that he did not grant special favors to supporters. The lack of proof makes this argument faulty. The other options would describe sound arguments.

Writing Practice, p. 116

Make sure that your argument includes supporting evidence but does not include emotional appeals or faulty reasoning.

> Answers will vary. Sample answer: To gain experience before going to culinary school, I decided to take a year off after high school to work in a restaurant. Although I enjoyed cooking, I had no professional experience. I needed to learn the basics. I knew that I would not have time to master all the techniques while studying nutrition, marketing, hygiene, bookkeeping, and government regulations. During my year away from school, I gained the experience I needed, so I was well prepared to start on the path to become a real chef.

Lesson 6.3

Building a Case, p. 118

1 B The fact that the company cannot afford mandatory sick leave is evidence given to support the claim that employees should vote against the legislation. The other answer choices provide information about the legislation or an opinion held by the company, but these statements do not give reasons to support the claim.

2 B The fact that this company already provides sick leave for employees demonstrates its commitment to employee health.

3 C The effect on employee benefits and job security is directly relevant to the audience. The other options are general information about the company.

4 A The financial information shows that the new law would be too costly for the company and that it would force the company to lay off employees. This information is relevant to the claim that employees should vote against the new law. The other options are not relevant to the claim.

5 C The author provides several pieces of evidence directly related to the company's cost for sick leave.

6 D The author provides relevant evidence and links the employees to the results of this legislation. This makes the claim persuasive.

Evaluating Evidence in Various Texts, p. 120

7 B Reagan uses this example from history as relevant evidence for his claim that his actions are necessary. The other options are other elements of an argument.

8 A Reagan states that the private sector is more successful at running social programs in order to justify his claim that the Department of Education and other social programs can be cut from the budget. The other statements are not directly related to the claim.

9 D

10 C The promise to not raise taxes is relevant to the claim. Reagan believes that not increasing taxes will help people and businesses recover from the recession. The other statements are not relevant to the claim.

11 D The lack of specific examples makes the evidence insufficient. The other options do not describe how the lack of specific examples categorizes the evidence.

12 C The president briefly provides relevant evidence that the recession caused the budget deficit (it lowered revenues and increased costs), but those two details are not sufficient evidence to support his claim.

Writing Practice, p. 122

Make sure your argument has sufficient and relevant supporting evidence for your claim.

Answers will vary. Sample answer: Food stamps are an important social service program that should continue to be fully funded by the government. People who are in the terrible position of choosing between paying for their rent and buying groceries have no opportunity to get ahead in life or to help themselves. This problem affects not only the unemployed. People who have jobs that do not pay enough to cover living expenses also can end up needing food stamps to make sure they and their families are well fed. If the government wants people to help themselves, it must first make sure that these people do not go hungry and that their most basic needs are provided. Only people whose basic needs are met can take advantage of opportunities to better their lives.

Lesson 6.4

Understanding Validity and Reasoning, p. 124

1 A The author claims that suffrage for women should not be granted. All the other statements are evidence that he presents to support his claim.

2 A

3 C The defeat of the Sanford bill can be verified in historical records. The other statements are the author's opinions.

4 D The evidence that is used to support the claim is not reasonable because it cannot be verified. It is not logically sound because it is based on opinions rather than facts. The other descriptions of this author's evidence are inaccurate.

5 B The writer's argument as a whole is biased because it is based solely on his unsupported opinion; therefore, it is invalid. Even his factual evidence about the reasons for the suffrage bill's defeat cannot be fully verified. There may have been other aspects of the bill that were not acceptable and that led to its being voted down. The other descriptions of the author's argument are inaccurate.

Evaluating Validity and Reasoning in Texts, p. 126

6 A Obama's tax cut is a verifiable fact. The other sentences are opinions. Words such as *best* and *want* are clues that these statements are opinions.

7 C Obama uses Romney's plan to support his claim that trickle-down economics doesn't work at all. He describes the plan as "fairy dust," and he says that it didn't work (in the past) and that it won't work (in the future). The other statements support Romney's plan.

8 C Obama is connecting the idea that the economy improves when the middle class has more money to spend with the idea that taxing the middle class does not help the economy. The other ideas do not logically support Obama's claim.

9 B Obama connects his ideas logically and produces verifiable facts, providing sound reasoning and valid evidence for his claim that he should be reelected to continue the progress he started.

10 C The last sentence states that Obama has a plan, which supports his claim that he should be reelected. The other sentences describe the opponent's actions but do not directly support Obama's claim that he will be the best person to move the economy in a positive direction.

Writing Practice, p. 127

Make sure your speech includes facts, reasons, and examples as evidence to validate your claim. Your evaluation of your claim should state why your claim is valid and your reasoning sound.

Answers will vary. Sample answer: Our schools need a representative on the school board who knows about the issues that current students face. I have two children in the school system, one who utilizes special-education services, so I have direct experience with the issues and needs of a variety of students. I have also spent much of my free time volunteering in my children's classes, speaking with teachers about problems they encounter, and looking for solutions to those problems. As a parent and a volunteer, I am an ideal candidate for the position of school board representative.

My argument is valid because I have given examples of my experience that are directly related to the position I seek. My reasoning is sound because I logically relate my evidence to the claim that I am an ideal candidate for school board representative because I know about current school issues.

Lesson 6.5

Evaluating Arguments Founded on Logical Reasoning, p. 129

1 D The author claims there are too many causes of obesity for doctors to be able to suggest just one solution to solve the problem. The other answer options are evidence and reasoning that the author uses to support the claim.

2 B The author makes the assumption that obesity is a medical problem that needs to be solved. The other answer options define terms and explain causes of obesity.

3 B The explanation of the set-point theory serves as a deduction in a series of deductions that support the claim that obesity is a complex problem to solve. The other answer options are other parts of an argument.

4 A

5 D The author formulates deductions from the results of the studies and uses them to support the argument. The other options do not support the author's claim.

Evaluating Arguments Based on Hidden Assumptions, p. 130

6 D The author claims that Shakespeare's work should have obscene words removed to clean it up and to make it more beautiful. Choice A can be inferred from the title of the book that the excerpt comes from, but it does not state the author's claim. Choices B and C are statements that the author makes to build his argument.

7 B The author bases his argument on the unstated assumption that offensive words lower the artistic quality of literature. The other answer options are stated ideas.

8 D The author's argument depends upon the reader accepting the belief that changing literature does not damage the original work or change it in an unacceptable way.

9 C The author bases the idea that Shakespeare's writing would be more beautiful if it were censored on the invalid assumption that censors can alter literature without damaging it.

10 A Although the author presents the idea that Shakespeare's work is defective as a fact and he assumes that everyone will agree with him, it is his personal opinion.

Language Practice, p. 131

1 B

2 C

3 D

4 A

Make sure you provide logical reasoning based on your hidden assumption.

> Answers will vary. Sample answer: Please be sure to clean and put away dishes that you use in the company kitchen. Clean countertops, start the dishwasher if it is full, and check the floor for any stray garbage that needs to be put into the wastebasket. Place any leftover food in the refrigerator, but remember that it will be removed each Friday to ensure that food is not left in there too long. Check that the table is clear before you leave the room. If everyone participates, the kitchen will remain clean.

> My hidden assumption is that people want to have a clean kitchen in their workplace.

Lesson 7.1

Comparing Texts on Similar Topics, p. 135

1 D Both passages are about Mammoth Cave. The genre of the first passage is memoir; the second passage is a nonfiction, informational text. The format of the first passage is all text, but the second passage includes text and tables. The first passage has a first-person narrator; the second passage has a third-person narrator.

2 B Knowing that passage 1 was written in the late 19th century helps readers understand why words such as *torch* (paragraph 1), *oxen* (paragraph 2), and *lantern* (paragraph 3) were used. The other choices might provide readers with information, but they would not affect understanding of the text.

3 A Passage 2 provides information about the park and fees associated with visiting. The information is more general than historians or conservationists would need. The text addresses all park visitors, not just families.

4 C Passage 1 uses vivid, connotative language to describe Mammoth Cave. Its main purpose is to entertain readers with fascinating information about the cave. Passage 2 provides facts and pricing information about the park. Its main purpose is to inform. Passage 1 might have also been written to inform readers about the cave's wonder and beauty and to persuade readers to visit the park, but passage 2 is strictly informational.

Comparing Fiction and Nonfiction, p. 137

5 C Passage 1 is a factual account of the torture methods used during the Spanish Inquisition. Passage 2 details the thoughts and feelings of one of the torture victims. Neither passage mentions the people who created the Spanish Inquisition, the purposes behind its formation, or the events that led to its end.

6 B Passage 1 is entirely fact-based; passage 2 details the narrator's emotions and thoughts during his experience. Passage 1 does not reveal the author's opinion about the methods of torture, does not detail the torture experienced by one man, and is not written from the point of view of the inquisitor. Passage 2 describes the experience of only one prisoner.

7 D Passage 1 is an informational text written mainly to inform people about what happened during the Spanish Inquisition. It was not written to help, to persuade, or to entertain readers.

8 D

9 B "The Pit and the Pendulum" presents the inner emotions and struggles of the prisoner to help readers identify with him. These are characteristics of fiction.

Writing Practice, p. 138

Make sure the first account focuses on facts and details about the event. The second account should include language, such as vivid descriptions or persuasive words, that is commonly used in the genre you have chosen.

> Answers will vary. Sample answer:

> Account 1: Kelly met her husband on April 26, on the 5:25 bus from Beele Street. Although the driver of this route was usually late, he was punctual that afternoon. Kelly, wet from the unexpected rain, ran to make it to the bus in time. She touched her pass to the electronic reader and then stepped

down the aisle, water dripping from her drenched clothing. A lurch caused her to bump into a fellow passenger. Kelly apologized, and the man smiled. After that day, they rode together daily without more than a "hello" until the afternoon of June 1, when she asked the man about himself. Many more conversations followed.

Account 2: The 5:25 was actually on time that afternoon, so I dashed—and splashed—through puddles for the last block. My favorite weatherman hadn't predicted rain, so I was soaked to the bone but sweating at the same time. As I shuffled my way down the slick aisle toward the back, the driver pulled sharply away from the curb and sent me staggering into the arms of a tall, broad man wearing a neat overcoat. After uttering an involuntary expletive, I stuttered an apology. Then I gazed up at his face, trying not to stare too hard at his bright blue eyes and sun-kissed skin. He gave me a wide smile, and somewhere up in heaven a choir of angels broke into song.

Lesson 7.2

Identifying Genre, p. 141

1 C Passage 1 is an essay; the author's viewpoint is clearly stated, and facts back up this viewpoint. Passage 2 is a historical article; it contains facts and figures, rather than opinions, about a historical topic.

2 A The purpose of both passages is to inform readers about an aspect of Japanese culture.

3 A Passage 1 is an essay describing the development of the Japanese tea culture, and Passage 2 is a historical article highlighting facts related to Japanese immigration to the United States. The dates and topics in the passages are details of content, not literary techniques. Passage 1 does not contain a plot.

4 B Passage 1 explains why tea became such an important part of Japanese culture. Passage 2 discusses US immigration rules that affected the Japanese. The other statements are incorrect or only half correct.

Comparing Texts from Similar Genres, p. 143

5 B Passage 1 is a nonfiction account written from first-person point of view, so it is a memoir.

6 A Lewis writes about his experience in nature with amusement, and Muir seems amazed by the variations in California's climate and scenery.

7 D

8 C Both authors use the first-person point of view to tell their narratives.

Writing Practice, p. 144

Both of your paragraphs should be about the same topic—you, but the paragraphs should have different styles of narration. Both should contain factual information, but your viewpoint should be clearly presented in the autobiography.

Answers will vary. Sample answer: Marilyn Jordan spent her early life in St. Louis, leaving the only home she'd ever known for a brand new life in Iowa with an overworked husband, a beat-up Chevy, and not nearly enough winter clothes. Iowa in January was cold, and Marilyn wasn't sure she'd ever get the chance to leave their tiny apartment on the edge of town. She needed friends, she needed a job, and she needed something to do. Petersen's Department Store seemed like the perfect fit.

We subscribed to the newspaper from the very first year of marriage, and in those early days nothing made me happier than to hear the *thwack* of newsprint against our thin front door at 6:30 every morning. Chuck would bring in the paper and then head to work. Nestled in bed, I would scan what was considered news in the little Iowa town we now called home and then search for a reason to get up and do something with my day. Eventually I started paging through the want ads. One morning I noticed that Petersen's was hiring in the men's department. I could do a job like that.

Lesson 7.3

Comparing and Contrasting Two Arguments, p. 146

1 D The author implicitly conveys the claim in the first paragraph (lines 1–8) by explaining how a human embryo is much like embryos of other species. In the second paragraph (lines 9–13), he says, "I do not think we could ask nature for more complete proof that human beings have evolved from one-cell ancestors as simple as modern protozoa. . . ." He concludes the fourth paragraph (lines 27–30) with ". . . we cannot do away with the facts of structure and development and fossil history, nor is there any other explanation more reasonable than evolution for these facts." Answers A, B, C are details that support Crampton's claim.

2 C Crampton supports his claim with facts about the fossilized remains of *Pithecanthropus*.

3 D

4 B Crampton believes that Darwin's theories of evolution and natural selection are valid; therefore, he would believe that unused traits disappear as a species evolves.

5 A Dennert begins by saying that "Darwinism is doomed to decay." Then he goes on to cite an article showing that Darwinism cannot be defended because it cannot be proved. Dennert uses answers C and D to support his claim. He does state that Darwinism goes against Christianity, but this is one of his reasons for opposing Darwinism. It is not his primary claim.

6 B Dennert refutes Crampton's argument, so he is disputing Darwin's theory of evolution.

Analyzing Evidence in Two Arguments, p. 147

7 C Crampton uses the *Pithecanthropus* to show that apes evolved (for example, their skulls changed shape) until eventually the ape-man evolved to become a human. Crampton does not say that other well-regarded scientists supported Darwin's theory. Crampton does not use the example to show how highly evolved humans are; rather, he uses it to show how closely related humans are to apes. He believes that *Pithecanthropus* is the missing link for understanding evolution.

8 A Crampton uses scientific research and analysis as the basis of his evidence. He does not use expert opinion, heresay, or witness statements.

9 B Dennert uses only opinion to defend his claim. It is not based on logic because it does not take into account evidence that supports the theory of evolution. His argument merely explains the opinion of another writer. He does not cite research or a record of events.

10 C The evidence of a "missing link" is used as proof that Darwinism has basis in fact. Although Crampton mentions the other points, those statements do not contradict Dennert's claim.

Writing Practice, p. 148

Make sure that your essay addresses the entire prompt, including a comparison of the two arguments and your opinion about the topic. Your writing should include evidence to support your viewpoint.

> Answers will vary. Sample answer: My neighbor, a teacher, is in favor of using tablet computers instead of textbooks in her classroom. She explained that tablets actually cost less than textbooks. They prepare students to use technology productively, just as they will when they get a job. Tablets offer technological tools that make them more engaging than textbooks. She also pointed out that one tablet is much lighter than many books, so the risk of injuries to students is greatly reduced because students will no longer be forced to carry extremely heavy backpacks full of books. My father argued that tablets were just gizmos that will distract students from learning. He explained that he thinks students will spend their time surfing the Internet, so they won't learn the material as they would reading from a textbook.
>
> I find my neighbor's argument to be the most persuasive. It is hard to dispute evidence, even when it contradicts personal beliefs.

Lesson 7.4

Comparing Textual and Visual Genres, p. 151

1 **A** The assassination of Abraham Lincoln is the topic of all three texts. The formats and the genres of the three texts are different. The newspaper article and the time line do not have a narrator.

2 **D**

3 **B** "O Captain! My Captain!" is a poem. The author's purpose is to show the reader how the nation felt after the untimely death of President Lincoln, through vivid descriptions, figurative language, and sensory details. The author was not writing to persuade, to inform, or to explain.

4 **A** The time line visually communicates information about the timing of events after Lincoln is shot, whereas the poem and article focus on the effect his death had on the American people. The time line does not contain interesting facts about events prior to Lincoln's death. The texts do not describe the events following his death in concrete detail, and they do not focus on events leading up to his death.

Evaluating Differences between Textual Genres, p. 153

5 **C** "The Story of an Eye-Witness" uses vivid descriptions to evoke compassion. "Evacuating Yourself and Your Family" offers facts, information, and practical advice about what to do during a disaster.

6 **A** Although readers might have experienced a natural disaster, want to learn about the weather, or work for the Federal Emergency Management Agency, the intended audience is people who might need to prepare for a future natural disaster. The passage contains information that can help readers plan for an evacuation. It does not talk in detail about past natural disasters, weather in general, or working for FEMA.

7 **C** The purpose of this text is to entertain and inform. The use of a narrative allows the writer to provide rich descriptive details that appeal to the reader's emotions. The passage does not explain key concepts about earthquakes. Although the narrative is told sequentially, conveying the sequence of events is not the author's main purpose. The passage is not meant to persuade readers about earthquake preparedness.

8 **B** Passage 1 has a broader scope than passage 2. Passage 1 provides details about how to prepare for and carry out an evacuation during several kinds of natural disasters. Passage 2 describes one event.

Writing Practice, p. 154

You should have written in two formats. The purpose of the first paragraph is to explain how to play a sport or do a performance. The purpose of the second text is to entertain the reader with a narrative about a game or performance.

Answers will vary. Sample answer: Basketball is a game played between two teams of five players on a court. Players on each team try to capture the ball and shoot the ball through a hoop to score points for their team. The opposing team tries to keep the other team from scoring. The game is divided into four periods. At the end of the four periods, the team that scored the most points is declared the winner. Many rules govern play. For example:

- Players may not carry the ball as they run; this is called traveling. Instead, players must bounce, or dribble, the ball or pass it to a teammate.

- The ball must be kept inside the boundaries of the court.

- When they are trying to steal the ball from an opposing team member, players must not make physical contact.

It was the fourth period, with only 10 seconds left, and the Tigers were one basket behind. With the Tigers on offense, the orange-uniformed players expertly passed the ball from player to player, but the quick-footed visiting Sharks tenaciously blocked every attempt to advance to the basket. Finally the Tigers' center planted himself at the three-point line and shot the ball. My fellow fans and I shot up from our seats and screamed as we watched the ball soar in an arc and then bounce off the rim of the basket. The ball hit the floor as the final buzzer sounded. A collective wail arose from the stands as the Sharks hugged one another in victory and the Tigers hung their heads, once again shut out of the championships.